*The Picture Book Comes
of Age*

The Picture Book Comes of Age

LOOKING AT CHILDHOOD THROUGH THE ART OF ILLUSTRATION

by Joseph H. Schwarcz and Chava Schwarcz

with a Foreword by Betsy Hearne
The Center for Children's Books
University of Chicago

AMERICAN LIBRARY ASSOCIATION
Chicago and London 1991

Designed by Charles Bozett

Composed by Ampersand Publisher Services, Inc.
and typeset by World Composition Services on a Mergenthaler
Linotron 202 in Palatino

Printed on 60-pound Glatfelter, a pH-neutral stock,
and bound in B-grade Arrestox cloth by
Edwards Brothers, Inc.

The paper used in this publication meets the minimum requirements of American National
Standard for Information Sciences—Permanence of Paper for Printed Library Materials, ANSI
Z39.48-1984. ∞

Title page illustration is taken from *Kirsty Knows Best* by Annalena McAfee and illustrated by
Anthony Browne. Illustrations copyright © 1987 by Anthony Browne. Reprinted with permission of Alfred A. Knopf, Inc. and Julia MacRae.

Library of Congress Cataloging-in-Publication Data
Schwarcz, Joseph H.
   The picture book comes of age : looking at childhood through the
art of illustration / by Joseph H. Schwarcz and Chava Schwarcz, with
a foreword by Betsy Hearne.
      p.   cm.
   Includes bibliographical references and indexes.
   ISBN 0-8389-0543-9 (alk. paper)
   1. Illustrated books, Children's—Themes, motives.   2. Illustrated
books—20th century.   I. Schwarcz, Chava.   II. Title.
NC965.S28 1990
741.6′42′09045—dc20   90-37809

Copyright © 1991 by the American Library Association. All rights reserved except those which
may be granted by Sections 107 and 108 of the Copyright Revision Act of 1976.

Printed in the United States of America.

95 94 93 92 91   5 4 3 2 1

Contents

Illustrations

Photograph by Hugo Jehle (1983). Used with permission.

In Memoriam: Joseph H. Schwarcz, 1917–1988

I met Joseph Schwarcz in 1965 through a children's literature course at the University of Chicago. He was on leave from his faculty position at the University of Haifa, where he later became head of the Department of Teacher Training and of the School of Education. Our friendship thrived on passionate discussion of the art and stories forming the 1960s renaissance in children's books, and, later, the innovations of the '70s and '80s. He displayed in class and in conversation the qualities that distinguished all his contributions to the field: original insight into the creative process, thoughtful assessment of artistic and literary effects, a profound respect for childhood, and a scope of interests that crossed national boundaries. His international perspective was hard won. His studies at the University of Vienna were interrupted by the annexation of Austria to the German Reich in 1939, when he emigrated to Israel. During World War II, he served as a counselor at the Youth Aliyah home for special children in Jerusalem, after which he began a career in teaching and teacher training that would span a diverse range of activities on behalf of children, especially those affected by conflict, deprivation, and disability, which he knew firsthand.

Joseph taught for fifty years as if he were born to it. He was wise, humorous, and creative, with a compassionate awareness of the vulnerability and pain of youth and, in more extreme cases, the psychopathology of childhood. He constantly generated new material to refresh his and his students' thinking. His fieldwork and experience with young people forestalled any academic isolation. A list of his inexhaustible work on committees, conferences, and editorial boards would require many pages. A few selective examples include his efforts on behalf of the Society of Christian-Jewish Cooperation in Düsseldorf; the founding of the Internationale Gesellschaft für Polyaesthetische Erziehung in Salzburg; a world congress of the International Society for Education through Art in Sevres; a jury for the Janus Korczak Centennial award for children's art (on behalf of the Holocaust Museum, Kibbutz Lohamey Haggetaot); the Center for Research and Development of Arab Education; a University of Haifa team assisting schools in emergencies resulting from the October war; a symposium on education in special subject areas for culturally deprived youth jointly sponsored by Temple University (Philadelphia) and Haifa University; and a University of Chicago conference on the illustrator as storyteller.

From self-directed investigations as well as formal avenues of scholarship, he derived a belief in art as curative, and his first area of concentration was the analysis of children's paintings and drawings. From there he branched into the exploration of illustration and its relationship to text in the picture book, about which he lectured extensively in Europe, the United States, and the Middle East. Joseph brought a psychological approach to examining the visual structure and subjects of art, but his mode was one of subtle interpretation rather than definitive judgment. His thesis on machine animation in children's book illustration was a turning point in developing his ideas about reading the language of pictures for symbols and signs of environmental aesthetics. His cross-disciplinary methods were innovative, and his emphasis on visual language was especially unusual in the context of a Jewish tradition that has relied on the word rather than on the graphic image. In addition to the metaphorical language of children's book illustration, he addressed other topics, ranging from modern advertising graphics to the educational functions of creative drama and ways of countering stress among children whose self-images are affected by war and handicaps.

Joseph not only published articles in English, Hebrew, and German, but he also viewed as essential the consideration of children's books in those and many other languages in order to avoid ethnocentric bias. His first book, *Ways of the Illustrator: Visual Communication in Children's Literature*, was published by the American Library Association and included in the *Choice* list of outstanding academic books in 1982. Joseph's proposal for *The Picture Book Comes of Age* stated:

> The large number of superior [picture] books being published, the wealth of approaches they reflect, the variety of new styles and techniques being tried out, and the wide range of age groups being addressed offer the opportunity of identifying motifs and themes which reflect the developmental needs of both younger and older children, the dynamics of their inner and outer worlds, and the conditions that circumscribe their existence.

His intention was to

> —contribute to increasing public awareness of the picture book as a potentially powerful medium which relates to children's experience on levels supporting humanistic responsibilities
> —help the adult viewer/reader (parent, librarian, teacher) to explore and evaluate picture books in the context of the child's development
> —encourage the creation and propagation of high-quality picture books treating significant themes.

The original plan included three sections. The first section was to be on the representation of the physical, including chapters on the significance of body language, styles of characterizing the individual, ways of expressing consistency of personality, and facets of human interaction. The second section was to be on the representation of the psychological, with chapters on love and anxiety in the supportive family, coming to terms with familial stress, the search for identity and the quest for autonomy, and existential stress. The third section was to be on the representation of the societal, treating the aesthetic dignity of the environment, the quality of urban life, awareness of special groups in society, the threat of war and the quest for peace, and the hubris of power.

After submitting sections of Parts II and III, Joseph died unexpectedly after a brief illness. Without the guiding hand that shapes and reshapes a book-in-transition to some final form, it seemed presumptuous to determine how he would have proceeded. A series of essays, connected as organically as possible, was the only way to rescue the valuable work he had done. To that end, several contributors deserve special recognition for helping prepare this manuscript. Without Chava Schwarcz's commitment in assembling sections, interpreting notes, selecting illustrations, procuring permissions, and traveling to the United States for consultation, the book could not have become a reality. Tina MacAyeal, the ALA editor involved with the project at the time of Joseph's death, believed in it strongly enough to direct the manuscript through posthumous publication, and Mary Huchting saw it through production. Barbara Duree's sensitive copyediting clarified Joseph's text without changing meanings or intruding on his vision, a time-consuming job that required delicate interpretation. The International Youth Library in Münich, the Max-Planck Institut für Bildungsforschung in Berlin, and the Swiss Institute for Juvenile Literature (Schweizer Jugendbuch Institut) in Zürich offered work havens at crucial points in Joseph's research. Erika von Engelbrechten at IYL and Reinbert Tabbert at the Pedaguogical College in Schwäbischgmünd were especially helpful. Special mention also goes to the illustrators, from Bologna to New York, who held discussions with him about their art.

Thanks to all of these individuals, Joseph's unique perceptions will extend beyond his lifetime.

Betsy Hearne

1

Visual Communication in Picture Books

Before considering the subject of visual communication in children's literature, it is necessary to restate a few generally known facts and observations.

Visual perception is, so scientists assure us, our most important sense. Since the beginning of the species, the perception of shape, color, light, and movement appears to have played a decisive role in the survival and in the biological, psychological, and social development of the human race. Those neurologists, psychologists, and even philosophers who endeavor to ascertain the relative prominence of our various senses speak of a hierarchy of senses and frequently accord the highest place to *visual* perception, mainly because of the wide range of three-dimensional depth and the extraordinary power of differentiation of our eyes.

Two more specific findings concerning the nature and functions of our senses are relevant here. One is the recognition that our sensory perceptors are not merely passive receptors of the input streaming toward them. On the contrary, they actively and almost unceasingly scan and explore the myriad impressions we are continually exposed to, and select from them according to our needs. For our eyes, the scanning covers a few billion messages per second—so they have to work hard to sort out which part of this abundance we shall grasp, either because of the strength of the input or because of its pertinence to our subsistence or to our mental and emotional life. There is a host of psychological and cultural issues attached to these questions of attention and perception. (Let me just note that the obverse side of these conditions is that visual *communication*, as opposed to visual perception, has to strive hard to gain our attention.)

The other finding is this: increasingly, psychologists, especially those

This chapter is an adapted version of the key lecture held at the symposium "Towards Understanding: Children's Literature for all Southern Africa's Children" (July 1987) held at the University of the Western Cape, Capetown. This lecture was published in *Towards Understanding: Children's Literature for Southern Africa* (Capetown: Maskew Miller Longman, 1988), 14–43.

belonging to the school of Gestalt psychology, who investigate the role of art and other complex forms of visual communication are becoming convinced that visual perception is intimately involved with thinking.[1] They postulate that thinking is not solely an abstract or verbal process but that it is tied up with sensory perception. Weismann, one of the prominent researchers on art in this context, offers a simple example to demonstrate the fanning-out influence of visual perception. On principle, he distinguishes among three kinds of seeing: *functional, associative,* and what he calls *pure.*[2] A man is walking along a corridor when a ball suddenly rolls toward him. "Attention!" he thinks, "I'll stumble if I'm not careful." This is an example of *functional* thinking. Another man, the moment the ball rushes in his direction, thinks rather fondly, "Doesn't it bring back the many hours I spent playing ball when I was young?" This is *associative* thinking. A third man would glance at the ball and think, "How gracefully this ball rolls along, like a dancer!" This is *pure* thinking, in Weismann's terms, because it is attentive to the object perceived rather than to the subject who is perceiving. This anecdote shows in a nutshell how our perception affects our mental and emotional life. It also manifests how effective and finely honed an instrument visual perception is. Frequently, if not mostly, visual perception operates on various levels at once. Consider another example: one can look at the sun just as it sets and receive a functional piece of information about the approaching end of the day; this information may immediately be processed into a feeling of joy; it may, in another person, arouse a sense of dissatisfaction with the day's achievements. And it may, at the very same moment, call forth associations with past experiences, with poems, with religious symbols, and so forth.

These examples refer to perceptions of reality. Conditions are not too much different when we turn to pictures, those two-dimensional representations of a three-dimensional world. It is very rare for a picture, any picture, to be no more than the clearly limited and defined representation of the information included in it. (The traffic light is probably the best example of unadulterated, exact information. Yet even changing traffic lights create different feelings in different drivers.) Pictures are never that simple. Their structure, proportions, configurations, colors, angles of lighting, perspective, and many other components hold allusions, associations, and overtones, which may eventually turn into metaphors and symbols expressing points of view;[3] usually even the creators of pictures—whether they be painters, photographers, filmmakers, or children—are not aware of all the possible implications.[4]

1. Rudolf Arnheim, *Visual Thinking* (Berkeley: Univ. of California Pr., 1971); *Art and Visual Perception* (Berkeley: Univ. of California Pr., 1974).

2. Donald L. Weismann, *The Visual Arts as Human Experience* (Englewood Cliffs, N.J.: Prentice-Hall, n.d.).

3. John Berger, *About Looking* (New York: Pantheon, 1985), selected chapters.

4. John Berger, *The Sense of Sight* (New York: Pantheon, 1985), selected chapters; Abraham A. Moles, *Information Theory and Esthetic Perception* (Urbana: Univ. of Illinois Pr., 1968).

This rich fabric of sensory input and the impressions inferred from it—functional, aesthetic, and spiritual—are characteristic of human existence. Our personal lives, our civilizations, and our cultures are based on this fabric. At this point it would be intriguing, and tempting, to pursue a vitally interesting subject, namely, the relationship between the two hemispheres of our brain and their mutual roles. Though many aspects of this relationship still need to be clarified, it seems quite certain that the left hemisphere governs analytical, abstract, logical thinking; the right one, spatial (i.e., visual), inventive, creative, and synthetic thought processes. In other words, in order to safeguard the development of the child's whole personality, we have to ensure a more or less balanced progression of the young person's verbal and sensory, emotional and intellectual capabilities. Although the issue is eminently relevant to our subject, I shall not pursue it further at this point, but shall turn instead to visual communication.

The role of visual communication in human evolution and culture is commensurate with the dominance of visual perception. From the most elementary information to the loftiest ideas expressed in art, from gestures intimating ephemeral moods in interaction with others to headlines screaming at us and advertisements beguiling us, films enchanting us, and TV embracing us, and, yes, children's books attracting us by their playfulness—visual communications, optical illusions, and messages in configurations of shapes and colors surround us, beckon to us, and often practically enwrap us. For well-known reasons, visual transmitters have become, for better or for worse, *the* encompassing, potent communication agents of our era.

Increasingly, then, children in all societies and cultures are being exposed to a barrage of messages that continue to grow in strength, both technologically and economically. Most of these messages, whether crude or sophisticated, whether functional or aesthetic, are intended to entertain or motivate adults, but they radiate brightly toward children as well.

It is here that the importance of the picture in children's literature comes in. Before continuing, however, I have to remove a half-truth embodied in what has just been said. The truth, as we all experience and know it, is that most of the powerful contemporary media usually combine two or more means of communication—visual, verbal, aural, kinetic—in their effort to develop their potential appeals. Words, pictures, sounds, and motion are employed for the creation of complex images, as they have been throughout history. However, technology has intensified the process. The coordination of word and picture, especially, is a mainstay of today's communication. I shall never be able to subscribe to the frequently cited adage about a picture being worth a thousand words. It works the other way 'round, too, at times. It is the combined appearance of words and pictures that counts in so many media. Therefore, from now on when speaking of pictures, I shall be referring to "illustrations," that is, pictures accompanying verbal texts.

Why should pictures be of such prime importance in children's books? From among the many reasons that could be adduced, I wish only to repeat, in this context, two observations made a few minutes ago. First, we should strive to develop the whole range of the child's personality; verbal, abstract, spatial, visual, and other sensory capabilities have to be stimulated, provided for, and guided. Second, because there are so many media around—most of them geared to adults yet exerting much influence on children—it is of supreme concern that we should support media that are specifically created and developed for young people. Among these, the illustrated children's book is no doubt the most vigorous and promising.[5]

When word and picture come together to produce a common work—the illustrated book—it is actually two languages that join forces. The verbal one progresses in linear fashion, with every word, every line, every page coming before or after every other one: this sequential order of the text guarantees comprehension. The picture, on the other hand, is an area, a surface usually representing space, with all its parts and details appearing in front of our eyes simultaneously. There we are at liberty to pick our way, perceive contents and meanings at our discretion, with no prescribed direction. These two different languages are, to some extent, learned spontaneously by experience. But more comprehensive knowledge comes with guidance.

In the thousands of illustrated children's books in existence—with thousands of new ones coming out each year worldwide—text and illustrations combine in so many fashions that it would prove difficult to categorize them. The mutual roles accorded to picture and word are practically unlimited. In the past, a number of basic conceptions existed about how illustrations were to be incorporated into or alongside the text. In the second half of this century, new forms of composition, arrangement, assemblage, and integration have been invented and applied. In the course of this development, the role of the illustration has become continually more variegated and more important. Children's book illustration has for the last few decades been thriving with almost incredible energy. If sixty years ago, illustrators were sometimes ashamed to admit they were doing work for children's books, today's children's illustrator is being recognized as belonging to a new genre of artists whose excellence and inventiveness are comparable to those of persons creatively active in other branches of the visual arts.

Let me be cautious: the processes I have just indicated characterize some countries more than others; but then, in any development, certain forces lead the rest, and in the present case, the international influences exerted are quite strong. One other cautionary remark: there are huge quantities of mediocre, bad, and trashy illustrated children's books around everywhere. But we have to live with this state of affairs. They signify not the end of the world, but rather an opportunity for the beginning of discernment. For it is fortunately also true that there are more and more excellent children's books being published as time goes on.

5. Joseph H. Schwarcz, *Ways of the Illustrator: Visual Communication in Children's Literature* (Chicago: American Library Assn., 1982).

An illustration—whether it be simply decorative, or descriptive in the sense that it repeats what the text tells, or narrative in the sense that it interprets—reaches beyond the text and may even contradict it. Any illustration either interacts with the text or interferes with it. The impact of an illustrated story differs from that of the same story without illustration. Different illustrations for one and the same text result in changed moods and appeals. Also, illustrations of various types mix in the same book; there are very few books that contain only decorative, or descriptive, or narrative illustrations. Besides, illustrations are bound to be perceived in different fashions by different viewers. The illustration is a complex and exciting art form.

To understand the appeal of that form, it is essential to realize that the illustrations in children's books are a *serial* art form. We have to relate to the whole sequence of pictures found in the particular book we are contemplating in order to characterize and evaluate their contribution to the story.

Having come thus far, I propose to focus on what is, to my mind, the most significant phenomenon in the context—the one for which we still have no other term but *picture book*. This kind of book, where text and pictorial narrations accompany each other, alternate, and intertwine, deserves, I believe, close attention. The picture storybook is an irresistible medium. Over a long period, it has persistently, unremittingly continued to overstep the limits set for it by successive definitions and interpretations of its nature. It is in the picture storybook that the two means of expression and communication work together most intimately, to the point where the cooperation and competition of printed word and picture is so essential that one alone is unable to carry out the full intention of the work. The picture storybook adopts every art style in existence. It strives to overcome cultural boundaries and to offer entertainment and enlightenment in a metanational framework.

In the course of its development, the picture book is well on its way to becoming a genuine new art form, one based on combinations and confrontations of verbal narrative texts with series of illustrations in practically unlimited variations of content, context, and style. What is true of any art form also applies here: superior picture books characteristically communicate on diverse aesthetic levels; they employ metaphoric and symbolic expression; their contents can be interpreted in various ways, which may lead to the disclosure of previously concealed meanings or to new meanings acquired over time.

I assume that very few people are still under the impression that the picture storybook exists only for small children. It definitely is of great importance to the very young: it informs them; it makes them laugh and cry. But the picture storybook has grown up, diversified, and improved in creative quality, in variety, and in scope during recent decades. Nowadays, the simplest and sunniest, but also the most serious and complex experiences and themes are being treated in picture books in aesthetically, psychologically, and educationally satisfying fashions. In particular, the countries that have developed the picture book to a high artistic level also commit it to serious motifs and themes. A stage has been reached where significant picture books are being created that are of interest to adults, not only as parents, or in any professional capacity, but as persons open to the influence of the arts. These books embody different appeals, mean different things, and speak in different tongues to young people and to adults.

The picture-book field has also generated a new type of person—the author/artist who creates both the story and the pictures and who is thus in a position to choose *what* to express by *which* technical and stylistic means. The works of such authors/artists contribute a fascinating chapter to the cultural scene of the latter half of the present century.

This "growing up" process of the picture storybook—the extension of its range—is probably less surprising than it seems when one remembers that motion pictures, television, and comics, to mention the most prominent media that adults are involved in, are very akin to the picture book: they, too, are based on the close collaboration, at times even the symbiosis, of picture and word. Just as movies and television reach downward and children form part of their audiences, the picture book pushes upward in the opposite direction. Needless to say, such processes are *one* aspect of changing childhood.

The fact that illustrated children's books are an intriguing field of creativity and at the same time an arena of mass production, that these books are vehicles of entertainment, of enlightenment, and of humanization, does not, of course, make them automatically beneficial. Children's literature is apt to serve all kinds of masters. Alternatively, it can evolve very well without any masters directing it. Therefore, as I use the term *beneficial*, I have in mind "being of benefit in an open society," a society that strives to minimize discrimination and to care for the development of its members. In this context, before considering the desirable versus the undesirable elements of any particular matter concerning children, I must clarify, if very briefly, the model of childhood that guides me and, obviously, the illustrators and picture-book makers whose work I appreciate.

In this model, growing up is a dynamic evolution, in the course of which the child undergoes continual modulations in every conceivable respect. As the organism stretches and young persons go through stages of development, changes take place not only in their physical, emotional, and intellectual powers but also in the textures of their relationships, their terms and conditions of interaction, and their degree of dependence on others. Growing up means enjoying pleasure and laughter and even happiness in being dependent on, and loved by, adults and other children. It also means tension and unrest and anxiety, because it is not easy to live with adults while strengthening one's own need for autonomy and finding one's place in society. Good authors and artists reflect these various facets of childhood on levels comprehensible, consciously or unconsciously, to children; they reflect the perpetual, ever recurring process of seeking a balance between conflict and harmony that the human personality is in need of, a process that lies at the root of literature and the arts.

Having emphasized the growing importance of illustrated children's books and having given my view of the nature of childhood, I shall submit a few opinions on selected aspects of illustration in children's literature, with the intention of underlining what one should nurture and what one should beware of. Far from putting forth a kind of compendium of "do's" and "don'ts," I will emphasize certain general lines of development, drawing on my experience and some familiarity with the children's book scene in a number of countries.

I have already stated that I am ready to accept the fact that mediocre and bad, as well as good, books exist and find their way into the hands of children, mostly through adult mediators. Although on a broad, general basis I abide by that statement, as I delve into specifics, I shall have to revise it in part. The main reason for this revision is that the illustrated children's book, the picture book, is a medium of mass communication, and therefore one of the mass-produced consumer goods. It should not surprise us, then, that the picture book also exhibits a number of the less commendable characteristics of such a medium. A number of these characteristics worry me, particularly because they are likely to be found even in books that are very well executed.

My main complaint, or accusation, is that there exists a surfeit of books which are, in structure, composition, and overall presentation, elaborately repetitive. In examining a sizable sample of books, one becomes convinced that there are certain plots, situations, and constellations and their pictorial representations that are duplicated, reproduced over and over again, with small variations, in any country and language one may think of. "Typical" chains of events and "typical" behavior patterns are reproduced, affirmed, and reaffirmed with exasperating faithfulness. Now I know quite well, as everyone does, that certain attitudes, patterns, and relationships exist that are typical of children at certain age levels, or, rather, stages of development, in certain familiar situations, in specific societal circumstances and frameworks, and so on and so forth. Every simple textbook in developmental or educational psychology will tell us so. Yet, the same textbook will also inform us that individuals will conform only partially to these general patterns and will grow and change in ways slightly, or considerably, differing from their peers. Stories for children should present both the typical and the individual. They should not be turned, as happens too often, into just more reproductions of blueprints.

This typicality troubles me especially in relation to what is called "body language." In too many books, people are represented in unnatural poses in pictures. The expressions of the persons depicted do not change much throughout the book, the body language is over-explicated—that is, gestures are theatrically underscored; the depiction of motion is stiff; hands, arms, and legs are drawn without coordination. Interaction between persons lacks credibility—people frequently do not look at each other, or they relate in other ways while they speak to each other; eyes are void, unconcentrated, forlorn. It is very difficult to draw and paint human beings—but please bear in mind that children learn interaction and body language not only from reality, but from media as well: *we are dealing with the picture as part of the child's social experience.*

The same stereotyping appears in the representation of landscapes, buildings, vehicles, and animals. In leafing through books, one gains an impression of a synthetic, bright world in which puppetlike protagonists act out pseudo-dramas infused with innocent, stereotyped happiness. An overall spirit of easy triviality—"don't be afraid; you will not be required to grapple with really demanding surprises"—reigns, not unlike in the TV serial.

Continuing this line of thought, I want to note two well-known and generally accepted phenomena, being fully aware that I shall thereby cause some brows to be raised.

The first is what I call the Disney School. No doubt Walt Disney was a genius who enriched our century by creating and introducing a whole array of inventions for our entertainment and amusement. Yet I am wary of certain manifestations of his contribution, and especially that of his studio and followers, to the illustration of children's books. Specifically, I refer to two style forms. The first presents children and adults and animals in an idealized form: everybody is beautiful, possessed of glamorous eyelashes, innocent to excess, or else is colorfully, dramatically wicked. Similarly, the background, landscapes, interiors, and objects are precious, dainty, and superclean. It is all synthetically stylish. The other style form is the world of the grotesque, goggle-eyed, silly-mouthed, aggressive, violent creatures who consistently cheat and pursue each other. By now, the Disney School has become entrenched in practically all countries where children's books are produced. It is not at all difficult to understand why these two style modes have become so popular, even apart from the fact that they are easily imitated: synthetic beauty responds to the falsified idealization of childhood that many adults prefer to accept rather than a more complex view. The grotesque creatures, on the other hand, appeal to legitimate aggressive feelings harbored at times by both children and adults. The problem is the banal acting out of these feelings. These styles do not enhance the figures and objects to which they turn their attention. Being rooted in artistic traditions such as Mannerism, Grand Guignol, and Art Nouveau, they offer overstated perfection, at times approaching the hysterical. Even when their moods are gentle, relaxed, and funny, they convey an essentially Manichean message, suggestive of the static, opinionated view that the world of humankind is divided into two camps—one good, one evil. If we were speaking of a few books here and there, there would be no point in mentioning these exaggerations. But their redundancy spans the globe, and their quantity spells influence.

Another kind of book that should be approached with circumspection is the picture story about animals. Yes, I know that animal stories are adored by most of us. I am aware that they are anchored in myth, in folklore, in the fable, and in the parable. I hasten to add that there exists a large number of significant animal picture stories. More than that, I am convinced that children feel close to animals and love them dearly because of their funny, feathery, and furry presence and their abundant kinetic energy, and also because children have little trouble understanding the relatively simple behavior of animals, and, finally, because children can identify with the vulnerability of small animals. So far, so good. And again, some—even quite a lot—of such books would be fine. But stories having an animal, any kind of animal—wild, domesticated, anthropomorphous, stuffed—as their hero, proliferate. In some of those countries that have developed the picture book to a high artistic level, the yearly production of picture books for various age groups includes a third or more of animal stories. That constitutes an overdose. It is partly a case of exploiting an appeal obtained without great effort. Illustrators know facile ways of drawing and painting cute and heartwarming animals. All that is needed is an inventory of not-too-many gestures and expressions, and of textures, and hundreds of redundant adventures can be recapitulated. Why would I think that there is a problem attached to these seemingly harmless stories? The problem lies in the fact that animal heroes are actually put before children as likely objects of identification. Animals are lovely and even serious beings, but in most stories featuring them, their actions, reactions, and thoughts are suitably simple. Let me be precise: I appreciate animals, and certainly fantasy beasts and monsters, as supporting cast—with the child as superior being. However, animals as heroes of stories are, often in a way, kind of one-dimensional human beings. Again we find that the run-of-the-mill stories of this kind support adult illusions of children as uncomplicated persons. I readily agree that animal stories should form part of children's experience; but, as with so many instances referring to psychological and educational considerations, quality and, especially, proportion are the decisive factors. Too many trite cats, dogs, bears, and elephants constitute an exploitation of juvenile susceptibilities.

Yet another issue that concerns me very much is the representation of girls and women in picture stories. I firmly believe in the urgent need for progress toward the equality of women in society. The process is a slow and cumbersome one, even under the best of circumstances. It is interesting, and sad, to note that even in countries that have progressed comparatively far in changing attitudes toward women and their status, picture books still tend to represent women in traditional, secondary roles. When, for example, the text says "Everyone is busy with their work," the picture will show a woman holding a broom; the same is true of girls' pastimes, and more consequentially, girls' roles in the plot and their pictorial representation—usually, girls are less central than boys.

Why should I devote so much time to, why should I bother so intensely and extensively about these stereotypical books and their illustrations? Because they have an unconscionable influence on attitude formation or on the perpetuation of attitudes that should be altered or at least mitigated. The attraction of these books lies in their colorful, frequently satisfactory execution and in the ease with which their plots and their protagonists can be comprehended. Yet, although many responsible adults have an imperative personal need for embracing a simplistic view of childhood, children are neither dolls nor puppets, nor are they angels or fiends or animals. They are, first and foremost and all the time, individual human beings. They do not act and react in undifferentiated fashions and should not be treated in such fashions. Christine Nostlinger, the great Austrian writer for children and youth, once said that as long as children are treated as irresponsible babes, so long will children's literature be considered an irresponsible medium. At the least, children's literature should not lend support to this conception.

The prevalent danger inherent in the genres of the books we are referring to is their power to inculcate stereotypes. By accumulative implication, they convey a sense of prefabricated, didactic uniformity. The American critic Patricia Cianciolo wrote a few years ago that conformity in the illustration is a vice.[6] I should go one step further: when trivial conformity takes over, it turns indoctrinary; it exerts mental pressures. It tends to eliminate ambiguity and open-endedness. It underpins regimentation. It stunts the growth of the individual and does not strengthen progressive attitudes.

Let me attempt to put this idea in perspective: any society educates its young generation toward *common* values, attitudes, and behavior patterns, for society's and the individual's mutual benefit. Formal education systems carry out this responsibility over long periods. Teachers, counselors, librarians, institutions, textbooks, curricula, and methods all serve to realize society's intentions. It is a difficult task, which can succeed only if much dedication, planning, and work are invested in the undertaking. Even so, to this day no existing educational system has been able to solve the dilemma of how to balance two basic objectives—to prepare young persons for their future social roles and at the same time to ensure individual growth. As often as not, the common, the typical, the general take precedence. Maybe this is as it should be.

Yet, given these conditions, I propose that we should refrain from conceiving of children's literature and its visual communications as being mainly another agent of *formal* education. We should accept it as a specific,

6. Patricia Cianciolo, *Illustrations in Children's Books* (Dubuque, Ia.: Brown, 1974).

open-ended art form, though one definitely connected to psychological concepts and educational values. If this sounds like tightrope walking, that is the impression I wish to convey.

These observations confront us with the question of *what, then, are the aspects of the illustrated book to be encouraged and stimulated?*

Good picture books should embody one or more of the following concepts:

Entertainment Value. Whatever the age range to which a book wishes to appeal, it should be able to attract and satisfy its audience with a certain vividness, even if the subject is weighty. Children have a right, as have adults, to be amused. Playing with words, shapes, colors, and compositions, not to speak of varied plots, and mixing reality with fantasy create opportunities for a smile, for a humorous intermezzo; tension can be relaxed and attention regained by arousing curiosity, by building up surprise.

Meaningful Human Interest. Whatever the framework—realistic or fantastic, epic or dramatic, and so on—characterization should be lively. As far as the ingenuity of authors and artists reaches, persons appearing in picture stories should have some of the diversity of living human beings. Whether the events represented and the persons experiencing them be simple or complex, whether the text and pictures be easily grasped or hard to comprehend, the way these persons act and speak and look should have a ring of sincerity. The story should have some real human interest and human concern, some warmth and criticism, too, originating in an authentic involvement with children and their world, with their joys and their pangs of anxiety, their relationships with adults and their groping search for meaning in life. Whether the plots, relationships, and developments narrated and represented are lifelike or surrealistic, pedestrian or hair-raising, they should not be employed to teach preconceived notions, but rather to demonstrate open-ended experiences. The accumulated impact of scores of picture books should lie in aiding their audiences to discern the interplay and the blend of confidence and insecurity, of failure and achievement, of conflict and harmony that make up human existence.

Societal Significance. My demand for a sincerely felt, imaginative depiction of body language and of interactions and relationships also applies, of course, to the social plane. This kind of depiction should start with books for the very young. In this context, the picture provides, at all age levels, the opportunity to widen children's horizons and to guide them toward deeper comprehension of the facets of social relationships and the intricacies of the social scene. These endeavors will succeed well if they are structured and executed in ways that will aid children to develop, through empathy with protagonists, elements of their own identity and future potential social roles, and to appreciate the viewpoints of other people. Word and picture can lead children from *dialectic* attitudes, which justify only one opinion, toward *dialogic* attitudes, which admit and accommodate several points of view; for dialogic attitudes are closer to the nature of human growth.[7]

It is important to note that for older children and teenagers, picture stories dedicated to social issues are published in an increasing number of countries. I have been working on articles about books treating questions such as the vicissitudes of contemporary urban life, social action by children for disadvantaged groups in society, and the quest for peace and the threat of war. These books arouse response by convincingly communicating their messages. With few exceptions, they reflect social issues in children's experiences. Thus, young people may be aided (it is always a matter of potential impact; nothing is ever guaranteed) to open up their personalities to the complex societal realities surrounding them; to recognize other persons, other groups and strata, other people and cultures; and to involve themselves—in their imaginations, for the time being—with concepts of social action.

Aesthetic Appeal. What we need in picture books is not only quality, but also variety. Any style of narration—realistic, fantastic, utopian, satiric—is welcome. Similarly, the whole range of styles found in modern art—realistic, expressionist, fantastic, surrealistic, satiric, even abstract—is used and should be willingly accepted. No style is preferable to any other. It is a fallacy to believe that because so many people prefer realism, it is more desirable or effective than other modes of writing or painting. Even communist countries have long ago abandoned their insistence on realism in art for children, and the whole treasure chest of contemporary art has been opened up there, as everywhere.

If and when children are able to encounter a few grains of any of these four ingredients—entertainment value, meaningful human interest, societal significance, and aesthetic appeal—in a sizable percentage of their picture books, the educational aspects will take care of themselves. Variation and individualization will outdo stereotyping and indoctrination.

Having outlined the more commendable and the less admirable fashions and models of the picture book, I have to make one point clear: I consistently aim at intensifying awareness, enhancing knowledge, and encouraging guidance—and never would I advise the use of censorship. In any form, censorship is an unworthy instrument of control. Also, in my experience, it backfires in the long run. It is preferable to have "bad" books around and let them be contested by the better ones. When the exemplary works cannot be contrasted with the inferior, they are in danger of becoming boring. The task lying ahead for all of us is to modify the public's taste, not to limit the audience's choices. And do not forget that censorship has a way of patronizing the mediocre, because it is safer than the excellent.

7. Heinz S. Herzka, *Play as a Way of Dialogical Development* (Leiden, Netherlands: Postacademisch Onderwijs Sociale Wetensschappen, n.d.); "The Dialogics of a Doctor-Patient Relationship" in *Doctor-Patient Interaction,* ed. Walburga von Raffler-Engel (Amsterdam and Philadelphia: John Benjamins Pub., 1989), 159–80.

Guidance, to be sure, needs patience and strong nerves. Yet several instruments can be conceived and developed to further the cause of quality and intelligent approaches. Certainly, in our efforts at evaluating stories and pictures for children, we shall never be able effectively to separate our aesthetic, literary, and artistic measures from our educational ones. Nor should we. However, we should only hesitatingly let our educational opinions get the better of our aesthetic judgment. *The attempt to turn children's literature into an engaged agent of progress without turning it into a propaganda tool means coping with a complex array of checks and balances.* We have to nurture the child's experience without trimming it too much. Let us not treat children's literature as a well-kept garden, thus robbing it of its nature as a windswept field.

2

A Close Look at a Picture Book

One must take a close look in order to discover what can be found in, and culled from, a picture book. Further, the careful scrutiny of one particular book will aid in the analysis of others. To serve as a paradigm illustrating the use of such an approach, I have chosen E. J. Keats's *Whistle for Willie*,[1] which came out in 1964 and has, I believe, stood up well to aging, with the possible exception of some of the social aspects hinted at.[2]

In this story, little Peter frets because he has a dog, Willie, whom he cannot call because he does not know how to whistle. Peter attempts again and again to whistle, and with every failed attempt, his dismay grows. But he tries all the more, and, in the end, a real whistle suddenly comes out. The proud boy parades his skill before his father and mother. That is all: it is a very short story relating what is apparently a slight matter. Yet when we dwell upon the book, our impressions expand. First, we may notice that Keats the author has accompanied his concise, sober text with illustrations, created in luminous, persuasive colors that alternate between glowing and subdued hues, and executed in a mixed technique of gouache and collage. We can see that Keats the artist has combined components selected from three art styles. For persons and some objects, he employs a stylized realism, with body language strongly emphasized. Expressionistic elements, such as the traffic lights or the boy's oversized face when he whistles to show his admiring parents, appear when Peter gets excited. Semi-abstract features characterize the background—rather large color areas reminiscent of Matisse. No doubt, the pictures dramatize the story far beyond the calm, verbal recitation. The illustrations dominate; they cover the whole page, and the text is placed within their confines, at the convenience of their contents and structures. Why does Keats choose to lavish such glowingly dramatic colors on a simply told, amusing experience? Well, the story may not be so simple, nor merely amusing.

Let us make use of what could be called "a diagram of emotional states"

1. Ezra Jack Keats, *Whistle for Willie* (New York: Viking, 1964).
2. Compare Schwarcz, *Ways of the Illustrator*, 183–84.

in order to visualize what goes on in Peter's mind. The horizontal line stands for emotional balance, or evenness; the curve indicates Peter's fluctuating moods. At the beginning, Peter is moody because he cannot whistle. When he sees another boy whistling, he gathers courage and tries, but nothing happens; his mood sinks lower, and he starts turning around and around. As Willie appears, Peter hopes and tries, with no result, and his disappointment grows. As he walks home and reaches his own doorstep, hope returns, and two more attempts follow, but still no whistle emerges. Now Peter feels really low when Willie comes. With his fifth try, Peter succeeds and feels "high." We understand that the boy must have spent some quite agonizing hours, with the intervals between his attempts seeming longer and his frustration deepening, until his determination prevails.

Following up these preliminary observations, we should be able to discover, using a step-by-step, page-by-page analysis, how Keats communicated this chain of events and what he wished to accomplish. On the first double page, Peter leans against the traffic post at a despondent angle. The houses on the far side of the road are abstract rectangles; on the nearby wall, the bricks appear from beneath the crumbling plaster; yet while this crumbling, in fact, signifies deterioration, the wall is strikingly illuminated. The opening sentence, "Oh, how Peter wished he could whistle," rests in the center of a crimson space. In the second picture, the boy on the far side who whistles for his dog stings Peter into action. After his first failure, Peter withdraws into acting out, trying to get dizzy; the houses along the street retreat, and the horizon widens under a billowing yellow sky. In the following picture, Peter becomes more intoxicated; the lights fly out, and the street starts spinning around (fig. 1). Dizziness seems to liberate Peter and to give him new strength.

So, in the fourth picture, when Willie comes, Peter hides in a carton and

Fig. 1. Ezra Jack Keats, *Whistle for Willie*
From *Whistle for Willie*. Copyright © 1964 by Ezra Jack Keats. Reprinted by permission of Viking Penguin, a division of Penguin Books U.S.A. Inc., and The Bodley Head

tries whistling again. Peter's failure is borne out by Willie's diffident walk away and by the background becoming even more abstract—all large rectangles in subdued colors. The fifth picture glows again in a rather melancholy violet and deep orange, while in the next one, as Peter approaches his house, the colors and objects are more realistic. In these two illustrations, Peter does not appear at all; only the chalk line indicates the path he takes. The line tells us that he walks haltingly; it seems that he wants to be home and safe but does not relish the thought of arriving there without being able to whistle. Following the line very closely, we detect what goes on in his mind. The line functions as a defense mechanism; drawing it binds anxiety and gives Peter time to master his feelings, to daydream, and to think things over. At first, the line wobbles, hesitant; gaining strength, it continues straight ahead; but some residual hesitancy is expressed by the changing colors when Peter picks out more pieces of chalk. He is encouraged and even dares to draw circles around two girls and the signpost in front of the barbershop. As he approaches his house, the line tells us that Peter is undecided once more—the line slows down, wobbles; loops appear, and Peter exchanges his colors even more frequently, to gain time, to gain inner conviction. Arriving at his door, he straightens up and blows and blows—to no effect.

Yet this time he does not turn away immediately—is it the safety offered by home, or the strength gathered on the long walk home? When, in the seventh picture, he puts on his father's hat as a magical act of identification—one that should make him feel more grown up and skilled—the act does not work. However, when his mother sees him, she gently plays his game, barely stifling her smile, and Peter still has the courage to pretend that he is his father setting out to look for his son.

Once he is outside (leaving behind him the tranquility of the flowery wallpaper), frustration takes over. Peter is deeply dissatisfied with himself. In the eighth picture, he retreats into an intense daydream that the artist lights up with luminous colors, though it takes place on a sidewalk running along a dilapidated wall smeared and scratched and covered with graffiti. Peter walks along a crack, employing another ubiquitous defense mechanism whose purpose is to bind anxiety and especially auto-aggressive feelings (by stepping on or avoiding a crack, one avoids a possibly dangerous outbreak of one's own aggression: "If you step on a crack / you'll break your mother's back"). Yet, as we see Peter walk down the sidewalk some time later, anxiety overpowers him, and walking along the crack is not a strong enough device to escape this feeling (fig. 2). On the wall he sees his shadow (the age-old symbol of the uncanny aspects of one's personality); he is scared, tries to run away from it, even jumps off his shadow—and the following scene shows what a vigorous jump it is, how fed up he is with himself, and how much energy he has stored up. But now the quieter colors of the ninth and tenth pictures lead Peter toward the turning point, back to the street corner of his first failure.

First he walked along a crack in the sidewalk.
Then he tried to run away from his shadow.

Fig. 2. Ezra Jack Keats, *Whistle for Willie*
From *Whistle for Willie*. Copyright © 1964 by Ezra Jack Keats. Reprinted by permission of Viking Penguin, a division of Penguin Books U.S.A. Inc., and The Bodley Head

The carton is still there. Willie approaches (against that abstract, moody, undecided background of the tenth picture), Peter dares, and this time a whistle comes out. In the eleventh picture, a happy Peter demonstrates his achievement to his admiring parents and an attentive Willie. The final picture of Peter and his dog returning from the grocery store unifies the story. The first picture showed Peter and the traffic lights on the left-hand side, with Peter leaning to the left; while in the last one, the wall is on the left, and Peter strides toward the traffic lights on the far right. Many psychologists consider an orientation toward the left in visual messages an expression of withdrawal or introversion, and movement to the right a representation of outward direction.

Whistle for Willie is a well-wrought story. Its surface structure is based on clear verbal and visual rhythms, seemingly innocent of complexities. On a deeper level, the story touchingly demonstrates the way in which psychological processes can be expressed verbally and visually; feelings, moods, thoughts, and attitudes take narrative and iconic shape. The book also demonstrates a very satisfying interaction between text and illustration.

Psychologically, we are told that circumstances demand an achievement of Peter. When it is not realized, stress sets in because of competitiveness (with reference to the other boys) and shame (with reference to the parents and to Willie). Failure generates anxiety. But early in this sequence of inner developments, adaptive responses arise—both imaginary and real activity, and both "fight" and "flight," as researchers on stress term this latter behavior. In the end, Peter wins out. All this might appear to be a small matter in adult eyes, but not so in a child's. The story also relates a threefold learning process reinforcing self-confidence—experiences leading toward success in mastering a skill, in applying assertive behavior, and in the use of imagination to gain strength for influencing reality.

Considering the aesthetic elements and structures, we should note that throughout the story, we, the audience, are never told exactly what goes on in Peter's imagination. We are only shown the outer symptoms and their mechanisms—the traffic lights, the chalk line, the hat, the crack, the shadow, and so forth—behind which Peter's imagination reinforces him to a point where he is able to return to action.

The precise, dry verbal account, heightened by few punctuation marks, is void of metaphors. On the other hand, visual metaphors follow one another. In creating them and entrusting them with the story's essence, Keats cuts across his own style forms. Starting with the crimson backdrop for Peter's initial exclamation, the backgrounds form a *semi-abstract* extended metaphor for the evolving human affective phases, with the oversized wallpapers complementing this function. The traffic lights flying out and away are an *expressionistic* metaphor—objects reflecting what goes on inside a person—for Peter's vertiginous spinning around. The utterly *realistic* chalk line turns out to be a double metaphor: it stands for the boy's progression in space and time; at the same time, it serves as a projective drawing encoding the psychodynamic aspect of his walk. The blowup of Peter's vigorously blowing cheeks is, in the context of that picture, an expressionistic rendering of his happiness, but the face is painted with warm, realistic exactitude. We realize that these are metaphors as we become aware—*if* we become aware—of the difference in the functions they fulfill and discover which of the functions they fulfill more satisfactorily. The backgrounds scarcely depict streets and buildings. They are not "literal" and not "figurative"; they undergo constant changes in size, position, and color. They barely signify streets and buildings, and they do so only because some of their shapes remind us of houses, sidewalks, etc., relative to Peter's and Willie's movements and on the basis of our own past experience. Their color schemes offer psychological connotations, for whose meaningfulness we are biologically and culturally conditioned: red might mean, . . . gray and mauve might mean, . . . and although peeling plaster and graffiti hint at a neglected area, the shining bricks and the colorful walls tell us that in Peter's experience, this is the setting for his activities, where his daydreams and his excitement happen. Or consider the traffic lights. Ordinarily they represent order, unequivocal orientation. Here they serve as a representation of Peter's wish and efforts to become giddy, to lose balance. Or the chalk line: it certainly serves as a representation of Peter's movements. Had Keats wished to leave it at that, he would not have excluded the boy from those two pictures. He would have shown him several times, expressing his internal and external oscillations by the same forceful use of body language applied throughout the book. As it is, in addition to the literal function of representing the traces Peter has left on the sidewalk, the line assumes the function of standing for Peter, of being a metaphor of body language and also a metaphor of the motivation for these gyrating traces. Then, Peter's head and face, in that moment of joy, are the kind of metaphor called "pars pro toto" (a part standing for the whole); the accent is on the lips and cheeks that produced the whistle, on the chest where the air for the whistle came from, and on the ears that listened and proved that it is true—the rest of him is negligible; and so, boundless pride and admiration can meet at a suitable angle.

How many words did Keats the author save by preferring to express these events and processes through visual metaphors; how much more condensed, and surprising, are the metaphors that express these ideas; how much joy does their charm provide, as we start guessing their intention, their meaning! It says much for Keats's intuitive wisdom that, balancing the metaphorical wealth, he represents the three magic actions (putting on father's hat, walking along the crack, and jumping off Peter's shadow) in the simplest way possible.

The overall narrative continuity is sustained mainly by the rich tapestry of backgrounds whose shifting and recurring geometrical configurations achieve the unifying effect of scenery. The other form of continuity is provided by the lively, highly dynamic portraits of the boy, who weaves in and out of these backgrounds.

For children, this is a fine story, acquainting them with a quick, inventive, assertive boy who believes in himself. He may fail and be quite sad for a while, or furious at himself. Yet, he takes up the challenge and stays with it; he knows how to achieve his purpose by acting and reacting, in his imagination and in the environment, led by a sense of basic trust and a need for achievement. The story both amuses and instructs. Many children will not, and need not, become aware of the complexities it harbors. In the minds of many others, some of its ideas, its visual beauty, and its advice to children will crystallize and sink in over time by way of empathy with Peter.

Although we will never be able to resolve the question of how much intuition and how much conscious awareness of psychological issues went into its creation, this book is one of the earliest picture books to treat stress meaningfully.

Because of the story's human appeal, the pleasant quality of its design, the significance of its structures, and the variety of motifs it touches upon, it is also an early instance of that emerging phenomenon—the picture book that has something to say to the adult, aesthetically, psychologically, and educationally.

CHILDREN'S BOOK CITED

KEATS, EZRA JACK. *Whistle for Willie.* New York: Viking, 1964.

3

Stress and the Picture Book

Themes of stress and anxiety have increasingly appeared in picture books published during the last few decades. These stories are child-appropriate, entertaining, fictional experiences that present the child with situations and processes reflecting aspects of stress and anxiety and ways of responding, acting out, and coping with stress problems, usually leading toward successful solutions. The books are created by authors and artists who know something about the way in which children attempt to master the realities of their lives, as Sendak once put it.

We have to establish immediately that in this view stress is not a "dirty" word. It is not a concept referring to states that children should not know about, to matters not to be brought up in their presence or in conversations with them, and, therefore, not to be treated in children's literature, in order to leave unclouded the assumption that childhood is a predominantly carefree time. Such notions are still prevalent, especially in the wishful thinking of adults. Certainly, childhood is often a very happy period, but it is never carefree. Stress is one of the conditions of our lives. For children, it is one of the conditions of growing up. It is one of the natural reactions of our minds and bodies, of our whole organism, to feelings of inadequacy when we are unable to meet demands made on us by others or self-imposed demands, or when people in our environment do not accept us as we are, and, in consequence, we can neither accept ourselves nor the people and conditions in our environment as they are. The reactions to stress can take the form of mild emotional unrest, or they may create an upheaval that violently grips mind and body. Stress creates a need for adaptive behavior, for activities performed in reality and in fantasy, activities whose purpose is to restore our self-confidence, or at least to reduce the imbalance we find ourselves in.

Children's bodies and minds continually grow and change and are prone to developmental and existential stresses. These can be defined as responses, partly conscious and partly unconscious, to situations and processes occurring in the normal course of life, whether originating in internal, organismic stimuli, or arising from external pressures usually emanating in the close environment. Feelings of inadequacy can come from many directions and take many forms—a sense of failure, of frustration, of worry, of loss of love, or of a crisis imminent or already acutely experienced. The symptoms are tension and anxiety. They trigger adaptive, more or less desirable and effective responses, such as a retreat into passivity, alienation, a craving for love, aggressive behavior, assertion, and others. In the course of trying to minimize their psychological imbalance, children often interchange and vary their conscious and unconscious strategies for escaping anxiety. They are motivated in this effort by their feelings about and observations of their own changing moods, and those of the environment. The child's world contains characteristic and powerful stressors, such as those arising from family relationships, from illness, and from death. Stress factors found in society include achievement demands; peer-group constellations; alienating circumstances in social, especially urban, living conditions; and war. However, we should not forget that a number of essential stress factors are inherent in the child's maturing personality: the child who has an intense need to be loved and cared for, to be close to "someone who loves him most of all,"[1] to be sheltered, and to be dependent also insists on experiencing adventure and danger, and wishes to become independent. The natural search for identity and the necessary quest for autonomy, the experience of discovering oneself and one's own powers, create conflicts and tensions necessary for growth.

A degree of stress is, therefore, an inevitable, inescapable condition of human existence, embodying essential developmental stimuli. Yet stress also entails manifold human suffering that has to be noticed and aided and, as far as possible and advisable, relieved or at least alleviated. Providing this supportive concern, among other things, is what loving a child means. Temporary stress situations and stress processes are necessary. However, an overload of recurring stress situations or chronic stress is a burden that stifles mental and physical health. Such a burden detracts from that measure of happiness which is the child's birthright.

Some stress factors appear in a child's life suddenly and harshly, as in dramatic crises. Other stressors operate quietly and persistently. The latter are frequently more significant, one reason being that they may last longer, and another, that children are unable or unwilling to articulate problems. They adapt, for better or for worse, by acting or acting out, or by dreaming and daydreaming. Adults become aware of such symptoms rather than of the underlying reasons and motifs, mainly because adaptive responses to stress differ greatly from one child to another. The stress response to the impact of stressors is a nonspecific one. Adults are often motivated to react to the symptoms—to punish, to threaten a loss of love, and even to add new demands.

This is the situation in which play, daydreaming, dreams, artwork, and

---

1. Maurice Sendak, *Where the Wild Things Are* (New York: Harper, 1963).

other creative activities have a role, as do films, books, and picture books: these media help by generating symbolic communication from and toward the child.

Remarkable writers and artists working in the field of picture books are continually enlarging the scope and variety of themes and motifs and are producing books of great artistic distinction. The aesthetic quality and psychological subtlety of these storybooks call for attention, because they give genuine expression to the child's conscious and unconscious thoughts and emotions. The illustrator and, particularly, the author-illustrator present with great symbolic force unconscious processes only hinted at in the text. True, this approach is not so new, since literature and the arts have for a long time proffered topics, metaphors, and symbols for the growing child's experiences. The innovation lies in the maturation of the picture book as a serious medium of communication, one that has taken on humanistic responsibilities.

Many authors and illustrators treat themes of stress and anxiety and present children with imaginative ways of working out their own problems. These authors use various genres to get their visual and verbal messages across to the child. For instance, there are many versions of the classical fairy tale with modern pictures, such as Luděk Maňásek's,[2] Mercer Mayer's[3] and Binette Schroeder's[4] illustrations for *Beauty and the Beast* (fig. 3); various editions of Grimm's fairy tales[5]; the genre of the contemporary fairy tale, such as Sendak's *Outside Over There*,[6] Van Allsburg's books (fig. 4),[7] and Herzka's *Do in den roten Stiefeln*[8]; the genre of the realistic story—for instance, Keats's Peter stories[9] and Isadora's *Ben's Trumpet*[10]; the magic-realistic story, where reality and fantasy both clash and intertwine, as in Burningham's Shirley books,[11]

2. J. M. Leprince de Beaumont, *La belle et la bête*, illus. Luděk Maňásek (Prague: Artia, 1969).

3. Marianna Mayer, *Beauty and the Beast* (retold), illus. Mercer Mayer (New York: Four Winds Pr., 1978).

4. J. M. Leprince de Beaumont, *Beauty and the Beast*, illus. Binette Schroeder (London: Walker, 1986).

5. Jakob Grimm and Wilhelm Grimm, *Dornröschen*, illus. Felix Hoffmann (Aarau and Frankfurt: Sauerländer, 1959); *Der Däumling*, illus. Felix Hoffmann (Aarau and Frankfurt: Sauerländer, 1972); *Hundertundein Grimm-Märchen*, illus. Felix Hoffmann (Aarau, Frankfurt, and Salzburg: Sauerländer, 1985); *Dornröschen*, illus. Bernadette (Mönchaltorf and Hamburg: Nord-Süd Verlag, 1984). *Frau Holle*, illus. Bernadette (Mönchaltorf and Hamburg: Nord-Süd Verlag, 1985); *Schneewitchen (Snow White)*, illus. Bernadette (Mönchaltorf and Hamburg: Nord-Süd Verlag, 1989).

6. Maurice Sendak, *Outside Over There* (New York: Harper, 1981).

7. Chris Van Allsburg, *The Garden of Abdul Gazazi* (Boston: Houghton, 1979); *Jumanji* (Boston: Houghton, 1981).

8. Heinz Herzka, *Do in den roten Stiefeln (Do in the Red Boots)*, illus. Heiri Steiner (Zürich and Stuttgart: Artemis, 1969).

9. For instance, Ezra Jack Keats, *The Snowy Day* (New York: Viking, 1962); *Whistle for Willie; Peter's Chair* (New York: Harper, 1967).

10. Rachel Isadora, *Ben's Trumpet* (New York: Greenwillow, 1979).

11. John Burningham, *Come Away from the Water, Shirley* (London: Jonathan Cape, 1977); *Time to Get Out of the Bath, Shirley* (London: Jonathan Cape, 1978).

Fig. 3. Binette Schroeder, *Beauty and the Beast*

Binette Schroeder, *Beauty and the Beast*, by Mme. Leprince de Beaumont & Binette Schroeder © Ill. by Binette Schroeder 1986. London; Walker Books Ltd., 1986

Fig. 4. Chris Van Allsburg, *Jumanji*

Illustration from *Jumanji* by Chris Van Allsburg. Copyright © 1981 by Chris Van Allsburg. Reprinted by permission of Houghton Mifflin Co.

Viorst's book about the little boy who sees monsters,[12] and Schindler's book *Sleep Well, Have Pleasant Dreams*[13]; and classical stories, such as *Alice in Wonderland*, with modern pictures (fig. 5).[14] A comprehensive compendium attempting to list books dealing with stress exists. I believe that this compendium is very valuable for parents, teachers, librarians, counselors, and social workers. It indexes more than 450 psychological topics and briefly annotates 1,031 books, many of them picture books, relevant to those topics. It includes books published up to 1975. The stream of books that has appeared since then has caused two additional volumes to be compiled and published in 1981 and 1985, respectively.[15]

Over and above offering quality, such books demonstrate the courage and the high measure of involvement (with, not infrequently, a personal need) exhibited by their creators in taking up sensitive, difficult, irritating, passionate, and sometimes shocking themes, and executing them pleasurably. Thus, the authors and illustrators make children smile and think things over; suggest to them new avenues of amusing, often humorous entertainment; and encourage them to entertain new ideas in support of their own imaginary and concrete efforts to improve or even master their inner and outer realities. On the surface, these books deliver beauty, surprise, fun, adventure, and drama; on a deeper level, they illustrate—in words and pictures, and in metaphors and symbols—another form of drama for the workings of the child's unconscious. Providing appeals on each level in different ways, these stories endeavor to embolden children to experience vicariously, and to learn what stress may mean and how it can be dealt with—for instance, these picture books show that other children have to stand up to stress, too. Moreover, and probably most importantly, many of these books earnestly strive to lead children and adults toward understanding, either intuitively or cognitively, how other stressed children mobilize their physical and mental defenses and powers and succeed in turning tension and anxiety into growth stimuli, into impulses propelling them toward self-confidence.

Most, though not all, such books are superior examples of a growing, diversifying, lively, and, in the cultural context, daring trend. Many focus children's attention on a specific motif. The protagonists manifest a twofold, often alternating response to stress—they retreat into fantasy and, having gained strength, assert themselves by advancing into activity, both imagi-

---

12. Judith Viorst, *My Mama Says There Aren't Any Zombies, Ghosts, Vampires, Creatures, Demons, Monsters, Fiends, Goblins, or Things*, illus. Kay Chorao (New York: Atheneum, 1973).

13. Edith Schindler, *Schlaf gut, Träum schön (Sleep Well, Have Pleasant Dreams)* (Ravensburg, Germany: Otto Maier, 1982).

14. Lewis Carroll, *Alice's Adventures in Wonderland and Through the Looking Glass*, illus. Markéta Prachatická (Chicago: Wellington, 1989; originally published in Prague: Albatros, 1982).

15. Sharon Spredemann Dreyer, *The Bookfinder: A Guide to Children's Literature about the Needs and Problems of Youth, Ages 2–15*, 3 vols. (Circle Pines, Mich.: American Guidance Service, 1977, 1981, 1985).

Fig. 5. Markéta Prachatická, *Alice's Adventures in Wonderland and Through the Looking Glass*
Markéta Prachatická from *Alice's Adventures in Wonderland and Through the Looking Glass* by Lewis Carroll. Ill. © 1982 Markéta Prachatická. By permission of Wellington Publishing 1989. Originally published Prague, Albatros, 1982.

nary and real. This is the road along which these stories wish to lead children toward success in overcoming stress and growing up a little.

It is fair to state that this trend was initiated with Sendak's *Where the Wild Things Are* (1963).[16] The story has been so extensively researched and evaluated that there seems to be no need to go into detail here. Let us simply note that it was *Where the Wild Things Are* which, more than any other book, put on the agenda of picture books unfamiliar, somewhat uncomfortable, and yet irrevocably compelling ideas on how much goes on

16. Sendak, *Where the Wild Things Are*.

in the minds of children that we will never (maybe should never) know, on the importance of a retreat into fantasy, and on the extent to which children are able to help themselves. Let us remember, too, that Sendak's was practically the first major book to represent, so outspokenly and continuously, psychodynamic processes by aesthetic means and to achieve perfect execution of that aim. It took adults by surprise, which is astonishing, considering that the story translated psychodynamic concepts and strategies that depth psychology had known and revealed for two generations. Yet, art can convince where research may not reach.

CHILDREN'S BOOKS CITED

BURNINGHAM, JOHN. *Come Away from the Water, Shirley*. London: Jonathan Cape, 1977.

——. *Time to Get Out of the Bath, Shirley*. London: Jonathan Cape, 1978.

CARROLL, LEWIS. *Alice's Adventures in Wonderland and Through the Looking Glass*. Illus. Markéta Prachatická. Chicago: Wellington, 1989. orig. Prague: Albatros, 1982.

DE BEAUMONT, J. M. LEPRINCE. *Beauty and the Beast*. Illus. Binette Schroeder. London: Walker, 1986.

——. *La belle et la bête*. Illus. Luděk Maňásek. Prague: Artia, 1969.

GRIMM, JAKOB AND WILHELM GRIMM. *Der Däumling*. Illus. Felix Hoffmann. Aarau and Frankfurt: Sauerländer, 1972.

——. *Dornröschen (The Sleeping Beauty)*. Illus. Bernadette. Mönchaltorf and Hamburg: Nord-Süd Verlag, 1984.

——. *Dornröschen (The Sleeping Beauty)*. Illus. Felix Hoffmann. Aarau and Frankfurt: Sauerländer, 1959.

——. *Frau Holle*. Illus. Bernadette. Mönchaltorf and Hamburg: Nord-Süd Verlag, 1985.

——. *Hundertundein Grimm-Märchen*. Illus. Felix Hoffmann. Aarau, Frankfurt and Salzburg: Sauerländer, 1985.

——. *Schneewittchen (Snow White)*. Illus. Bernadette. Mönchaltorf and Hamburg: Nord-Süd Verlag, 1989.

HERZKA, HEINZ. *Do in den roten Stiefeln (Do in the Red Boots)*. Illus. Heiri Steiner. Zürich und Stuttgart: Artemis, 1969.

ISADORA, RACHEL. *Ben's Trumpet*. New York: Greenwillow, 1979.

KEATS, EZRA JACK. *Peter's Chair*. New York: Harper, 1967.

——. *The Snowy Day*. New York: Viking, 1962.

——. *Whistle for Willie*. New York: Viking, 1964.

MAYER, MARIANNA. *Beauty and the Beast* (retold). Illus. Mercer Mayer. New York: Four Winds Pr., 1978.

SCHINDLER, EDITH. *Schlaf gut, Träum schön (Sleep Well, Have Pleasant Dreams)*. Ravensburg, Germany: Otto Maier, 1982.

SENDAK, MAURICE. *Outside Over There*. New York: Harper, 1981.

——. *Where the Wild Things Are*. New York: Harper, 1963.

VAN ALLSBURG, CHRIS. *The Garden of Abdul Gazazi*. Boston: Houghton, 1979.

——. *Jumanji*. Boston: Houghton, 1981.

VIORST, JUDITH. *My Mama Says There Aren't Any Zombies, Ghosts, Vampires, Creatures, Demons, Monsters, Fiends, Goblins, or Things*. Illus. Kay Chorao. New York: Atheneum, 1973.

4

Love and Anxiety in the Supportive Family

How do children find out that their parents love them? Is it not much easier to become aware that someone does not love you? How do parents instill in their children the belief that they support them, and that they support them because they love them? To guide us as we look at picture books and attempt to respond to what we find there, what we need in approaching these questions is not an incisive treatment of the issue, which has to be left to the psychologists, but a brief clarification of concepts. How do parents extend support? When we ask them, they tend to say, by offering security, by helping the child to develop a feeling of trust that in any circumstances he or she will be cared for and loved. Counselors and psychologists will probably stress that children have a strong need to be accepted as they are; these experts will suggest that parents should be sparing in temporarily withdrawing love from their children, for whatever reason, because a loss of love hurts children much more strongly than adults assume. Most sensible adults know that children respond favorably to their parents' strong but not pushy attention to their children's interests and achievements. Children also need their parents' sympathy and understanding when confronted with failure. They want praise, and they long for protection in situations causing them hardship. They ask in many overt and covert ways to be assisted in coping with the anxieties rising within them from a hundred sources and reasons, and not to have them explained away. The main source of anxiety is that as children continue to develop, they have to adjust to the changes in themselves and in the outer world.

When the question "How can you find out that your parents love you?" is put to children, the answers are naturally more tangible. When someone loves you, say children, they hold you; they caress you; they look at you in a way that shows their feelings; they talk to you, kindly or sternly, but they take the time to talk to you; when they care for you, they will notice that you want to be encouraged or comforted; they make you believe you can count on them. Smaller children will say "being spoiled" makes you feel loved, and "chocolates" and "when they buy toys." One girl said, "My dad sometimes writes 'I love you' on a slip of paper, and then I feel good." And again and again, being kissed, being caressed, being embraced. Contact—physical, visual, and verbal—is what makes children feel safe and wanted.

The responses refer to attitudes, relationships, and conduct. Which of these ideas and emotions relating to love and support are picture books able to present, and how? It seems that over a long period, and practically everywhere, the family has been depicted in rather sterile ways.[1] Stories once were trivial and represented conventional concepts, even if the innumerable animal families are included, though the latter tend to exhibit more dramatic action. But times are changing. Several years ago, Jeanhenry, a Swiss researcher on children's literature, wrote an article titled "Let's Talk a Little of Tenderness," in which she drew attention to a profound transformation that had, in her view, taken place over the last few years in picture-book representations of relationships between adults and children.[2] Wishing to state the point as clearly as possible, she chose to concentrate on, and demonstrate, one particular situation—moments of tenderness and mutual assurance. She concluded that in picture books of the 1980s, the expression of feelings by way of spontaneous, unreserved bodily contact can be found often, differing much from the stiff, inarticulate body language that characterized earlier books.

She cites many illustrations showing parents and grandparents and children kissing and embracing, children reaching out and touching adults, children being carried and held closely—a new, dynamic, responsive emotionality had penetrated into illustration. This trend indicates a significant development concerning adult attitudes toward children, with picture-book makers responding to the trend and, without doubt, also informing and leading it. It is, says Jeanhenry, as if adults in picture-book illustrations have given up the stance of addressing children from the border of the page or even beyond it. She succinctly and elegantly concludes:

> Tenderness is like a light and volatile perfume. One dabs two drops behind each ear, a little on the wrists there where the heart pulsates; you have to come close to sense it, and its memory stays on . . . but to avoid time effacing it, for memory to guard its traces, this interplay of gestures that expresses [tenderness], has to be repeated a hundred times over.[3]

This "light and volatile" passage embodies an important truth: love is an ongoing communication of enduring relationships. Supportiveness makes sense only if the child can perceive it over long-lasting periods. Recognizing this fact will facilitate our understanding of what role the picture book may fulfill in this context. Evidently, the picture book is a fair and suitable

---

1. A famous example is discussed in Barbara Bader, "A Second Look: The Little Family," *Horn Book* (March/April 1985): 168–71.

2. Josiane Jeanhenry, "Einige gedanken über Zärtlichkeit, über liebevolle Zuwendung" ("Let's Talk a Little of Tenderness"), *Jugend Literatur* (Feb. 1986): 20–29.

3. Jeanhenry, "Einige gedanken," 21.

medium for presenting forms and expressions of contact—physical, verbal, and visual; of active and interactive behavior; of processes of changing relationships; of moods. By its very nature, it is most effective in the representation of brief instances. The short range is a limitation that is actually advantageous. The rare picture-book stories that attempt to cover longer periods are likely to lose their forcefulness and their immediacy, and to become overly didactic.

LOVE THAT GOES WITHOUT SAYING

A number of valuable books celebrate the family atmosphere created by good, devoted parents. Before examining some of them, I wish to confess that somewhere deep in my heart I have a weak spot for books that convey the flavor and taste of thoughtful, loving parents who are happy that they have children of their own, by including the parents as an integral part of the background against which the story is told, as a self-evident element of the child's experiential environment. In such stories, parents do not loom too large. They may even show up only occasionally, almost incidentally, staying behind the scenes for most of the time. When they appear, it seems that they add just a light touch to the plot and background. But obviously, their inclusion and appearance are intended to mean much more than that: by what they say and the way they look and act, parents put a stamp of approval, of acceptance, on the ideas and deeds of their offspring.

Let's look at some examples. Peter's wondrous experience of *The Snowy Day* is all his own.[4] Yet, when he comes into his warm house, full of excitement, his mother takes off his wet socks while he tells her about his adventure; there are no complaints on her part as she listens attentively (fig. 6). Similarly, brief participation characterizes both of Peter's parents in *Whistle for Willie*.[5] In *The Snowman*, the parents, though taken aback as their eyes follow their son as he rushes up and down, in and out, building a snowman who later comes to life, never interfere with his actions and his dreams, thus silently backing him in what he does (fig. 7).[6] The textless book *Rain* relates a brother and sister's thrill at going out into the heavy rain, encouraged by their mother.[7] On their return, they are received with affection by their mother and then joined by their father. In *Barnaby and the Rocket*, the boy prepares for a bonfire; first, he begins building it by himself, but slowly and quite naturally, the project grows into a family experience, with everyone sustaining Barnaby's excitement.[8] At times, parents stay behind the scenes altogether: Max's mother (*Where the Wild Things Are*) is never seen (Sendak wished to leave her countenance to children's own

4. Keats, *The Snowy Day*.
5. Keats, *Whistle for Willie*.
6. Raymond Briggs, *The Snowman* (New York: Random, 1978).
7. Peter Spier, *Rain* (Garden City, N.Y.: Doubleday, 1982).
8. Lydia Pender, *Barnaby and the Rocket*, illus. Judy Cowell (London: Collins, 1972).

Fig. 6. Ezra Jack Keats, *The Snowy Day*
From *The Snowy Day*. Copyright © 1962 by Ezra Jack Keats. Reprinted by permission of Viking Penguin, a division of Penguin Books U.S.A. Inc., and The Bodley Head

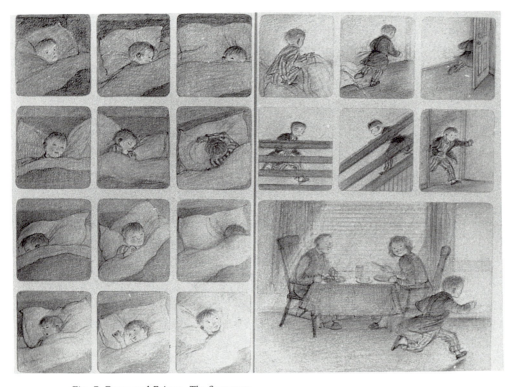

Fig. 7. Raymond Briggs, *The Snowman*
From *The Snowman*, by Raymond Briggs. Copyright © 1978 by Raymond Briggs. Reprinted by permission of Random House, Inc.

imaginations); only the smell and then the view of the supper she has prepared show that she cares and that her love has not suffered by the clash of her and her son's tempers.

My liking for this seemingly lightweight but actually meaningful introduction and participation of parents in picture books stems from a conviction that parents should, in fiction as in real life, let their children play out a part of their daily lives *without* looming too large, without being dramatically involved. In the stories just mentioned, parents fulfill a role by staying (metaphorically, not pictorially) on the sidelines, serving, so to speak, as a barometer (come rain, come snow) of the mood prevailing in the home. They project an attitude of trust and nonpunitive support. Need we point out that even so, anxieties are always around the corner in a child's life? Peter of *The Snowy Day* dreams that the snow has melted away. The boy in *The Snowman* wakes up to see his friend melting.

But, of course, parents are vitally involved in their children's existence, and vice versa; therefore, their mutual relationships are tremendously important, and so is familial barometric pressure. So it is fitting, even necessary, that storybooks should take up the theme of mutual relationship, representing its facets and constellations, and thus offering a better understanding of how parents bestow a sense of security on their children.

THE SHELTERING FAMILY

The subtle, individualized depiction of each member of a family is a basic element in characterizing their mutual relationships. Trivial faces weaken a story's impact.

I Go with My Family to Grandma's presents a special, rare concept and structure—the grand panorama of a large family.[9] Five families go on a holiday visit to their grandpa and grandma's place. The time is the first decade of the twentieth century. The whole experience is based on themes and rhythmic variations: five cousins, a girl in each of the five families, are the "reference people," through whose eyes the event is recorded. This device also helps to introduce another rhythmic element—each family lives in a different borough of New York City, and each girl's name begins with the same sound as the name of the borough she lives in. As the rally progresses, each girl, along with her family, sets out on a different vehicle: Millie, from Manhattan on a bicycle; Bella, from Brooklyn on a trolley; Carrie, from Queens in Papa's wagon; Beatie, from the Bronx on two trains; Stella, from Staten Island in Papa's car on a ferry. The illustrations, surely created in close cooperation with the author, take up and expand these rhythms, adding a few visual ones of their own, to create the panorama. A first rhythm appears in the number of children in each family, respectively,

9. Riki Levinson, *I Go with My Family to Grandma's,* illus. D. Goode (New York: Dutton, 1986).

2 + 4 + 4 + 6 + 8 (including twins) = 24. A second rhythm is that each family's outing begins with a somewhat smaller illustration, taking up a third of the large double page, which shows how the day begins and how the children prepare. A third rhythm arises from the carefully attentive, faithful depiction of clothing fashions, traffic vehicles, buildings, and street scenes; repeated five times, these scenes achieve distinct local color for each family—a period piece. Thus, clearly perceptible socio-economic differences that have arisen among the five branches of the second generation are brought out. A fourth rhythm is called forth by interlacing two strands of development that take place in time and space: one recurrent direction of movement is established by one family after another getting up, setting out, and converging upon Grandma's, with each arrival duly acknowledged and joyously celebrated by the increasingly larger company that has already gathered. At the same time, another movement takes place within the grandparents' home: as successive branches of the tribe arrive and affection is showered upon them, the growing crowd continues moving progressively through the house, from the entrance through the parlor to the dining room, where the table is being set for dinner, to the kitchen, and, after everybody has arrived, into the backyard, where there's a large tree for the festive family picture to be taken by the attendant photographer (fig. 8). Obviously, the earlier people arrive, the more fun they have. They appear in the following order:

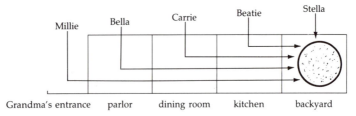

The result of all this commotion is bliss. Apart from minor trouble with some of the children, stress is absent. A general feeling of being wanted, sheltered, and comfortable encompasses thirty-four souls. Taking a cue from the author's alliterations, the pageant is nostalgic, not naive; romantic, but not routinely so; vivid, but not vain. It offers an example of what critics of children's literature (mainly European ones) tend to refer to rather deprecatingly (often justifiably so) as a "sane," artificial, overly idealized world. It is a mood, though, which all of us, children and adults, have a need for and should be permitted to enjoy here and there, once in awhile on a weekend, especially if it is presented to us in such a humorous vein and with such intriguing execution and is removed into the past.

Another work to be briefly considered here is composed of two small, textless volumes by Ormerod—*Sunshine* and *Moonlight*.[10] They take us into

10. Jan Ormerod, *Sunshine* (Harmondsworth, England: Puffin/Penguin, 1985); *Moonlight* (Harmondsworth, England: Puffin/Penguin, 1982).

to Grandma's.

Fig. 8. Diane Goode, *I Go with My Family to Grandma's*

From *I Go with My Family to Grandma's* by Riki Levinson, ill. by Diane Goode. Illustrations copyright © 1986 by Diane Goode. Reproduced by permission of the publisher, Dutton Children's Books, a division of Penguin Books USA Inc.

the contemporary nuclear family. The spirit characterizing the books finds expression in a stirringly sensitive portrayal of the parents and their daughter. Body language serves to represent the commonly difficult situations— either beginning or terminating the day—that cause headaches and tears in a multitude of households. What Ormerod depicts is simple, but it evokes a desired state rarely attained. The simplicity arises from the warm, realistic style and the clear, seemingly effortless structuring of the events. The impression of a genuine relationship originates in the unhurried pace at which the two sequences, waking up and falling asleep, unfold. For, although both in the morning and at night some time segments are speeded up (for example, undressing in *Moonlight*), and others are slowed down (such as leaving in *Sunshine*), mainly by altering picture sizes, the overall mood is leisurely. While the three persons enact a commendable, even enviable version of two ubiquitous rituals (fig. 9), they also demonstrate to each other, silently (the welcome absence of words contributes to the effect) and almost solemnly, how much they care for each other, have patience with each other, and enjoy being a family. The two small volumes reverberate with overtones of mutuality achieved by characterization and textures: the joy the three obtain from being together (fig. 10); the quiet understanding that exists between father and daughter at the supper table and in the

Fig. 9. Jan Omerod, *Moonlight*
From *Moonlight* by Jan Omerod (Kestrel Books 1982), copyright © Jan Omerod, 1982

Fig. 10. Jan Omerod, *Moonlight*
From *Moonlight* by Jan Omerod (Kestrel Books 1982), copyright © Jan Omerod, 1982

morning before Mother is awakened; the satisfaction both parents derive from their vividly active child; the delicate love Father and Mother show for each other. This motif—the parents' love for each other—as an element in the family's happiness is also brought out well in some of the families in *I Go with My Family*. . . . Unfortunately, it is a motif that appears very rarely in in-depth picture books. One possible reason may lie in the fact that children are emotionally involved in various ways with one parent more than the other, a constellation for which good picture-book makers seem to have a passionate empathy. Yet, an awareness of their father and mother loving each other, supporting each other, and enjoying each other's company can strongly reinforce children's sense of security. The display of such feelings should not be left to the pages of mediocre or trivial books.

For the children inhabiting these three books—*I Go with . . .* , *Sunshine*, and *Moonlight*—the family is a happy place. Not so for Rosa, the protagonist of several of Vera B. Williams's stories.[11] We will leaf through three of them—*A Chair for My Mother, Something Special for Me,* and *Music, Music for Everyone.* These are stories for older children. They present a one-parent family. It is satisfying to note that here, as in a growing number of picture books, the one-parent family is represented as a common phenomenon of society.

The background is Rosa's life with her mother; her grandmother, who lives with them, and an aunt and uncle, who live nearby, complete the family. They stick together and help each other emotionally and economically. Mother is a waitress in a small diner. She works hard and often comes home tired. Rosa helps out in the diner once in a while and puts part of her earnings in the big jar on the shelf, where Mother also drops the change from the tips she gets (fig. 11). Grandma adds more coins. The jar, its

Fig. 11. Vera B. Williams, *A Chair for My Mother*
From *A Chair for My Mother* by Vera B. Williams. © 1982 by Vera B. Williams. Reprinted by permission of Greenwillow Books
(A Division of William Morrow & Co.)

becoming filled and being emptied, is a central object in the home and in the stories, indicating that it is not easy to make ends meet, a state Rosa is constantly and sensibly aware of.

The plots of the three books connect with ease. In *A Chair for My Mother,* the jar is emptied, and the three women—Grandma, Mother, and Rosa—go out and have a wonderful time choosing a comfortable chair for Mother so she can rest when work has exhausted her (fig. 12). This joyful experience

11. Vera B. Williams, *A Chair for My Mother* (New York: Greenwillow, 1982); *Something Special for Me* (New York: Greenwillow, 1983); *Music, Music for Everyone* (New York: Greenwillow, 1984).

Fig. 12. Vera B. Williams, *A Chair for My Mother*

leads Rosa to reminisce about the misfortune that befell them when their old apartment burned down and their neighbors helped them furnish the new one. In *Something Special for Me,* the coins in the jar are spent on a birthday present for Rosa herself. After deciding on several presents and at the last moment turning down what she chose, Rosa is reduced to tears. The final choice is an accordion, a choice that makes her happy. *Music, Music for Everyone* starts out with distress: the chair is often empty now during the daytime. Grandma is sick and does not sit in it very often; she is usually upstairs in bed. All the family takes care of her. The jar is empty because Mother spends all her money to help Grandma get better. By now, Rosa is quite good at playing the accordion. Inspired by Grandma, she teams up with three girlfriends. They start a band, practice, play at a neighborhood party, and are overjoyed with their success. Some coins are dropped into the jar on the shelf.

The verbal style in the three books is a marvel. This style also denotes one of the not-too-frequent cases where a relatively ample text does not impair the balance between the verbal and the visual narrative in a picture book. The stories flow along, related in unaffected language. Description, narration, and dialogue combine so naturally that shifts often go by almost unnoticed. The point of view is definitely Rosa's. She looks at life and understands much about it. Yet her healthy instincts and her thought-fulness allow her to be satisfied with her own life. After all, some important goals are reached; for that, she can always trust her ma and grandma. As Rosa sees it, life is not so bad, among other things because it's a women's world, where one person quickly understands another. Several situations, and especially the dialogues, reflect the hushed pride the women take in running their own lives, the sympathy they feel for one another, and the closeness they are in need of.

The pictorial style can be said to be realistic, mellowed by elements of the naive and heightened by strong colors. The lower-class character of Rosa's environment is brought out well by signs of austerity and of style. But, mindful of Rosa's acceptance of her circumstances, the illustrator en-wraps her world in warm hues. The illustrations jump around, with rapidly changing points of view and perspectives; this approach could create some difficulties in adjusting one's attention when progressing from one picture to the next. Yet, the problem scarcely arises; the pictures are pleasing and effective because the artist is consummately skillful with the composition of her illustrations. She knows how to balance out the visual forces of line, space, and color, whatever the content—an achievement that is demon-strated in one picture after the other. The scenes are convincing; so are the relationships. A special expressiveness flows from the close-ups of an often pensive Rosa and in moments of intimacy with her mother, such as the last picture in the first book as she falls asleep in Mother's lap in the new chair, and in the second book, when Mother chases her, or when Rosa starts to cry and Mother comforts her, with their heads touching and Mother meanwhile putting the money back into her bag (fig. 13). In the background we can see the musical instrument store—and children leafing through the book for a second time knowingly smile long before Rosa herself zeroes in on the accordion.

We are able to find out more about Rosa and about the artist if we view the three stories as consecutive chapters of one book. Williams establishes a unifying structure for the three volumes. The left-hand page contains the illustration; its colored background is carried over to the right-hand page, where the text appears. Rather low on this page rests a vignette, to my mind neither really necessary nor attractive, which repeats or complements or provides details on the theme depicted in the illustration. Both pages are surrounded by constantly varied small borders, echoing the hues of the adjacent illustrations. These two features underline the naive aspect of Williams's style. In *A Chair . . .* , the borders and vignettes are rather prim and tame. The overall structure (of the two opposite pages) is, in this volume, interrupted only once, when text and pictures stretch across two pages to let us see the long procession of neighbors bringing their gifts for the new apartment. In *Something Special . . .* , the vignettes are unchanged, but several borders come alive, commenting, not just repeating, what goes

Fig. 13. Vera B. Williams, *Something Special for Me*
From *Something Special for Me* by Vera B. Williams. © 1983 by Vera B. Williams. Reprinted by permission of Greenwillow Books (A Division of William Morrow & Co.)

on verbally and visually on the pages they frame. When Rosa almost selects the skates as her birthday present, the border dances with a wheeling, looping line; when she almost opts for the tent, thinking of the trips she, Mother, and Grandma will be able to make, Rosa is surrounded by white clouds in a bright sky. Structure is abandoned once in this volume; this time the text takes over a double page.

In *Music, Music . . .* , the structure as a whole and its components loosen up. At first, when Grandma is sick and the chair is empty, small mosaics make up the borderline, expressive of hesitancy. As Rosa walks up the stairs with a plate of soup, a flowery line bespeaks her love for Grandma; but as we proceed toward the band practicing and then the excitement of the party, the borders become bolder, widen, intrude into the page, and take over the illustrative functions. Sweeping stripes circumscribe the pages as Rosa brushes Grandma's hair, and encircle the four girls playing their instruments. When Rosa wonders about Grandma's health, other static little squares reappear. In other words, from the first through the third volume, borders evolve from being almost purely decorative into being part of the narrative.

As, in the latter part of the third volume, we approach the night of the party, the staid structure of the double page becomes dynamic, flexible, and colorful, with strongly varying compositions following each other. Naive styling retreats in favor of a more fantastic vein. The recurrent portraits of the four girls are increasingly sensitive and beautiful reflections of the spirit of companionship and the impact of music. Another beautiful achievement lies in the successive portraits of Rosa. Just as in the text her thoughts, interests, and activities undergo changes, and in the third story her mother somewhat recedes, so in the illustrations, judging by her looks, her face, and her gait, Rosa is subtly growing up. It is very satisfying to recognize that the artist's evolving style parallels her protagonist's growing-up processes—form reflects and expresses content.

The apparently simple, down-to-earth nature of the text and pictures is, at first sight, as convincing as it is easily perceived. An appreciation of its quality comes a little later. In Rosa's case, stress and anxiety stem from social circumstances rather than psychological relationships. She is aware of Mother's strenuous job, worries about Grandmother being sick, and takes part in the frightful experience of the fire that destroys their apartment and their belongings. The incisive motif, a "basso ostinato," is the constant concern over whether ends will meet. This money consciousness is objectified by the jar, which is at the same time the fount of joys that can be attained with patience, in good time. Stress and anxieties are eased by relatives and neighbors; even Mother's boss is kind and helpful. Nobody seems to complain too much. Thus, Rosa is able to like and accept her way of life. She, too, still feels sheltered.

Stories presenting socio-economic backgrounds comparable to those in Williams's books are rare, and it is even more unusual to find that neither protest, nor promise of a change in circumstances, is included in the plot. The sincerity characterizing this attempt at interpreting the life of lower-class people constitutes a value in its own right. Williams does not intend to idealize poverty, but to show that even in severe conditions, human supportive relations may thrive.

One word on serialization: the picture book is by its very nature limited to treating short-range experiences. The limit can, as we have just seen, be overcome by the use of the precarious device of serialization, the design of staying with a protagonist over several books. In successful cases (as, for instance, in works by Bergström (fig. 14),[12] Stevenson,[13] Williams, or in Keats's stories about Peter), serialization may lead to the creation of intriguing, lovable protagonists.

However, all too frequently, fresh, original earlier volumes beget tired later ones dedicated to cashing in on popularity. In many series (as is

12. For instance, Gunilla Bergström, *God Natt, Alfons Åberg* (Stockholm: Rabén & Sjögren, 1978); *Aja Baja, Alfons Åberg* (Stockholm: Rabén & Sjögren, 1973).
13. For instance, James Stevenson, *What's Under My Bed?* (New York: Morrow, 1983).

Fig. 14. Gunilla Bergström, *God Natt, Ålfons Aberg*

Gunilla Bergström: *God Natt, Ålfons Aberg*. Text och build: Gunilla Bergström 1978. Reprinted by permission of the illustrator.

commonly found in cartoon strips and TV sitcoms), the protagonist and the supporting cast are fixed, never-changing types who live out repetitiously structured plots, mostly funny and entertaining. This typicality also appears, of course, in Stevenson's excellent Grandpa stories. True artists, like Keats at the time he created the Peter stories and knew when to stop the series, or Williams in the present volumes, lead us to expect unfolding characterizations, varying moods, and broadening relationships. We may become attached to a child-hero and his or her growing pangs and joys. We may become involved with a twofold experience—following the steps of a maturing child and a maturing author. In essence, the picture book is, however, a medium performing at its best when it communicates intensive happenings spanning relatively short time intervals. The Rosa books are happy exceptions to this rule.

. An unusual example of a supportive father can be found in *My Father Always Embarrasses Me*.[14] Mortimer's mother is an important television reporter, always busy and away from home. His father, being "only" a writer, "does nothing" but hammer away at a typewriter and take care of his son in an embarrassing way: kissing him in front of other kids, dressing in an

14. Meir Shalev, *My Father Always Embarrasses Me*, illus. Yossi Abolafia (Chicago: Wellington, 1990; originally published in Jerusalem: Keter, 1988).

awkward way, and singing loudly in the street (fig. 15). Only after Father wins an award for a fabulous cake he entered in a school baking contest does Mortimer become proud of him. The illustrations show a very warm and humorous relationship between father and son, the body language of the figures emphasizing the closeness more than the criticism on behalf of the child.

HAUNTING SIGHTS AND TRUSTWORTHY MOTHERS

Tensions often take the form of frightening dreams or daydreams, which serve to personify unsufferable generalized anxieties. The following three

Fig. 15. Yossi Abolafia, *My Father Always Embarrasses Me*

Yossi Abolafia from *My Father Always Embarrasses Me* by permission of Wellington Publishing, Chicago 1990. Originalli: Jerusalem, Keter Publishing House, 1988: Aba 'osehbushot.

books exemplify how stories may assist children in confronting and over-coming bad dreams, with the help of their mothers. Nick, the sophisticated little boy in *My Mama Says There Aren't Any Zombies, Ghosts, Vampires, Creatures, Demons, Monsters, Fiends, Goblins, or Things*,[15] is not so sure that Mama can be relied on. He sees and hears ghosts everywhere (mostly, to judge from the illustrations, they arise from the branches scratching the wall outside, or the wind howling around the corner, etc.) (fig. 16). Whenever he tells Mother about these things, she flatly denies that they exist. Nick really loves his mother, but she exhibits some of those vexing habits and ideas that parents can have: she always knows best, and she is absolutely certain of what she knows—most of the time, anyway. Every time that she is

Fig. 16. Kay Chorao, *My Mama Says . . .*

Reprinted by permission of Atheneum Publishers, an imprint of Macmillan Company from *My Mama Says There Aren't Any Zombies, Ghosts, Vampires, Creatures, Demons, Monsters, Fiends, Goblins, or Things*, by Judith Viorst, illustrated by Kay Chorao. Illustrations copyright © 1973 by Kay Sproat Chorao.

15. Viorst, *My Mama Says . . . .*

unwilling to accept Nick's word that these monsters pursue him, he immediately remembers yet another instance of the errors and mistakes she commits, and does not own up to, in daily life. He has a long list of such misdemeanors ready in his head, and he tries again to convince her of his fears—but in vain. The idea of monsters is simply beyond her understanding. Actually, in a way, Nick loves his mother all the more because of her mistakes, for this dent in her superiority justifies his own certainty that the cataloged frightening fiends are there. But in this partly playful and partly serious anguish, he is alone. Adults simply don't believe in demons that make life hard for children. Probably they don't want to know about this kind of suffering befalling their children, because they wouldn't know how to deal with it. No use telling them; they will fall back on their stock reply. Thus, Nick ruminates and rumbles on, and the goblins continue to visit him. But, as the story ends, Mother does not make a mistake. One of the creatures that moments ago still threatened Nick melts, transformed into the wrap Mother wears. She holds him close, and his exasperation gives way to tenderness. She turns into a Madonna figure, reminiscent of a Renaissance painting (fig. 17).

The book offers hilarious situations, with some sense of trepidation added because the monsters are quite impressive. Chorao's varying layouts and sizes are eloquent, and so is her lively portrayal of mother and child.

It is a well-known precept that parents should relate sympathetically to

Fig. 17. Kay Chorao, *My Mama Says . . .*
Reprinted by permission of Atheneum Publishers, an imprint of Macmillan Company from *My Mama Says There Aren't Any Zombies, Ghosts, Vampires, Creatures, Demons, Monsters, Fiends, Goblins, or Things,* by Judith Viorst, illustrated by Kay Chorao. Illustrations copyright © 1973 by Kay Sproat Chorao.

their children's nightmares and illusions and not deny them. If the present story does not violate such advice, it is precisely because, although Nick reports that Mother never admits to having committed an error, the illustrations give her away, distinctly showing that she is aware of having blundered or of being wrong, time after time. Nick, the sharp-witted boy, is sure (as are the children enjoying the book) to notice her expression every time. So, maybe being frightened is part of a dialogue with Mother and keeps her close. The story is a humorous example of what Viorst, who writes for both adults and children, once said about what a relief it is that we are all ambivalent creatures.

Meal One[16] is about a wild dream. Helbert wakes up, in his dream, with a plum in his mouth. Together with Mother, he hides the pit under the bed. It turns into a plum tree that grows and grows until its roots threaten to swallow Helbert's breakfast. As anxiety rises within him, he demands meal one from Mother. So, she turns the clock back an hour, and he can wake up once more—in reality this time—be hungry, and gently ride down to the breakfast table on Mother's back. The dream is filled with weird adventures involving the boy and his mother. They wrestle and run and try to deal with the tree getting out of hand. Seen through psychoanalytic eyes, oral, Oedipal, and phallic motifs mix and mingle in a boisterous fashion, and are all taken up just as boisterously and entertainingly by the large overpowering illustrations. Whether Helbert wakes up in a dream or in reality, the story seems to import, his mother can be trusted to be around and to help him.

A variant of this motif—a threatening daydream and a satisfying resolution of stress with Mother's help, on return to reality—is found in *Ciaobambola*.[17] This story suggests a way of working through a girl's feelings concerning her sex role, approached from a specific, feministic point of view. It is a rainy Sunday, and Giovanna (seven or eight years old?), in a languorous mood, would like to spend the day with her mother, reading, stretched out on her mother's bed. But this is Giovanna's birthday, and her aunt and uncle will arrive soon with a present. She fears that they will give her a doll, thus emphasizing her female role. Suddenly, she retreats into a swift dream: the relatives, grotesque, overpowering, "kind," appear and hand her Maribel, an elegant, large doll. Giovanna takes the doll, pushing herself further into femininity. While this morning she in reality wears pants, she now exchanges clothes with Maribel and turns into a young lady. All of a sudden, the now boyish Maribel runs off; Giovanna is utterly alone. Throughout the dream, her room becomes increasingly unreal, until she stands on a small piece of floor somewhere far out in a starry night. Frightened, she wakes up, cries for Mamma—who is at her side. Just then the

---

16. Ivor Cutler, *Meal One*, illus. Helen Oxenbury (London: Heinemann, 1971).

17. Adela Turin, *Ciaobambola*, illus. Margherita Saccaro (Milano: Ed. della parte della bambine, 1978).

aunt and uncle arrive, looking a little less like their dream caricatures, and present her with a bicycle (fig. 18). It seems that Mother let them know her daughter's wishes. Giovanna is supported by her mother, or rather influenced by her, in emphatically resisting an overemphasized conventional sex role. The large, picturesque illustrations bring out well the contrast between the harrowing dream and the intimacy between mother and daughter.

Fig. 18. Margherita Saccaro, *Ciaobambola*
From *Ciaobambola* by Adela Turin, ill. by Margherita Saccaro. Milano: ed. della parte della bambine, 1978.

While in *My Mama Says . . .* and *Meal One* only mothers appear and fathers are absent, we seem to assume that fathers exist; there is simply no need for them at the time the stories happen. With *Ciaobambola*, however, one is not so sure. In most picture books, the assumption is reinforced by our knowledge of the author's and the artist's convictions. But a more general observation can be attempted. While certainly no rule exists, it seems as though picture-book stories that tell about a child and his or her attachment to the opposite-sex parent often only imply the existence of the same-sex parent, who is absent, because he or she if actually present would disrupt the working through of the child's current problem. On the other hand, by corollary, stories featuring a parent and a same-sex child are likely to take place in one-parent families, even if this fact is not explicitly stated.

Here, then, are three much-needed mothers who have their own personal ways of coping with their children's wild dreams; three stories, humorous, yet not entirely innocent, about rising tension and tension released.

The books assembled here constitute a commendable selection of imaginative works suggesting how parents can strengthen their children's belief in themselves, a belief that comes into being mainly if a child feels that he or she is accepted or wanted. It is significant that in all these stories, physical tenderness and intimacy play an important role.

CHILDREN'S BOOKS CITED

BERGSTRÖM, GUNILLA. *Aja Baja, Ålfons Åberg*. Stockholm: Rabén & Sjögren, 1973.
———. *God Natt, Ålfons Åberg*. Stockholm: Rabén & Sjögren, 1978.
BRIGGS, RAYMOND. *The Snowman*. New York: Random, 1978.
CUTLER, IVOR. *Meal One*. Illus. Helen Oxenbury. London: Heinemann, 1971.
KEATS, EZRA JACK. *The Snowy Day*. New York: Viking, 1962.
———. *Whistle for Willie*. New York: Viking, 1964.
LEVINSON, RIKI. *I Go with My Family to Grandma's*. Illus. D. Goode. New York: Dutton, 1986.
ORMEROD, JAN. *Moonlight*. Harmondsworth, England: Puffin/Penguin, 1982.
———. *Sunshine*. Harmondsworth, England: Puffin/Penguin, 1985.
PENDER, LYDIA. *Barnaby and the Rocket*. Illus. Judy Cowell. London: Collins, 1972.
SHALEV, MEIR. *My Father Always Embarrasses Me*. Illus. Yossi Abolafia. Chicago: Wellington, 1990. orig. Jerusalem: Keter, 1988.
SPIER, PETER. *Rain*. Garden City, N.Y.: Doubleday, 1982.
STEVENSON, JAMES. *What's Under My Bed?* New York: Morrow, 1983.
TURIN, ADELA. *Ciaobambola*. Illus. Margherita Saccaro. Milano: Ed. della parte della bambine, 1978.
VIORST, JUDITH. *My Mama Says . . . .* Illus. Kay Chorao. New York: Atheneum, 1973.
WILLIAMS, VERA B. *A Chair for My Mother*. New York: Greenwillow, 1982.
———. *Something Special for Me*. New York: Greenwillow, 1983.
———. *Music, Music for Everyone*. New York: Greenwillow, 1984.

5

Grandparents and Grandchildren

In the last decade or so, picture books about grandparents have proliferated. They form part of a wider trend, the growing importance of old people in society. Demographic changes, the prolonged lives of elderly people, and, as a result, an ever larger percentage of the aged among the population have exerted an influence. These developments modify the situations and attitudes in many families: the presence of grandparents, whether near or far, becomes a significant element in the growing-up processes of their grandchildren, no doubt, with differences created by social and ethnic backgrounds. But picture books have taken up the subject enthusiastically, whatever the reasons for doing so.

Many of these books offer simple plots and relationships. In general, the grandparents depicted in one book do not differ greatly from those in another, or from grandparent characters found in earlier children's books. There is some logic behind this similarity. Old people's lives are less complex than those of younger people, though they have their own complications. The responsibilities of old people lessen, their social ties diminish, and they have a need to fall back on their families. Their existence tends to narrow down. This situation opens the way to an easy stereotyping of characters and plots. However, a number of good picture books offer maturer concepts of the manifold relationships that may exist between children and their grandparents; of children's ability to understand old people, to care for them, and love them; and of the meaning grandparents have to the children. A varied array of old people is found in the books we have in mind. Some of these characters are still going strong and independent; others are weak and barely able to take care of themselves; still others are utterly dependent on their families. In several stories, the health and stature of the elderly are diminished. Whether these characters are admirable, strange, or to be pitied, a mood of mutual intimacy characterizes the stories: children and grandparents are very meaningful to each other.

Let us start out with that most superb of all grandfathers, the figure created by James Stevenson for a series of stories in which he stars together with his grandchildren, Mary Ann and Louie. In each story, Grandpa tells the children a tall story with the intention of helping them overcome some fears that grip them, usually at nighttime. In *What's Under My Bed?*, for example, Grandpa asks the children if the story he has just finished telling them is too scary for them, an idea they deny.[1] But their dismayed faces belie their words. So they start seeing scary things and rush down to Grandpa, who tells them that the very same things happened to him when he was a child. As he exaggerates about the terrible noises and the monsters that appeared to him, the children are led to belittle them and explain them away, one by one, and in the process the children calm down. All ends with ice cream (fig. 19).

Fig. 19. James Stevenson, *What's Under My Bed?*
From *What's Under My Bed?* by James Stevenson. © 1983 by James Stevenson. Reprinted by permission of Greenwillow Books (A Division of William Morrow & Co.)

This synopsis cannot possibly give an idea of the vivid dialogue that takes place between the three partners, with Grandpa, that spry, wily old gentleman, leading Mary Ann and Louie on, while they believe that they are outwitting him, outghosting their ghosts, until they forget about their own apparitions—for tonight, that is. Text and pictures render the fast-changing moods of fun, excitement, and relaxation in combinations that differ perceptively from one page to the next. The picture size, the place-

1. Stevenson, *What's Under My Bed?*

ment of the text and illustrations, and the typography play a role in developing the story at a fast pace. It is a simple story; but one quickly detects that the text is the result of careful honing, with every word and phrase in place and quite sophisticated illustrations. Two time periods are involved— the present, with Mary Ann and Louis spending the evening with Grandpa, and the past, focusing on Grandpa's own experiences. In each time period, two modes of experience appear, reality and imagination. In other words, the pictures need to depict four alternating situations. By showing the present unframed, the artist fully frames Grandpa's reminiscences. Also, scary imagination is shown in larger pictures than sensible reality. Another fine point is that the children in the story only *hear* Grandpa's tale, while the child who views the illustrations *sees*, Grandpa as well, as a stumpy, incongruously mustachioed boy wandering through the halls of his own grandparents' mansion (fig. 20). That mustache—does it not indicate that Grandpa's boyhood scare might be a hoax, invented tongue in cheek for the benefit of Mary Ann and Louie, rather than a real memory? In the course of these exciting events, related by lively and intricate techniques, the two children's anxieties, the rather welcome shudders, are scaled up no less than three times—first by Grandpa's scary story, then by the chil-

Fig. 20. James Stevenson, *What's Under My Bed?*
From *What's Under My Bed?* by James Stevenson. © 1983 by James Stevenson. Reprinted by permission of Greenwillow Books (A Division of William Morrow & Co.)

dren's own imaginings, and finally by Grandpa's recollections. The anxieties are beautifully resolved at the end. It is worthwhile to compare the first and the last pictures in the book to gain an overview of the eminently satisfying tension and release. Fun, excitement, and security are offered expertly by the old man. This is one of the rare cases in which an accomplished cartoonist takes up his tools, usually sharpened to arouse adult audiences, and refines them to fit children's imaginations without, however, simplifying his style to a point where he would be playing down to the children.

Actually, though, this appealing, elegant grandpa is an exceptional figure in picture books. The other books we are going to look at portray grandparents in a more realistic, serious vein. *Jan and the Grandmother*[2] presents an old woman living alone with her cat. She is still independent, though apparently quite lonely. She has time on her hands; she looks out of the window for hours. On some days, she stands before her easel and paints, and painting makes her happier.

Jan, who must be eight or nine years old, loves his grandmother. She looks a bit strange, his friends say, but he doesn't care. However, she tends to forget things, more and more, and to misplace her key. Jan loves to visit her once a week (fig. 21), to listen to her recall her childhood, and to eat the meals she prepares for him. She herself eats, too—slowly. Then they play Chinese checkers. She has lots of time, as does Jan.

But then Grandma changes. She walks very slowly in the rain; she cannot find her glasses, so they cannot play Chinese checkers; when she asks the cat where the glasses could be, Jan gets furious and runs away. Coming home, he goes to his room and slams the door behind him. Not until evening is he able to talk to Mother about his disappointment with Grandma. When Mother explains to him how old people need more time for everything, he calms down and tries to accept Grandma as she is.

The story is told evenly and well. The large illustrations, done in strong colors, add depth. They depict Grandma's apartment, which is old-fashioned but well kept and roomy, reflecting her loneliness. Jan's own moods come out simply, roughly: the way he looks at Grandma's doings rather than at her, and the way he gets angry with her. Grandma herself is rendered as an impressive woman. Her elongated, haggard face shows that she must have been beautiful, yet the look in her eyes is sad, forlorn, expressive of how difficult it is for her to keep up with what she has to do, to remember, to continue living as if life were easy. Although she and Jan scarcely look at each other, their closeness is expressed in the pictures by several means. A turn of the head, a slanted shoulder, and the way Grandma is seen, through Jan's eyes, being busy in her apartment show

2. Gisela Degler-Rummel, *Jan und die Grossmutter* (*Jan and the Grandmother*) (Ravensburg, Germany: Otto Maier, 1978).

Fig. 21. Gisela Degler-Rummel, *Jan und die Grossmutter*
Gisela Degler-Rummel, *Jan und die Grossmutter*. © 1978 Ravensburger Buchverlag Otto Maier Gmbh.

how much the two care for each other. The illustrations, not the text, tell us that both know things will slowly deteriorate.

My Grandpa Is Old, and I Love Him Very Much is a study of the frailty of human nature and human relationships, and yet is a picture book easily understood and appreciated by young children.[3] Grandpa lives in a village. After Grandma dies, his family invites him to town, but the visit does not work out too well. Grandpa does not feel at home in town, so he returns to his village. The strength of the book lies in the pictures—realistic, deceptively simple illustrations of what happens in the family while Grandpa stays with them; but the pictures are also deeply sensitive, graphic renditions of what goes through the small grandson's mind. The boy, who tells

3. Wolf Harranth, *Mein Opa ist alt, und Ich hab Ihn sehr lieb (My Grandpa Is Old, and I Love Him Very Much)*, illus. Christina Oppermann-Dimow (Ravensburg, Germany: Otto Maier, 1986).

the story in the first person, spends his time with Grandpa, tries to help him and make things easier for him so he will not feel so much out of place. At the same time, the boy observes him closely (as is shown in the illustrations), quizzically at first and then with growing admiration for the old man's obstinacy. This running portrait of Grandpa, the boy, and their relationship creates continuity. The boy's emotional intensity comes out in the look on his face—his eyebrows raised, surprised when Grandpa sits down in Father's place at the table and nobody tells him not to, and when Grandpa talks with a full mouth; quite disgusted when Grandpa prepares for the night (fig. 22); wide-eyed when Grandpa yawns with his mouth open. But then the boy begins to respect Grandpa, who knows how to fix a dripping faucet and a toy car (fig. 23). Grandpa is restive and taciturn, however, and one day he gets up and leaves. The polite embarrassment that gripped the family throughout Grandpa's stay still reigns when they all accompany him to the railway station. But then, probably a few days later, the boy asks Mother when they will visit Grandpa.

Grandpa is shown as an old man, without embellishment (except for the dust-jacket picture, where he is made up for publicity's sake): his back is

Fig. 22. Christina Oppermann-Dimow, *Mein Opa ist alt, und Ich hab Ihn sehr lieb*
From Wolf Harranth/C. Oppermann-Dimow, *Mein Opa ist alt, und ich hab ihn sehr lieb*. Copyright 1981 by Verlag Jungbrunnen, Wein.

bent; his movements are wooden and awkward; he walks with a precarious gait; his hands are knotted, his face is wrinkled, and his eyes are usually sad. He is often helpless. And yet he is upright and determined and commands attention. That is why he is lovable.

While the full-page illustrations throughout the text are in color, a narrative touch is added to the book by two series of twelve small drawings in black and white. The first series depicts Grandpa's life until Grandma's death. The other, his days alone in the village until the family visits. Although these two panels are unnecessary, they add some background. Their appeal lies in comparison: before, the two grandparents sleep together in their big bed; later, Grandpa is alone. Before, he buys a whole loaf of bread; later, half a loaf. A joyful life becomes empty and sad. There is a large measure of truthfulness to be found in this story.

In *Now One Foot, Now the Other*, Bobby, a boy of almost six, is confronted with a harrowing experience.[4] Grandpa, his best friend, who taught the boy how to walk and helped him with his building-block towers, has had a stroke, is paralyzed, and has lost his power of speech. Bobby is aghast when his parents tell him that Grandpa will probably never again recognize him. But then Bobby sets out to help Grandpa remember, to talk, and to

Fig. 23. Christina Oppermann-Dimow, *Mein Opa ist alt, und Ich hab Ihn sehr lieb*
From Wolf Harranth/C. Oppermann-Dimow, *Mein Opa ist alt, und ich hab ihn sehr lieb.* Copyright 1981 by Verlag Jungbrunnen, Wien.

4. Tomie de Paola, *Now One Foot, Now the Other* (New York: Putnam, 1981).

move again—now one foot, now the other. By the end of summer, they walk as far as the end of the lawn. The illustrations focus on the interaction between Bobby and Grandpa and, occasionally, with his parents. They very clearly depict both the light and the serious moments of Bobby and Grandpa's changing relationship. Text and illustrations succeed in presenting this difficult theme at the level of five- to six-year-old children, with reasonable authenticity, including touches of humor and joyfulness here and there—no small achievement. Although some of the verbal and visual formulations are too smooth, and the developments related are quite improbable or extremely rare, the situations and relationships are real. The book is entertaining and conveys a simple sense of human purpose.

When one begins to search for stories about grandparents, their grandchildren, and their families, it is really astonishing how many can be found, how many questions are raised and answered, and from how many angles the theme can be approached. *I'm Going to Ask Grandma* has an ingenious slant: Max has everything one can wish for—loving parents and lots of playthings.[5] And yet he has a problem; Max is insecure and easily frightened. Frequently, dogs or people seem to grow into huge monsters, and Max runs away; or a small boy on a bicycle turns into a sort of Hell's Angels rider. These metamorphoses are shown in very effective pictures. Max thinks things over for a long time. Then he decides it is time to ask Grandmother—his mentor—for advice. She sits on a bench, framed by big flowers, doing some mending, with Max sitting by her side, a picture of contentment and concentration in glowing colors (fig. 24). Of course, Grandma has advice ready: whenever things or people start to grow and threaten him, Max should pronounce his full name. Max is skeptical, but her advice works. In *Timothy and Gramps,* the boy loves his grandfather but is quite bashful about him, until Gramps impresses Timothy's classmates with his stories.[6] *Through Grandpa's Eyes* relates a boy's visit with his grandfather, who is blind but who, by relying on his other senses, is happy and busy, together with Grandma.[7] *Grandma without Me* is an ambitious and optimistic combination of two issues: separation from a grandmother, and a parents' divorce.[8] Because of the parents' separation, the small boy's close relationship with his Grandma suffers in the short run, but things will surely work out again soon. Several books emphasize ethnic background: *When Grandpa Came to Stay* is about a Jewish grandfather's first visit to his family after Grandma has died.[9] *Nana Upstairs and Nana Downstairs* represents life in an Italian family through a child's reminiscences of a grandmother who has died (fig. 25).[10]

5. Margarete Kubelka, *Ich werde Oma fragen (I'm Going to Ask Grandma)*, illus. Hans Poppel (München: Ellermann, 1983).
6. Ron Brooks, *Timothy and Gramps* (Sidney and London: Collins, 1978).
7. Patricia MacLachlan, *Through Grandpa's Eyes*, illus. Deborah Ray (New York: Harper, 1980).
8. Judith Vigna, *Grandma without Me* (Niles, Ill.: Albert Whitman, 1984).
9. Judith Caseley, *When Grandpa Came to Stay* (New York: Greenwillow, 1986).
10. Tomie de Paola, *Nana Upstairs and Nana Downstairs* (New York: Putnam, 1973).

Mäxchen dachte lange über das alles nach. Dann nahm er sich vor:
›Ich werde die Oma fragen.‹ Die Oma wußte für alles Rat, nicht nur für
die Löcher in den Hosen, auch wenn Mäxchen zu viel Eis gegessen
hatte und es ihm schlecht wurde. Sie konnte Papierschiffchen
falten und lange Geschichten vom Großvater erzählen.
Die Oma hörte geduldig zu, als Mäxchen ihr die Sache mit dem
Größerwerden anvertraute. Man sah richtig, wie sie nachdachte.
Ihre Stirn wurde so runzelig wie die kleine
Ziehharmonika, die Mäxchen zum Geburtstag
bekommen hatte.

Fig. 24. Hans Poppel, *Ich werde Oma fragen*

From "Ich werde Oma fragen" by Hans Poppel and Margarete Kubelka, © 1983 Verlag Heinrich Ellermann, München.

Fig. 25. Tomie de Paola, *Nana Upstairs and Nana Downstairs*

Tomie de Paola, *Nana Upstairs and Nana Downstairs*, copyright © 1973 by Tomie de Paola. Reprinted by permission of Putnam Publishing Group.

A GRANDPARENT REMEMBERED

The motif of a grandparent remembered has sparked the creation of at least two valuable and beautiful books: *Granpa*[11] and *Mary and Her Grandmother*.[12] While other stories take place in the present, though with many flashbacks and, as in *Grandma without Me*, through glimpses into the future, these stories tell about the past. The stories show how the protagonists, in both cases girls, remember and retrace their long-lasting relationship with their respective grandparent until the grandparent's death—how a person revered, loved, looked at in wonderment, one who has all the time in the world for the grandchild and who can be told secrets, an ever-willing and ever-inventive playmate, gets weaker and responds less, and finally dies. Psychologically, the stories represent a time of mourning, and even a tinge of disappointment at being left alone, with grief overcome by working through the past. For this reason, the books are frankly and naturally nostalgic; thus, love and the spirit of a happy childhood are preserved. Both books present each girl's emotional intensity with careful, tactful restraint. But the girls differ as much as do the books and the styles and techniques of their creators. The girl in *Granpa* is small; she remembers romps and games, fooling around, and short conversations—a lot of activity with Grandpa (fig. 26). And the illustrations are mainly humorous sketches,

Fig. 26. John Burningham, *Granpa*
From *Granpa* by John Burningham. Copyright © 1984 by John Burningham. By permission of Jonathan Cape Ltd., Publishers.

11. John Burningham, *Granpa* (London: Jonathan Cape, 1984).
12. Bettina Egger, *Marianne denkt an ihre Grossmutter (Mary and Her Grandmother)*, illus. Sita Jucker (Zürich: Bohem Pr., 1986).

like snapshots ingeniously hung up by the imagination (including those of Grandpa remembering his own childhood). Mary is an older girl, and she calls up images of her grandmother that are solemn celebrations—paintings illuminated by blue-green and light brown lights—of a woman composed, warm and distinguished, and admired for the quiet support she gave her granddaughter (fig. 27). Only two pictures are grey-hued—Grandma's funeral near the beginning of the book, and the scene where Mother attempts to explain death to Mary and to calm her sorrow and her anxieties that her parents and she herself might die, too (fig. 28).

A word of caution is in order. There are picture-book makers who sincerely strive to the best of their talents to respond to this emerging social and psychological need, the need for children and grandparents to relate to one another. In their books, both children and adults are characterized well. Their joys, strengths, and intimacies, their shocks, weaknesses, and private tragedies are narrated slowly and allow the child-reader-viewer to have all the time needed to savor the story.

However, in many countries, there has been a spate of mediocre and outright inferior works with trivial plots; shallow, artificial characteriza-

Fig. 27. Sita Jucker, *Marianne denkt an ihre Grossmutter*

Sita Jucker *Marianne denkt an ihre Grossmutter* from *Marianne denkt an ihre Grossmutter* by Bettine Egger. Ill. by Sita Jucker © 1986 by Bohem Press, Zürich, Recklinghausen, Wien, Paris. Photolithos: E. Beverari/Verona. Druck: Grafiche AZ/Verona

Fig. 28. Sita Jucker, *Marianne denkt an ihre Grossmutter*

Sita Jucker *Marianne denkt an ihre Grossmutter* from *Marianne denkt an ihre Grossmutter* by Bettine Egger. Ill. by Sita Jucker © 1986 by Bohem Press, Zürich, Recklinghausen, Wien, Paris. Photolithos: E. Beverari/Verona. Druck: Grafiche AZ/Verona

tions; and difficulties and conflicts too easily overcome in expected ways. These makeshift treatments try to cash in on many parents' fears and insecurities when confronted with the infirmity of old age and with their own parents' relationships with their grandchildren. Triviality facilitates matters in the short term because problems seem to disappear without hurting anyone too much. But this is a deceitful portrayal; for in real life, stereotyped solutions do not often work. So librarians, teachers, and counselors should carefully examine the books they offer to children and their families who are curious to discover how other families feel about their older members.

Returning to the good and excellent books, we find that two moods generally reign: the humorous and the melancholy. More often than not, these two moods mix and create a framework for acquainting us with those old and very young persons who are held together by a special bond, one based on mutual trust, mutual need, and mutual support. Grandparents derive from this bond a relationship based on almost unconditional love, a role, and a function in life. Children feel secure with these old people who have time, are full of strange ideas, and are less demanding than their parents.

As works of art, these books, even the good ones, tend to be simple. The plots and language are concise, and the illustrations focus on essentials. The artists display good craftsmanship in the way humor and intimacy and the strong, lucid, visual characterizations portray the difference (by way of confrontation) between small children and old persons. But there is little verbal and visual metaphor; the composition is vigorous, but it omits the ambiguous, as if the very subject demanded uncomplicated treatment. Real depth is rare. Among the books mentioned in this section, only *Jan and the Grandmother; My Grandpa Is Old, and I Love Him Very Much;* and *Now One Foot, Now the Other* offer, by means appreciable to the child, a taste of the agony that silently grips those whose world narrows and whose self-esteem lessens. When parents are involved in the story, they are shown realistically—supportive, yet sometimes a bit helpless. Interestingly, in most books, a one-to-one relationship is portrayed—one grandparent and one grandchild (though in some stories a sibling is involved). Just as with stories about children and parents, storytellers in word and picture seem to know that children wish to have close persons for themselves alone, in reality and even more so in their imaginations, often to compensate for what reality does not offer. (So it should possibly come as no surprise that when even an artist as creative as Helen Oxenbury illustrates a book on both *Grandpa and Grandma*, the story seems too tame.[13])

For the child, the grandparent's world, as presented in these books, is essentially an enclave where stress is mitigated; it is a corner, a refuge, where one can behave in a less grown-up way than one is able and expected to elsewhere, and is criticized less. There is much physical closeness. Such opportunities for a temporary regression to earlier behavior patterns are extremely important for children's mental health, so grandparents also fulfill a psychodynamic role. They may aid in lowering anxiety and offering temporary security. They also strengthen children's self-confidence in various, even diametrically opposed ways: by helping their grandchildren to

13. Helen Oxenbury, *Grandpa and Grandma* (New York: Dial/Dutton, 1984).

help themselves (as in *What's Under My Bed?* or in *I'm Going to Ask Grandma*), by praising them (as when Mary's grandmother says that Mary skates better than everyone else, in *Mary and Her Grandmother*), and by letting them feel how precious their company is and how much the grandparents seek to make the hours together beautiful (as in *Granpa, Mary . . ., Now One Foot . . .*). When the grandparents become infirm and need physical and mental help, children are encouraged and strengthened by the tasks they fulfill and by the recognition that they are able to assist and to care for adults.

Yet, clearly, these stories intimate that the grandparents' pain, suffering, and growing weakness also arouse anxieties about illness, loss of love, and death. As in other essential spheres of life, close love and anxieties are never far apart.

The parents we have met in these stories try to help their children more by well-meant factual information and explanation than by emotional support, at least in the texts. The illustrations tend to express more compassion, as, for example, in the double portrait of Mary and Mother after Grandma has died: mother and daughter find comfort in being very close and sharing their sadness.

Judging from these books, we are able to deduce that knowing grandparents may provide many-faceted experiences that further personal and social growth. It is disappointing to find that so few picture books explore these parameters at a level suited to children of various ages. A few of those dealt with here demonstrate that such an exploration can be done successfully. But none of these works has a truer universal ring than *My Grandpa Is Old, and I Love Him Very Much,* in spite of its specific European background.

What we have found should also remind us of the advice proffered by psychologists writing on the subject. They counsel families and social workers and, implicitly, picture-book makers not to idealize grandparents' potential roles beyond a certain limit—a limit that is probably overstepped by many picture books which have not been mentioned here. We have to remember as well that very many children have cold, cantankerous, demanding, remote grandparents. It seems that no notable picture book has as yet taken up this variation of the theme.

However, in general, psychologists agree that the presence of grandparents enriches the child's family life.

CHILDREN'S BOOKS CITED

BROOKS, RON. *Timothy and Gramps*. Sidney and London: Collins, 1978.

BURNINGHAM, JOHN. *Granpa*. London: Jonathan Cape, 1984.

CASELEY, JUDITH. *When Grandpa Came to Stay*. New York: Greenwillow, 1986.

DEGLER-RUMMEL, GISELA. *Jan und die Grossmutter (Jan and the Grandmother)*. Ravensburg, Germany: Otto Maier, 1978.

DE PAOLA, TOMIE. *Nana Upstairs and Nana Downstairs*. New York: Putnam, 1973.

———. *Now One Foot, Now the Other*. New York: Putnam, 1981.

EGGER, BETTINA. *Marianne denkt an ihre Grossmutter (Mary and Her Grandmother)*. Illus. Sita Jucker. Zürich: Bohem Pr., 1986.

HARRANTH, WOLF. *Mein Opa ist alt, und Ich hab Ihn sehr lieb (My Grandpa Is Old, and I Love Him Very Much)*. Illus. Christina Oppermann-Dimow. Ravensburg, Germany: Otto Maier, 1978.

KUBELKA, MARGARETE. *Ich werde Oma fragen (I'm Going to Ask Grandma)*. Illus. Hans Poppel. München: Ellermann, 1983.

MacLACHLAN, PATRICIA. *Through Grandpa's Eyes*. Illus. Deborah Ray. New York: Harper, 1980.

OXENBURY, HELEN. *Grandpa and Grandma*. New York: Dial/Dutton, 1984.

STEVENSON, JAMES. *What's Under My Bed?* New York: Morrow, 1983.

VIGNA, JUDITH. *Grandma without Me*. Niles, Ill.: Albert Whitman, 1984.

6

Longing for Love, Contending for Love

Some children are lucky in that they have parents who convey clear signs and proofs of love and care. No doubt, even these children have to cope with their parents, to vie for attention, to give in to parental demands. They may, like Nick of the goblins in *My Mama Says . . .,*[1] have some trouble with their mothers or with both parents. But basically they are secure. Other children are less lucky and, consequently, less happy. In their eyes, too, parents are both wonderful and difficult people to live with. The parents want to be trusted implicitly. Are they to be trusted? They want to be loved by their children. Do they know how children can give expression to their love? They certainly think they know how to bring up children. But do they know how to love them? The parents are very preoccupied with themselves. They are armed, very strongly, with their routine methods of dealing with children. Children often wish they didn't need their parents so much. But they do. And, just as fervently, they want to need them. In a sense, coping with parents is a pervading issue, one that is indecisive, ambiguous, and puzzling. Aspects of the dilemma accompany and occupy each child over long years of affection, anguish, and stress.

BEING LEFT ALONE

Sometime in very early childhood, when infants begin to develop memories, separation anxiety appears. Children cry when Mother goes away for even a short time, for the child can remember that she was present just before but is not yet able to remember that she will return or that states can alternate. And several years later, the attachment to the parents, and especially to the mother, is still so vital that children easily and quickly interpret the situation of being left alone as a loss of love. Even though they are given sensible, understandable explanations, they search for ulterior reasons. Being left alone is an emotion of many shades. Consider these two brief stories about small girls. *Staying Home Alone on a Rainy Day* presents

1. Viorst, *My Mama Says. . . .*

62

the situation in miniature.[2] Mother has left her little girl for just a short time, to do some shopping. At first, Allison feels grown up. But then it starts to rain, and the house grows dark. She tries to keep herself busy, but being busy doesn't help. That noise—is it her mother returning? The phone rings, but she is too afraid to answer it. Could it have been her mother, she thinks after it stops ringing? Then the rain stops, and through the window Allison can see her mother, running home, her arms full of packages. So she does care, thinks Allison, and fleeting doubts recede.

The illustrations create the flavor of the book. When it starts to rain, fog covers the windowpanes, and Allison becomes restive and feels cut off. Then misty patches of color cover the piano and the kitten; uncertainty, not only the rain, blurs Allison's view. When she is scared of the ringing phone, the illustration shows her dramatically retreating behind the large blue window curtain, clutching its folds (fig. 29). Red patches of color that Allison discerns in the fishbowl remind her of a mother fish and a baby fish swimming together; where is her mother? Toward the end of the story, two pictures show Allison standing by the window and rubbing off the mist— we see her lovely, anxious face from the outside, as if through Mother's eyes as she returns. The sun shines through the window and in Allison's heart, as her mother hurries home. But the book jacket and the very last picture emphasize the story's essence—they show a pensive girl pressing two fingers together, trying to stay her anxiety (fig. 30). Some of Iwasaki's books come across as a bit too sweet. This one, however, has a compelling velvety texture that perfectly enwraps the girl's restlessness.

Mommie's Scarf is a textless book composed of eight expressively staged photographs.[3] A small girl's mother has gone away—for hours? for days? Although her father stays with her, she misses her mother. She is able to find some solace in the beautiful scarf that her mother has left at home. It now represents her attachment to Mother. It is carried everywhere—with the toys, on a walk with father, to bed. Moments of happiness and of anxiety are vividly associated with the scarf (fig. 31). It comforts and sustains the girl until her mother's homecoming is celebrated and the scarf returns to its ordinary function.

Staying at home alone has different connotations for older children; to them, it is a situation they have become used to. *Sleep Well, Have Pleasant Dreams* presents the experience as part of the search for self-reliance of a girl whose parents go out for the evening.[4] In their eyes, their daughter is a big girl now (she is seven or eight years old, judging from the illustrations). They kiss her good night and turn off the lights. Now the dark comes alive with anxiety-arousing noises. A large beast jumps on the girl's bed. A toothy monster occupies the living room. A little red man's merry patter

2. Chihiro Iwasaki, *Staying Home Alone on a Rainy Day* (New York: McGraw-Hill, 1969).

3. Gabriele Lorenzer, *Das Tuch von Mama (Mommie's Scarf)* (Ravensburg, Germany: Otto Maier, 1983).

4. Schindler, *Schlaf gut, Träum schön.*

Fig. 29. Chihiro Iwasaki, *Staying Home Alone on a Rainy Day*
From *Staying Home Alone on a Rainy Day* by Chihiro Iwasaki. Copyright © 1969. Reprinted by permission of McGraw Hill Publishing Co.

Fig. 30. Chihiro Iwasaki, *Staying Home Alone on a Rainy Day*
From *Staying Home Alone on a Rainy Day* by Chihiro Iwasaki. Copyright © 1969. Reprinted by permission of McGraw Hill Publishing Co.

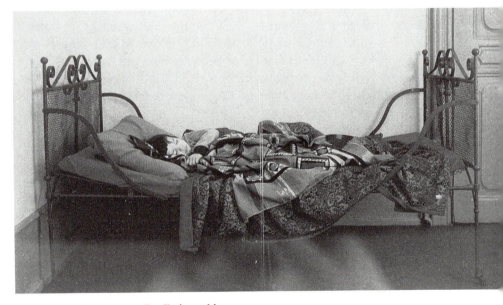

Fig. 31. Gabriele Lorenzer, *Das Tuch von Mama*
Gabriele Lorenzer, *Das Tuch von Mama*. © 1983, Ravensburger Buchverlag Otto Maier GmbH.

resounds on the kitchen table. The girl is afraid but will not give in. First, she hides under the blanket; then, she gets up, time after time, turns on the lights, and searches out the real source of every noise: the cat, the alarm clock ticking away, some apples rolling off the kitchen table. Later, she drowns out suspicious noises from outside the apartment by singing aloud. As she becomes more secure, step by step, she permits herself to be tired. She turns off the light for the last time, crawls into bed, and falls asleep. If you are expected to act grown up, you can either panic or fight back.

The illustrations bring out the contrast between the peaceful apartment— a Matisse-like interior—and the big monsters prowling in the dark. Strong colors reverberate with the girl's emotions, which oscillate between fear and self-assurance (fig. 32). The colors also disclose the intention of the book, about which the text is silent, and they do so mainly through the representa-

Fig. 32. Edith Schindler, *Schlaf gut, Träum schön*
Edith Schindler, *Schlaf Gut, Träum Schön*. © 1982 Ravensburger Buchverlag Otto Maier GmbH.

tion of the parents. In their daughter's eyes, the parents are a young, hand-some couple. In the beginning, when they prepare to leave, "Mother **says,** 'Sleep well, my big girl,' and gives me a kiss. She smells good. Father **pinches** my cheek and says, 'Have pleasant dreams, my big girl.' "

But the girl's tense face does not reflect this somehow manipulative **ring** of certainty. Does she think her parents really believe she will not be afraid and discover how to overcome her fears? In the end, the text says, "And the beast, the monster and the little man are gone"—while the picture closes in on the parents, who have come home. They are having a good look at their sleeping daughter (fig. 33). There are no easy smiles. Mother is seen from behind. Father's face has an odd look. Are they satisfied? Are they proud of their girl? Will she tell them, the next morning, how the evening passed, or will she choose to keep quiet? The story does not close

Fig. 33. Edith Schindler, *Schlaf gut, Träum schön*
Edith Schindler, *Schlaf Gut, Träum Schön.* © 1982 Ravensburger Buchverlag Otto Maier GmbH.

on an obviously harmonious note. A question mark, a silence hangs in the air. Growing up is a lonely affair.

ON ASSERTIVENESS AND CHANGE

Most children who feel neglected do not remain passive. They stand up and fight. Consciously and unconsciously, they seek strategies for how to win a share (or more) of love.

One author-artist has created two exemplary picture books demonstrating the struggle of assertive children for a place in the warm sun of parental attention and the changes they may achieve. Anthony Browne's *Gorilla*, one of the significant books of the 1980s, tells of Hanna, a quietly assertive girl, and her struggle for intimacy with the father she loves.[5] In her heart, she knows he is vigorous and active and lovable, much more so than the apparently subdued type who is busy with his work. She starts dreaming of gorillas; she wishes her father would go to the zoo with her. But he never has time. Then her birthday approaches, and suddenly her father does pay some attention to his daughter, giving her a toy gorilla as a birthday present when she goes to bed. The gift makes her angry, since she was expecting a real, live gorilla. But the gift triggers a dream. The gorilla grows, dresses in father's clothes, and takes Hanna out for the night—to the zoo and a super-gorilla film, with ice cream and cakes for Hanna and lots of bananas for himself, and a final romantic waltz at the doorstep—perfect wish fulfillment. But Hanna wants and gets more. When, in the morning, she tells her father of the night's events, he invites her to the zoo: now wish fulfillment crosses over into reality.

The story is related in brief passages. It begins in reality, with the exposition of Hanna's predicament and her first attempt at mastering it; it continues in fantasy, where the solution is worked through; and it returns to reality, to verify the solution in real life. The story includes the structural elements of fairy tales, inventively combining traditional motifs—such as magic, wish fulfillment, and animals coming to the aid of children—with the motif of father-reading-newspaper, one of the modern versions of father-abandoning-child! (Another is Father glued to the TV set; some picture-book fathers devote themselves to both the newspaper and the television!) On the narrative surface, this is an amusing account of how a birthday turns out to be pleasant despite initial disappointment.

On the psychological level, it is a drama acted out on two stages—Hanna's home and Hanna's imagination—with two actors appearing on each. The story starts long before her birthday and revolves around two themes: the complexity of father-daughter relationships and the role of fantasy in a child's pursuit of love.

In this book, the verbal narrative is the "score," albeit an excellent one.

5. Anthony Browne, *Gorilla* (New York: Julia MacRae Bks. and Random, 1983).

The music, so to speak, is performed both narratively and psychologically, in the pictures. One element in Browne's style is realism. He applies it here for a sympathetic portrayal of the *dramatis personae*. Hanna is one of the loveliest girls ever depicted in a picture book, with her eager face that brightens even more with strands of hair escaping from her ponytail. Her shoulders, her arms, and her hands have a natural, quivering expression throughout, whatever the mood. The gorillas and their relatives—the other apes—are sad, gentle creatures. Even Father, whether withdrawn or communicative, has the artist's understanding. Browne is also a punctilious hyper-realist who creates some spooky moods—such as the spotless, chilly kitchen with its ice-cold blue-and-white hues, with straight lines, straight angles, and small squares dominating, accented by sharp perspectives (all this scenery showing David Hockney's influence); other hyper-realistic highlights are Father's work corner, the animals' fur, and the table full of treats late at night.

Browne's surrealistic leanings, and power, come out very delicately in ominous shadows that become contradictory in some illustrations, such as in the kitchen and in Father's room.

Metaphoric visualization reigns, however. Throughout the book, gorillas dominate. Books, Hanna's own drawings, lamp shades, cereal boxes, the banister, playthings, reproductions, sights met in the night—does not even the hill under the moon, seen beyond the front door, look like a gorilla's head? Gorillas fill the home and the town, serving as a single-minded projection, as an extended metaphor of Hanna's longing, by now quite obsessive, for a virile, warm, and dependable father. These images not only decorate and transform Hanna's environment; here and there they act up: the ones on the lamp shade stop dancing and say good-bye when Gorilla comes alive. The wallpaper and electric sockets also have a say. There is practically no end to metaphors. There are the chairs, for instance; in the beginning, Father's is an obstacle that has not been overcome; at the end, Hanna's chair aids Father to traverse distance. Or consider the many stripes and grids, including Hanna's bed, which call to mind the idea of being caged.

As befits a drama, the book progresses in clearly outlined scenes that are intimately connected through the mesh formed by the metaphors. The first act begins with Hanna smilingly drawing gorillas on the title page and continues on the next page, where she reads about gorillas. Now she tenses up—the book she is holding doubles the defensiveness of her tightly closed legs; breakfast in the kitchen, as the attempt to reach Father creates a vertical axis; makes us feel as if her eyes are about to sear the newspaper, but Father continues reading, his face shut away. He and the newspaper are part of the horizontal axis formed by the cupboards and the refrigerator, in whose cold center his head rests. Father leaves for work; then comes two harshly moving pictures, the first as Hanna tries once again to approach Father, to cut through the stripes and angles crowding the corner, her sweater the only warm spot there; her back bends slightly forward, her arms, hands, and fingers form an overwhelming picture of conflict between an outflow of feeling checked by the immovable figure in the chair (fig. 34). The desktop, where one expects family photographs, is blank. A girl of nine,

Fig. 34. Anthony Browne, *Gorilla*
From *Gorilla* by Anthony Browne. Copyright © 1983 by Anthony Browne. Reprinted by permission of Alfred A. Knopf, Inc. and Julia MacRae.

looking at the picture, said, "It's as if the green curtain were coming down on all her wishes." In the second picture, Hanna, the day after, even dares to touch the chair, but the dark silhouette in the corner spells hopelessness; all her wooing will not coax her father out of his shell. She retreats into the TV corner—one of the most telling representations imaginable of a child's withdrawal and renunciation. Television makes for passivity. Yet, Hanna's fantasy is active—beyond the pretty flowers emanating from the set, the menacing jungle encroaches on the wallpaper.

The second act begins on the evening before Hanna's birthday. She walks up the stairs, goes to sleep, wakes up in the middle of the night, opens the small package containing the toy gorilla, and furiously throws it into the corner. Now magic starts—Gorilla grows. At the same time, the lights in the toy house brighten and twinkle. A moment of fear and an invitation to the zoo ensue. Down and out go Hanna and Gorilla.

The third act follows quickly, the trip that more than fulfills all wishes, with tenderness abounding, as Hanna is held and carried and touches and embraces Gorilla (fig. 35). Then comes a variation of the breakfast table scene, as Hanna and Gorilla sit opposite each other, with no newspaper separating them. The climax is the waltz in the moonlight, the very real kiss, and Gorilla's promise to see Hanna in the morning.

The last act finds Hanna waking up, smiling at the toy gorilla, and rushing down to tell her father, so fast that the artist is too slow to catch her; only a whiff of her descent is in the air. Father has changed; he wears bright clothes; he is close and strong; and he offers to take Hanna to the zoo. Did he plan this event before, or did he, taking up the hint in the dream, decide it on the spur of the moment? Can he act so spontaneously? We will never know for sure. The secret of a good story is that it knows how to keep secrets.

In case we are still skeptical of the identification of Father with Gorilla—even after we saw Gorilla borrow father's hat and overcoat, and after Gorilla promised Hanna that they would see each other in the morning—the book's

Fig. 35. Anthony Browne, *Gorilla*

penultimate picture features a banana sticking conspicuously out of Hanna's father's back pocket (fig. 36). If we are still unconvinced that the story is about Hanna's successful fight for her father's attention and about her belief that, withdrawn within his shell, there exists a warm person worth fighting for—the same picture has, on the wall, a drawing of a *human* father and his daughter: the need for "gorillaization" subsides. Then, the very last picture recapitulates the nightly walk with Gorilla, except that this time Hanna is with her father.

Some things do not change: although it is Hanna's birthday, her mother—like Max's (of *Where the Wild Things Are*)[6] father—is totally absent from both text and illustration. It would be unfair for the same-sex parent to spoil the Oedipal fight and fun. Some things do change: Max wouldn't have wished to tell his mother that he just gave up a kingdom for the smell of her supper.

We have so far interpreted the story from two points of view; the aesthetic

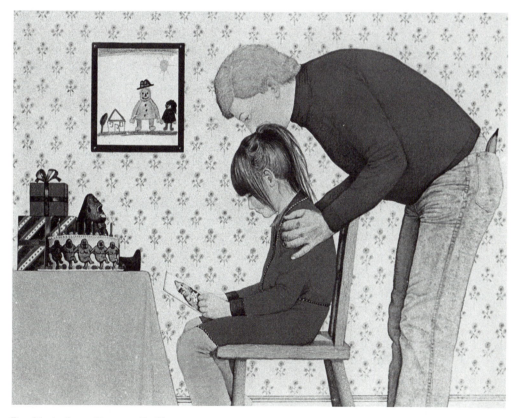

Fig. 36. Anthony Browne, *Gorilla*

6. Sendak, *Where the Wild Things Are.*

and the psychological. A third aspect can be detected, one related to cultural issues. The bureaucratic and the technological phenomena—father's work, the newspaper, television—represent a cold and emotionally unsatisfactory way of life. Hanna seeks redress by turning to the warmth of violent, instinctive forces. Yet, when these approach, they threaten to swamp significant values of Western civilization—the Mona Lisa, Whistler's portrait of his mother, Charlie Chaplin, the Statue of Liberty, and other pictures turn into gorillas. Even the classic waltz is transformed. Then moderation is achieved, when both extremes soften as they meet. Again, lest we are incredulous, the motif is fully brought out on the cover. What appears at first glance to be nothing but an expression of thrilling, innocent fun is also, deeper down, a surrealistically realized statement. The background is a restive city at midnight. Strange sights appear in the windows—a hanged man, for instance—and on the roofs, a tree, a bottle, a snail, uncertain figures, and King Kong catching airplanes. A sense of danger exists. In the foreground, turning toward each other, swing the two partners of the nightly trip—on a crazy, impossible branch growing out, of and binding together two distant trees. Hanna and Gorilla symbolize hope for a world where functional and intrinsic relationships, affective and intellectual aspects, and the primal and the mature have a chance of balancing each other instead of vying for sweeping ascendancy in a conflict that could lead to a drying up of civilization or to cataclysm.

Of course, this interpretation is relevant only to adults. Even to them, it might at first sight appear uncomfortable or arbitrary. However, the alternative lies in assuming that a superior artist who displays a genuine empathy for children's concerns in his many books would engage in quite tasteless jokes that are far above the heads of children and of no interest to them. It is, after brief initial misgivings, much easier to accept an in-depth approach. No doubt, Browne enjoys pranks, especially visual ones; he employs jokes, but they embody sarcastic meaningfulness. Besides, this motif—Browne's comments on the cultural scene—also appears in other books of his. So does another motif implicit in *Gorilla:* Browne's favorable opinion of women.

The excellence of *Gorilla* arises from the convincing fashion in which Browne combines the various means of his art. The story is told in concise paragraphs, the illustrations are flexible yet precise, and body language is applied exceedingly well. The result is drama. It is such a fascinating book because, notwithstanding the complex richness of its communications, we never lose sight of the central human motif that it serves—a young girl's need for tenderness.

The Visitors Who Came to Stay once more takes up the theme of the search for love, but in more entangled circumstances.[7] It also leads Katy, the

---

7. Annalena McAfee, *The Visitors Who Came to Stay,* illus. Anthony Browne (London: Hamish Hamilton, 1984).

protagonist, toward a maturer understanding of what mutual attachment might mean. Actually, at the outset, Katy has everything she believes she could want. Her father, William, is separated or divorced from her mother. He and Katy live alone in their house by the sea. Then, one day Father's girlfriend, Mary, and her son, Sean, begin visiting them; later, they come to stay. Katy feels lost, disoriented; the intruders take over the house; Mary occupies William's attention and draws him away from Katy. Sean drives Katy crazy with his pranks and trick toys, never missing a single opportunity to irritate someone. One day Katy can bear it no longer and tells Father so. Mary and Sean leave. Father and Katy resume their routine. But Father is very quiet, absorbed in thought. Even Katy, after a while, feels that something is missing. When Father suggests that they visit Mary and Sean in their house, she agrees.

The story, told by McAfee in a realistic, matter-of-fact vein, offers characteristically contemporary motifs, situations, and developments that are certain to stimulate Browne's creative imagination. Its sensibility would be even more effective if the story were somewhat briefer and the sentences, shorter. On several pages, the text distracts one's attention from the illustrations. Yet, the story is original and well carried through, including the open ending. Browne's inventive powers soar as he paints large pictures, most of them crammed with content and arresting detail, pictures imbued with his dedication to the hyper-realistic, rather static lucidity of appearances. In a way, each painting tends to be self-contained. No sense of continuity, of one illustration leading over visually to the following one, can be detected at first. The pictures are strangers to each other, in content, style, and narrative intention. However, a closer scrutiny reveals that coherence is not absent from the extreme oscillations of moods. Coherence, visual narrative, and continuity are achieved brilliantly, though not easily. Two strands of style represent Katy's changing states and moods. At first, and throughout most of the story, the more satisfied Katy is with things as they are, the more realistic the pictures are. The less secure or sure of herself she feels, the more crowded with surrealistic items the paintings become. In this book, as well, visual pranks, weird views, and jokes abound. Here, they are not accidental. A certain logic guides the artist's vision as he allows these stylistic moods to alternate, to mingle, and to interact with each other, until they exchange their functions near the end of the story.

Surrealism in this book means that Browne gives reign to his fascination with the work of Magritte, the well-known surrealistic painter. He does so both by emulating Magritte and by actually citing Magritte's paintings. Surprising as this emulation is, it is controlled by the artist in order to serve the narrative.

The first illustrations realistically present the almost compulsive order and cleanliness characterizing the secluded tenderness with Father. The mood softens as Father and Katy sit, all by themselves again, on the beach. When Katy goes on one of her rare visits to her mother, and she and her father are waiting for the train, the piece of sky seen through the viaduct at the station is suddenly much bluer than the sky above, and some white clouds swim in it, a first allusion to Magritte: Katy becomes tense when she has to separate from Father for the weekend. In the following picture, Mary and Sean arrive for their first visit. Bright light and strong colors intrude with them, contrasting with Father and Katy's subdued hues. Katy's security breaks down. The cupboard fills up, dramatically, with Magritte motifs. On the opposite wall, a (Magrittean) locomotive lets off steam. The clock makes a face, as does the teddy bear, and the cat escapes, horrified. Now weekends are filled with noisy fun: the carousel glows with absurdities, and flags at half-mast fly above—as Father embraces Mary. As the two visitors—invaders—come to stay, Katy feels strongly threatened by Mary's hamper full of clothes and by Sean's disgusting trick monster hand—just one of his innumerable gadgets.

The two following illustrations bring us to the nadir of Katy's feelings. One shows the four characters sitting at the breakfast table (fig. 37). It depicts the total lack of contact between the two children and the intense love William and Mary feel as they look at each other. The kitchen floor is littered with Sean's assorted trick toys. Inner and outer disorder complement each other. This picture has been incisively analyzed by Gertrude Herman.[8] She also relates that "a knowledgeable friend" has brought to her attention the fact that Browne used as his model a cover titled "Saying Grace," created by Norman Rockwell for the *Saturday Evening Post* of November 1951.[9]

Then another weekend arrives. The four of them spend it on a crowded beach (fig. 38). For Katy, the world around her becomes indecipherable. Wherever she turns, her gaze confronts strange people and objects. In this cohesively crazy world, people seem to be having a good time. Still, some signs are frightening, especially when compared with the first beach scene, when Father and Katy were there all alone; now the white cliffs beyond have changed into a finger; the ship, into a bus; and the seagulls are joined by a flying pig. However, in the picture's center sit Mary and William, their feet touching, in a pose that is a direct quotation from the great Impressionist Édouard Manet's pastoral painting "Le déjeuner sur l'herbe" (1867). As we look closer, we perceive that they, William and Mary, together with Katy (though she turns her back on them) and Sean, are the only four normal people on the beach. The stylistic forms affirm that this moment is the turning point in Katy's life. Now she can no longer put off becoming aware of what love might mean for adults. The learning process has begun, and it continues. One evening, as Father and Mary go out, the children see a romantic old movie on television, starring Clark Gable—is it *Gone with the*

8. Gertrude Herman, "A Picture Is Worth Several Hundred Words," *Horn Book* (July/Aug. 1985): 473.
9. Herman, letter to *Horn Book* (Jan./Feb. 1986): 3.

Fig. 37. Anthony Browne, *The Visitors Who Came to Stay*

Anthony Browne from *The Visitors Who Came to Stay* by Annalena McAfee, ill. by Anthony Browne, reprinted by permission of Hamish Hamilton Ltd.

Wind? The room Sean and Katy are in is realistic, decorated with flowery, faintly erotic tapestry. As Mary and Sean leave, somewhat later, the house resumes its hyper-realistic, clean-and-cool atmosphere—only the seagull out there is now (a worried sigh in Katy's heart?) a teddy bear. Peace fully returns: as Father and Katy sit, close together, in the pavilion on the beach, a real seagull flies by—time has stopped; the pavilion's clock faces have no hands.

But time does not stop; both Katy and her Father find that they miss the visitors. As we turn back one page and have another look at the geometri-

Fig. 38. Anthony Browne, *The Visitors Who Came to Stay*
Anthony Browne from *The Visitors Who Came to Stay* by Annalena McAfee, ill. by Anthony Browne, reprinted by permission of Hamish Hamilton Ltd.

cally accented kitchen, we detect that the cat (that symbol of the female) hurriedly escapes from it, as it did before when the visitors arrived. Now the rules in the game of styles change. Katy begins to feel alienated in her clean-and-cool, realistic house. She sits on a large question mark. Now the primly dressed girl in her school tie loosens up a little (but her haircut doesn't) and involves herself in thought. In the end, William and Katy stand in front of Mary's home, with Mary and Sean looking down at them from the window. House and front garden are dazzlingly overwhelmed by surreal elements. A flying fish wings through the air. But Katy is no longer intimidated. She wants to be part of the fun.

The narrative purpose of these illustrations is supported by the items adorning the left-hand pages bearing the text—large, unframed, hyper-realistic depictions of single objects that immediately and intimately connect with Katy's troubles are related on the respective pages: a photograph of herself with Father; a gleaming toothbrush for the weekend with Mother; Mary's hateful shoes; and others, page by page. The perfectionism that Browne lavishes on these mostly decorative, negligible items annoys, aesthetically, because of the out-of-proportion importance they assume when compared with the full-page illustrations on the right-hand side. Yet, through these objects, the artist accurately reflects the exaggerated, meticulous, petulant—annoying—attention Katy wastes on them throughout the story. Thus, the objects assume a narrative function.

In and out of these alternately overpowering and receding pictorial configurations wander the four people whose desire for love, fear of being left out, and longing for close relationships are acted out in the story. The four are sympathetically characterized as real, likable, unaffected persons. The turmoil is all in Katy's mind; her touch with reality becomes tenuous at an early stage, as the problems seem to be unsurmountable, and also later, as she is drawn to the visitors. For her, surrealism—that strange intoxication—is an attribute of Mary and Sean.

The idea communicated is clear. Katy, who believes that having her father all to herself is as natural as it is permanent, learns that life is unpredictable. In the end, she is both willing and able to share her father and, in turn, receive a family. She finds the courage to open herself up to the challenge, the ebb and flow of an as yet uncharted future. The visual analogy of this development is the stylistic distance traversed from the peaceful cover picture, with a small giraffe emerging from the sea, the tiny teapot on the rail, and the woman with the funny hat as the first slight warning signs of Katy's insecurity, to Mary's unreal, twinkling house, which now attracts Katy more than the strict way of life that she and Father have imposed on themselves.

Underneath runs the current of Browne's observations on the cultural scene. We can assume that these observations were attuned to McAfee's story, though there they are alluded to only obliquely. What we mean is this: why did Browne use Norman Rockwell's "Saying Grace" for one of the crucial scenes in this book? First of all, obviously, the fact that the picture's composition and configurations suited his purposes exactly must have caught his eye. In both pictures (Rockwell's and Browne's), four people are joined around a table. Strong contact can be felt along the horizontal axis; in Rockwell's, the young man on the left looks at and listens intently to the elderly woman saying grace; in Browne's, the eyes of William and Mary meet in a searingly frank expression of their mutual love. Rockwell's almost vertical axis shows two youngsters, each occupied independently; yet somehow the way their heads are inclined shows that they are drawn into the solemn mood. Browne's two children are out of tune with the moment; Sean, as usual, is frenziedly active with his tricks, feverishly trying to prove himself. Katy is frozen, disconnected, and declines to see what is going on before her eyes; she is almost hidden behind the cereal boxes; her mood is spelled out by the skeleton on one of the boxes and, more importantly, by the tabletop—while Rockwell's tabletop rests on a sturdy leg, Browne's is suspended in the air.

Browne's picture is *not* a parody of Rockwell's, although certainly we may imagine a twinkle in the former's eyes as he structured his own. Yet Browne maintains the mood of solemn concentration, though transforming it by entrusting it with a narrative purpose. However, surpassing these affinities, there is the fact that Rockwell was an American artist depicting a typical American scene. Now we can perceive Browne's version as the central link of an extended metaphor, a chain of allusions to the fact that Mary and Sean are Americans: the array of flags flying at half-mast over the carousel, with the British one lowest of all (in Katy's mind); the consumerism indicated in the text, expressed by Mary's rich wardrobe and Sean's huge number of gadgets—Groucho Marx's spectacles among them—and the fun orientation they represent, in both text and illustrations; the Empire State Building as a sand castle on the beach; Clark Gable; and no less than the White House with the American flag now flying high, to the left of Mary's house. Browne's comment can thus be understood as describing Katy's initial situations as British, staid, orderly, and balanced on the brink of being sterile. Into this pattern sweep the two Americans—disquieting, unsteady visitors who jolt the balance, introducing fresh, dynamic, though topsy-turvy unrest, which promises to be more conducive to human fulfillment than does seclusion. Once again, as in *Gorilla*, there is a meeting, a mingling, a possible conciliation of cultural attitudes: the extended metaphor is rounded off in the quiet, anticlimactic, last image of Katy's teddy bear wearing Sean's Groucho Marx spectacles—a synthesis?

THE MERITS OF COMPARISON

One is easily and justifiably tempted to compare *The Visitors Who Came to Stay* and *Gorilla*. Their similarities and differences are too intriguing to be left untouched. Besides, comparison can clarify a few more issues.

In both books, the protagonists are girls who fight for their father's love and against what they experience as neglect. As it turns out, in both cases, the fathers are, or become, attentive to their daughters' problems. Hanna's gives her the right present and then spends her birthday wit her. Katy's gives in to her wish, sending Mary and Sean away. Browne himself thinks that both books are alike to a certain extent in that both are about feelings.[10] In aesthetic terms, the resemblance lies in the masterfully sustained visual metaphorization of thoughts and emotions. As Browne puts it—it's a way of showing nonvisual things in a visual way. In both books, realism and surrealism vie with each other. In both, surrealistic elements communicate the psychological concept that strict order and cleanliness rather than safe-guarding a sane way of life serve as defense mechanisms that keep anxieties at bay and impair happier relationships and growth. Both books contain comments, even advice, on developments in contemporary civilization.

Browne aims at entertaining; he wishes to evoke smiles, to create fun. He applies exaggeration and satire. The jackets of each book clearly hint that he thinks the idea that reality can be fully rational is an illusion. But these fireworks are unable to hide his empathy, his warm emotional involvement with the characters whose experiences he portrays. Does he not think, by the way, that girls and women are more assertive, interesting beings than men?[11] Whatever level we focus on, we can discover optimism— a belief in desirable change and in freedom.

However, Browne himself insists that no narrative link joins the two books. He views *Visitors . . .* neither as a sequel to[12] nor as a follow-up[13] of *Gorilla.* The difference starts with the story, which in *Visitors . . .* was authored by McAfee. According to Browne, it was difficult to convince her that a story could be told in pictures as well as in words.[14] That is, the balance between the verbal and the visual had to be, and was, achieved in ways not applicable to *Gorilla.* There are other points of divergence. Hanna is younger than Katy, so that much of her happiness is bound up with her father, who responds to her need for a warm, intense relationship with him.[15] Katy, the older of the two, is closer to the stage at which she should be ready to transfer some of her affective ties to other persons, to enter new relationships. Her father gently coaxes his child, so it seems, toward such a development.[16]

Considering the volumes from the aesthetic point of view, it is important to emphasize two perceptible dissimilarities concerning the creative process and its results. In *Gorilla,* continuity is achieved by what we have called the drama occurring on two stages. By contrast, continuity in *Visitors . . .* is

10. Reinbert Tabbert, "Nichtsichtbares sichtbar machen" ("Showing Nonvisual Things in a Visual Way"). An interview with Annalena McAfee and Anthony Browne. *Informationen des Arbeitskreises für Jugendliteratur* (Jan. 1986): 8–13.

11. This assumption is certainly supported by some of Browne's later books, such as *Piggybook* (New York: Knopf, 1986) and *Kirsty Knows Best* (New York: Julia MacRae Bks., 1987).

12. See Tabbert, "Nichtsichtbares."

13. See Sylvia Marantz and Kenneth Marantz, "An Interview with Anthony Browne," *Horn Book* (Nov./Dec. 1985): 696–704.

14. Sylvia and Kenneth Marantz, "Interview," 703.

15. Hanna's father is not necessarily a single parent. See Tabbert, "Nichtsichtbares," 2.

16. Browne says he felt more sympathy, perhaps, with Katy's father than with Hanna's. See Tabbert, "Nichtsichtbares," 2.

sustained by what we have called a game of styles (with large roles for Margrittesque irony and significance accorded to objects).

The stories also belong to somewhat different genres. In *Gorilla*, the reader participates in both the real and the imaginary narrative events. He or she thus is involved in the fantastic journey. In this respect, *Gorilla* resembles, for instance, *Where the Wild Things Are*. In *Visitors . . .*, we, the readers, remain in reality. We are ignorant of the action going on in Katy's imagination. Only symptoms are communicated to us, metaphors of states of mind. In this respect, *Visitors . . .* resembles, for example, Keats's *Whistle for Willie*.

Browne has shaped two books devoted to related themes: a simple story created by himself, and a complex one, assisted by an author. Becoming aware of how one particular artist has ingeniously varied his creative approach offers us a deeply satisfying experience.

LOSING THE FIGHT

Sometimes children lose out in the struggle for their parents' affection. Certainly, in real life this occurs frequently. In an untold number of families, there are children who, although they are apparently being cared for, feel unloved and unwanted for reasons they cannot fathom. Maybe they disappoint their parents in some way, or perhaps relationships between the parents and within the family or social and economic factors may be involved. Often, it may be that parents are simply too busy. Very likely, the family is not acutely aware of the situation or does not care sufficiently to want to change it.

Myth and fairy tale know about this issue, though they tend to treat it in rather set ways; they offer compensatory, no doubt utterly significant fantasies, which, however, lead beyond the family. The picture book hardly ever takes up the theme with a contemporary background.

An exception is *Not Now, Bernard*.[17] In this story, the issue is crisp and clear-cut. Whatever Bernard does, he is able neither to attract his father's nor his mother's attention. They are simply busy—reading the paper or watering the flowers. Whatever he starts to say or do receives the same response, "Not now, Bernard"—even when he is threatened and then enveloped by the monster in the garden, and even when the monster bites Father and roars at Mother and makes himself at home in Bernard's room. Certainly, Mother cares for Bernard: even when he has changed into a monster, she puts his supper in front of the TV set, places his milk at his bedside, and solicitously turns off the light when he goes to sleep. Yet, even though the monster (Bernard) protests and angrily demands recognition of its monstrous character and behavior, unseeing routine will not be disturbed—not now.

17. David McKee, *Not Now, Bernard* (London: Andersen Pr., 1980).

McKee keeps a light touch. The matter-of-fact text and illustrations, in a dynamic graphic style, create a sequence of riotously funny exaggerations. Children certainly laugh and enjoy being reminded of how ever-busy their parents are and how unrelenting the sacred daily rituals may become. Readers derive satisfaction from sympathizing with Bernard when, losing hope of ever being able to make his parents look at him or listen to him for a moment, he loses his patience with them and becomes aggressive. However, when even by changing into a monster Bernard is unable to make his parents notice him, exasperation turns into despair. In the parents' eyes, his moods and his identity have no importance whatsoever. Such a reaction spells defeat. When even aggression fails to evoke a response, the gap between being brought up and being loved becomes too wide (figs. 39 and 40). Bernard gives up because he feels given up.

We can never be certain how children understand adult humor. McKee, one of the masters of satire in the picture book, surely also wants to criticize, tongue-in-cheek, the alienating force inherent in letter-perfect educational practices handled by busy parents. The story will arouse anxiety in some

"ROAR," went the monster behind Bernard's mother.

Fig. 39. David McKee, *Not Now, Bernard*

"Not now, Bernard," said Bernard's mother.

Fig. 40. David McKee, *Not Now, Bernard*
From *Not Now, Bernard* by David McKee. Copyright © 1986 by David McKee. Reprinted by permission of the publisher, Viking Penguin, a division of Penguin Books USA Inc.

children precisely because its seemingly innocent exaggerations will remind them of their parents' attitudes. This is a good, helpful book to use to initiate talks with children.

From Iwasaki through McKee, we have moved from stories relating how children long for tenderness that is absent only momentarily to others telling of children who have to make sure they get their share of intimacy by overcoming various forms and degrees of withdrawal and neglect, as they themselves feel and interpret it. Do the characters succeed? Will Hanna's father stay close to her? Will Bernard's parents realize, the next morning, that their child has changed?

In the books examined here, coping with parents relates both to the powerlessness of children and to their sources of power. Some children give up. Fortunately, most don't. Their innermost needs assert themselves. Their imagination comes to their aid. So does the imagination of picture-book makers who have the courage to help children to develop their own selves.

CHILDREN'S BOOKS CITED

BROWNE, ANTHONY. *Gorilla*. New York: Julia MacRae Bks. and Random, 1983.

——. *Piggybook*. New York: Knopf, 1986.

IWASAKI, CHIHIRO. *Staying Home Alone on a Rainy Day*. New York: McGraw-Hill, 1969.

KEATS, EZRA JACK. *Whistle for Willie*. New York: Viking, 1964.

LORENZER, GABRIELE. *Das Tuch von Mama (Mommie's Scarf)*. Ravensburg, Germany: Otto Maier 1983.

MCAFEE, ANNALENA. *Kirsty Knows Best*. Illus. Anthony Browne. New York: Julia MacRae Bks., 1987.

——. *The Visitors Who Came to Stay*. Illus. Anthony Browne. London: Hamish Hamilton, 1984.

MCKEE, DAVID. *Now Now, Bernard*. London: Andersen Pr., 1980.

SENDAK, MAURICE. *Where the Wild Things Are*. New York: Harper, 1963.

SCHINDLER, EDITH. *Schlaf gut, Träum schön (Sleep Well, Have Pleasant Dreams)*. Ravensburg, Germany: Otto Maier, 1982.

VIORST, JUDITH. *My Mamma Says. . . .* Illus. Kay Chorao. New York: Atheneum, 1973.

7

The Emergence of Identity

Throughout childhood, the individual's personality grows and expands. Slowly, yet forcefully, biopsychological processes, genetic inheritance, physical constitution, and life experiences lead the child toward a larger range of capabilities, expanding relationships, wider horizons, and a greater measure of consciousness of his or her own self and of independence. Different psychological persuasions employ a host of concepts, whose definitions and connotations overlap in intricate ways, to describe and interpret these developments. What is clear beyond doubt is that somewhere along the way, children's strong attachment to their parents, the need for close intimacy with them, diminishes. Parents continue to be essential in the child's life, but no longer are they the only significant other persons. The need to feel close and to be loved, and the growing need to discover and assert one's self—two enduring, not easily reconciled necessities in every human being's life—intensify conflicting tendencies in the child's mind. From the psychoanalytic point of view, these processes, originating in what Bettelheim has called Oedipal disappointment, have been compellingly delineated by Bettelheim within the context of his treatment of the importance of fantasy stories.[1] The search for individuality includes many interrelated aspects. In modes partly similar to those characterizing the fairy tale, the contemporary picture-book story attempts to entertain the child and to aid him or her by offering plots, relationships, and metaphors for the various facets of the search.

A MEASURE OF AUTONOMY

Striving for an increasing share of autonomous behavior, of being responsible for oneself, is an early element in the crystallization of the personality—an element that operates hesitantly and precariously at first and gains strength as the years go by. From assertive experiences, children derive a

1. Bruno Bettelheim, *The Uses of Enchantment: The Meaning and Importance of Fairy Tales* (New York: Vintage Bks./Random, 1977): 124–25.

sense of pleasure and of mastery—especially if the conflicts arising in the course of action are solved, more often than not, in a way certain to convince children that their parents support these basically rebellious actions. In some of the stories discussed earlier, we have met fictional heroes who do act autonomously. Max of the *Wild Things*,[2] Peter of *Whistle for Willie*[3] (and also, by the way, Peter in *Peter's Chair*, another story in Keats's Peter series),[4] and Hanna of *Gorilla*[5]—all successfully attempt to assert themselves. Yet, the primary objective of their action is to attain, through independent real and imaginary experiences, the attention and affections of their parents— though with Peter, the need for "environmental acknowledgement" surely also extends to the big boy who whistles for his dog. In *The Visitors . . .* , Katy asserts herself and is encouraged to understand that change is necessary for her own individual development to proceed—within the family.[6]

The girl in *Sleep Well, Have Pleasant Dreams*[7] (who, left alone at night when her parents go out, mobilizes her powers of self-reliance to overcome anxiety personified by the monsters she imagines and then perceives to have been exaggerations of her own mind) is actually much like the girl in *The Trek*,[8] whose mother has stopped walking her to school every morning. In a way, the two stories resemble each other. Both girls are propelled into action by stress imposed on them by their parents. Both prove that they can cope realistically with anxiety, through personification, with the help of their fantasies. Both relate their experiences in the first person. The girl in *The Trek* is getting used to walking alone. But even though a friend joins her, the experience is still scary. She works through her feelings by imagining the way to school as a trek through the jungle. Everywhere in her peaceful neighborhood, the bushes, trees, flowers, stone walls, even newspapers, turn into strange, beastly animals. Water flowing from a hose in front of a shop becomes a river the two have to swim across. But they make it. At first, the girl's voice betrays a slight grudge against Mother, who is not aware that they live at the edge of a jungle and sends her off, right into danger. But the girl decides to venture out, trusting only her own cunning. This dramatization encourages her to admit to herself that it is only her amazing skill that saves her, day after day. Overcoming such notable threats is much more rewarding and overcompensatory than simply facing reality, and it strengthens her sense of security.

The background for the girl's and her friend's bittersweet experience is a running stretch of a few streets and corners in a sedate neighborhood, where people go about their early morning business—and where, surpris-

2. Sendak, *Where the Wild Things Are*.
3. Keats, *Whistle for Willie*.
4. Keats, *Peter's Chair*.
5. Browne, *Gorilla*.
6. McAfee, *The Visitors Who Came to Stay*.
7. Schindler, *Schlaf gut*.
8. Ann Jonas, *The Trek* (New York: Greenwillow, 1985).

ingly yet expectedly in the girl's eyes, animals and, here and there, pieces of a "wild," savannahlike landscape appear (fig. 41). The artist employs the exhilarating wizardry for which she is well known to help the girl detect and shape familiar, funny, and weird forms of assorted fauna hiding all along the trail—all of which is triggered, as the title page indicates, by the view of the animals in the picture in the girl's bedroom, which we glimpse as she gets ready to set out for school, bending backwards, her eyes filling with anticipation. Ingenious application of visual allusions, illusions, and ambiguous figures, and the reversal of figures and backgrounds arouse the viewer's curiosity and draw him or her along until, after the girls have

Fig. 41. Ann Jonas, *The Trek*

climbed the mountain (i.e., the few stairs in front of the schoolhouse) and past the enigmatic parrot, the girls are exhausted and the parrot dissolves into a potted plant and a knob on the railing. The scary trek is over . . . for this day.

We noted above that the two books, *Sleep Well . . .* and *The Trek*, are similar in several respects. However, seemingly small nuances create different emphases. *Sleep Well . . .* is somewhat more serious than *The Trek*. Relying upon herself, the heroine explains away the monsters and falls asleep, tired and satisfied. It is quite clear, however, that she did not choose the situation as an opportunity for acting autonomously. She is intent on proving herself in order to please her parents. By contrast, the girl in *The Trek* conjures up the dangerous animals and their dwellings at will. She talks of "my" animals. She repeats the make-believe experience day after day. It serves to reinforce her desire to rely on herself and to forgo Mother's protection. She relishes the taste of that controlled tinge of anxiety.

It is interesting to compare the two books and to find out how two stories so close in concept succeed so well in communicating by texts and pictures, content and style, glimpses of their different meanings: one girl, still wholly embedded in the family, fights off monsters; the other manipulates the beasts as a means of striking out on her own. In *The Trek,* as in many other of her works, Jonas limits her texts to a minimal, precise exposition of situations and feelings, and paints quite sophisticated pictures that reflect the playfulness and inventiveness, the sensuous creativity characteristic of children. Jonas is as sensitive to the anxieties of children as to the secrets of visual perception and illusion. The combined impact is as humorous as it is psychologically authentic.

Julia, or A Present for Mother is about another girl who insists on acting independently.[9] The story records a school outing. Teacher takes her group of small girls on a trip through the woods and up a hill. Throughout the day, Julia lags behind and gets lost at every turn, worrying Teacher and the other girls (fig. 42). She wanders off because she becomes absorbed with the sights of leaves and animals and signs in the sky. Any view and sound is likely to entice her. The perils she encounters cannot deter her from endangering herself, because her inquisitive mind cannot refrain from any opportunity to look into things. The most textless story is swiftly carried along, one experience triggering the next one with convincing visual continuity. Identifying and following squirrels leads to an alarming moment as

Fig. 42. Wiltrud Roser, *Julia, oder ein Geschenk für Mutter*
Wiltrud Roser, *Julia, oder ein Geschenk für Mutter* © 1982 by Otto Maier Verlag Ravensburg. By permission of Wiltrud Roser

9. Wiltrud Roser, *Julia, oder ein Geschenk für Mutter* (*Julia, or A Present for Mother*) (Ravensburg, Germany: Otto Maier, 1982).

a wolf grabs Julia's satchel. Birds she feeds attack her; she stumbles down the rocks, falls on her face, frightens off the wolf's cubs, and finds her satchel; from now on, a small dog follows her. When they all reach the cafe on top of the hill to get ice cream, Julia is not willing to tie her dog up outside. She chooses to sit on the terrace, all by herself, clutching the dog. As a large balloon appears in the sky, she falls asleep and dreams of the pilot, who descends and invites her to join him. The sun sets, and they return home, boisterously satisfied. As Julia presents the dog to her mother, Mother, sighing deeply, is visibly displeased and taken aback.

The story is delicately funny, yet at the same time it insists vigorously on Julia's individuality. She is sensitive but also resolute in her need and intention of satisfying her own curiosity. Her creative interests lead her along. Her small experiences, about which the other girls would not know or care, are more dangerous but finer and more exceptional than theirs. Her wish to be different, to be herself, is strongly brought out. As the trip begins, on the title page, Julia stands slightly apart from the rest of the girls. Similar scenes recur during the day; as the group returns and all the other girls sing loudly, a closed-mouthed Julia walks in front, triumphantly cradling her dog (fig. 43). She is the determined outsider, vindicated by her strange experiences—including even the proverbial descent into the underworld, the wolf's lair, and the excursion into a satisfying daydream when she feels neglected for a moment. Her peers don't really mind her, nor understand her, it seems. Teacher is nice and attentive. Only the twins, double representations of nonindividuality, mock her as often as they possibly can. Keeping to herself provides Julia with surprising rewards.

At this point, we should mention Shirley. In two books *Come Away from the Water, Shirley* and *Time to Get Out of the Bath, Shirley*[10]—Burningham creates amusing stories and uses them to focus on a specific aspect of the quest for autonomy—the one Bettelheim has called the child's painful disenchantment with his parents.[11] In each story, Shirley wanders off and escapes, in her imagination, from Mother's insufferable cautionary chatter and (in the first story) from her father's apathy. She finds a treasure and is crowned a queen in the first tale (a psychological symbol of self-attainment), and vanquishes a king and his queen in water sports, in the latter. She pays no heed to her mother, who, in turn, has not the slightest idea of what goes on in her daughter's mind. The disillusionment is mutual; so is the lack of communication. Shirley's search for self-realization is removed from her parents' knowledge, empathy, and participation. The composition of the two books emphasizes this gap by operating on three levels. There is reality, Mother, and her monologue on the left-hand page. Shirley's fantasy journeys are revealed on the right-hand page (fig. 44). The third level, Shirley playing on the beach or in the bathtub, respectively, bodily enacting

10. Burningham, *Come Away from the Water, Shirley* and *Time to Get Out of the Bath, Shirley.*
11. Bettelheim, *The Uses of Enchantment.*

Fig. 43. Wiltrud Roser, *Julia, oder ein Geschenk für Mutter*
Wiltrud Roser, *Julia, oder ein Geschenk für Mutter* © 1982 by Otto Maier Verlag Ravensburg. By permission of Wiltrud Roser

her fantastic feats, is invisible, recorded only in Mother's observations; thus, the emotional distance is augmented: "Now there's water everywhere!" says Mother in *Time to Get Out . . .*, as she wipes the bathroom floor (fig. 45). Of course, Shirley has just pushed the king into the water, and he has made a big splash. "You won't bring any of that smelly seaweed home, will you, Shirley," says Mother as Shirley sails off for Treasure Island in *Come Away . . . .* While Roser's Julia does not mind being protected, both on the trip and at home, as long as she is allowed some leeway for doing precisely what she is motivated to do, the stress imposed by Mother's attention and Father's inattention drives Shirley, who is older, off and away.

BEING DIFFERENT

The last two protagonists we have met also reflect another aspect of the evolving personality—the need to find out, to try out how one's self is

Fig. 44. John Burningham, *Come Away from the Water, Shirley*

From *Come Away From the Water, Shirley* by John Burningham. Copyright © 1977 by John Burningham. Reprinted by permission of Jonathan Cape Ltd.

Fig. 45. John Burningham, *Time to Get Out of the Bath, Shirley*.

From *Time to Get Out of the Bath, Shirley* by John Burningham. Copyright © 1978 by John Burningham. Reprinted by permission of Jonathan Cape Ltd.

different from others: Julia, from her peers; Shirley, from her petty parents, and, in a way, from who she is in the present.

In this context, the works of Leo Lionni come to mind.[12] Several of his lyrical fables, or parables, suggest a persistent, though diverse, preoccupation with the motif of identity and self-realization by way of creative play with visual configurations. Lionni has created both stories that have an unthreatened protagonist, such as *Frederick, Tico of the Golden Wings,* and *Cornelius,* and others that have a protagonist whose existence is temporarily endangered, as in *Little Blue and Little Yellow, Pezzettino,* and *Swimmy.*

Among all these heroes, Frederick, the poetic mouse, is the one most certain of himself. He knows he is different; he is not able to gather grains

12. Leo Lionni, *Frederick* (New York: Pantheon, 1967); *Tico of the Golden Wings* (New York: Pantheon, 1964); *Cornelius* (New York: Pantheon, 1983); *Little Blue and Little Yellow* (New York: Astor Bks./McDowell, Obolenski, 1958); *Pezzettino* (New York: Pantheon, 1975); *Swimmy* (New York: Pantheon, 1963).

and roots—only words, colors, and sun rays. He has the inner conviction that these nonmaterial goods will one day be helpful to his fellow mice. He is content to be an outsider. When, in deep winter, his colors and words strengthen the hungry mice's morale, social recognition (you are a poet!) makes him blush. *Frederick* is the most unequivocally profiled of Lionni's stories. Frederick, the individualist, is placed, from the first and in picture after picture, separate from the working mice against a background characterized by potatolike forms (stones, mice, etc.) in shades of gray with occasional outbreaks of stronger colors (fig. 46), especially in the winter, when Frederick conjures up images of colors in his fellows' imaginations. He sits alone; he turns his back on his peers, and toward the end, he addresses them from high up; even the expression in his eyes varies from theirs—it is unfocused, contemplative, until the wintry moment when, his glance dominating the scene, he delivers his message. Under the circumstances, the mice certainly exhibit remarkable tolerance, ultimately rewarded, toward this elitist member of their society, for only now can they understand what he meant when he refused to participate in their efforts. They adore him. Lionni stresses Frederick's importance by the hundreds of his signatures adorning the endpapers. Frederick has an outsider's identity, but his self-realization is bound up with his society. If only we knew how Frederick will act next summer!

Tico in *Tico of the Golden Wings* arrives at his identity in more indirect

Fig. 46. Leo Lionni, *Frederick*

From *Frederick* by Leo Lionni. Copyright © 1967 by Leo Lionni. Reprinted by permission of Pantheon Books.

ways. At first, he has no wings; then, he acquires golden ones, but the
other birds are not pleased. He is lonely and exchanges his feathers for
ordinary black ones. Now he is accepted by the other birds because he is
just like them. But Tico (speaking of Lionni, it seems) knows better. He
knows that everybody is different. Everyone has his or her own invisible
golden dreams. Swimmy, the fish, in the book of that title, on the other
hand, is favored by fate *because* he is different. He is the only black fish in
a red school and the only one not being eaten by the big fish. He is lonely,
so he will not rest until he finds another red school of fish and teaches them
to swim in formation, pretending to be like one big red fish, with Swimmy
being its black eye. In this way, they will be saved. Swimmy actually
achieves self-realization by giving up his own separate identity. *Cornelius,*
the crocodile, gets into trouble because he walks upright from birth and he
is rejected by the other crocodiles. When he learns more tricks from the
monkeys, all the crocodiles imitate him; his curiosity is "in"; now he is
accepted. These heroes demonstrate that there are various ways of becoming a special being and, at the same time, making one's peace with the
crowd and also fulfilling a social role.

In *Little Blue and Little Yellow,* the two friends get mixed up in each other's
personalities and experience a few painful minutes, until they sort their
identities out again. *Pezzettino,* that strange little piece, is not sure he is
himself; maybe he is a small piece of somebody else? He sets out to find
out. As he asks one being after another (One-Who-Runs, Strong-One, and
others), if he possibly is their little piece, they affirm that they are complete,
with no piece missing. Finally, the Wise-One sends him to an island where
there is nothing but heaps of pebbles. Pezzettino trips and breaks into lots
of little pieces. Now he is certain that he, too, is made of little pieces and
is, therefore, a whole being. He picks himself up, all the pieces of himself;
arriving back home, he shouts, "I am myself." His friends do not quite
understand what he means, but since he seems to be happy, so are they.
Philosophically, there is more to this story than we shall discuss here. One
could go on. In *The Greentail Mouse,* field mice learn from the city mouse to
put on masks and threaten each other; when they take off the masks, they
feel it is good to be, peacefully, themselves again.[13] Then there are stories
such as *Alexander and the Wind-Up Mouse*[14] and *Let's Make Rabbits,*[15] in which
inanimate animals wish for, and attain, real-life personalities.

These Lionni heroes know that identity is a very precarious possession.
It grows slowly, and it easily gets lost; its development can arouse misgivings in the environment. The outsiders may attempt to adjust, or they
may become models for their society because they are different. They all,
however, are individualists who cannot develop and live except by being

---

13. Leo Lionni, *The Greentail Mouse* (New York: Pantheon, 1973).
14. Leo Lionni, *Alexander and the Wind-Up Mouse* (New York: Pantheon, 1970).
15. Leo Lionni, *Let's Make Rabbits* (New York: Pantheon, 1982).

different. A few make amends to their puzzled fellow beings, who cannot fathom why these individualists bother so much with their own selves and their own experiences (just as Julia's peers and Shirley's parents cannot). In the end, identity and self-security are worked out—except for Swimmy, who loses himself in order to create an organized society. Along the way, these sensitive beings suffer deep existential anxiety, imposed by loneliness, social pressure, and their own fragility. Occupied as they are with who they are, they acknowledge social integration. However, Lionni does not let us doubt that he thinks of them as superior beings because of their power of introspection and their creative insight. In surprising transformations of styles and techniques, and in masterly fashions of color and form, Lionni, the eminent aesthete among picture-book makers, insists on creating his parables about animals, toys, and pieces; there is no place for reality versus imagination; his world is a romantic and humorous fantasy. But these anthropomorphous creatures speak quite incisively to the human child and adult on how bewildering, interesting, *and* important it is to become oneself.

In *Kirsty Knows Best*, being different refers to several interwoven questions.[16] In real life, Kirsty is an outsider, rejected by her peers; in fantasy, she soars above them. Her fervent belief is that she can be different from the person she seems to be. In Kirsty's life, the quandary of not being satisfied with who she is reaches deep.

The book lets us participate in what appears to be an ordinary school day. When Kirsty is awakened by Mother's shrill voice, she looks at her with shortsighted eyes. Through a dismal breakfast (it's a poor home) with Mother scolding her for daydreaming, the gloomy road to school, boring lessons, an irate teacher with cold eyes, playtime spent alone (for Nora, who bullies her and sneers at her for daydreaming, makes sure that Kirsty will be left out), Kirsty's day leaves much to be desired—the more so since, after school, she will return home to her unemployed father and to her mother, who is bored by her work operating a cash register in the supermarket.

Daydreaming is Kirsty's way of coping with reality, of opting out of it whenever it becomes too oppressive and lacking in promise. The promises are ready in her imagination; Kirsty knows better than to trust reality, which is why the passages depicting the girl's day as it drearily moves along are interspersed with others telling of her glorious fantasy experiences that correct reality's mistakes. It is a distinctive feature of Kirsty's existence that her endeavor to "corriger la fortune" (correct fortune) includes her parents; she does not intend to disengage herself from them but to free them, too, from silent despair.

So it is that Kirsty wakes up as a princess, only to be rudely called by

16. Annalena McAfee, *Kirsty Knows Best*, illus. Anthony Browne (London: Julia MacRae Bks., 1987).

her mother into the kitchen. Yet, breakfast turns into a party for the three of them. When Nora sneers at her on the road, Kirsty switches to a pseudo-Chinese landscape with Nora pulling her ricksha. Now the parents are drawn in to the fantasy, and their dreams are acknowledged. Mother's fame spreads as she rises to be a superstar. Father—who at the moment Kirsty dreams for him is still reading the paper in bed, with a rubber water bottle at his side (he has no job to get up for), and who likes to tinker in the toolshed at night—is a genius on his way to changing the future of mankind. Toward the end of the story, when school becomes insufferable; the lesson drones on; and during break, Nora spits out hate-inspired half-truths about Kirsty's father being a slob, her mother a drudge, and Kirsty herself as thick as an out-sized brick, Kirsty knows better. Sweet vengeance takes over, going beyond this single day. As Nora shriekingly carries on, in Kirsty's vision she turns, by stages, into a thickening toad and explodes. Meanwhile, Kirsty is a butterfly winging its way up and away. These changes—the swift passages from one world to the other—are not by any means related in a simple fashion. Nothing about this book is pedestrian except for the poverty of home and the dead weight of school. Both the verbal and the visual account, and their combination, are wrought and polished with attentive competence. They surprise, entice, haunt the reader, and leave him or her wondering how and why.

The story, though one can scarcely speak of a plot, has much balance. The real-life scenes are rendered in prose that is clear and exact in description and dialogue, with the recurring refrain of "But Kirsty . . ." whenever we are about to move over into the imaginary realm. The daydream sequences are rhymed poetry, adorned by illuminated initials. McAfee endows Kirsty's changing existence with distinction. For the illustrations, Browne calls up colorful and complex images expressed in a selection of his styles and modes. The changing faces of the people in the story are a careful study in human expressiveness. The environment shocks. Beyond that, Browne matches Kirsty's illusions with allusions, her dissociations with associations, and her mental ruminations with his visual ones—with clues strewn all over.

In the first picture, Princess Kirsty wakes up in her Renaissance bedroom, with some Gothic elements included, smiling and planning for an auspicious royal day (fig. 47). She is pretty; no eyeglasses are in evidence. The portrait of "An Unknown Youth" (after a miniature by Nicholas Hilliard, c. 1588) adorns the wall. Still, the artist's brush introduces several incongruities into the splendid room, indicating that Kirsty's escape from the present is not fully achieved. A modern alarm clock stands on the night table; the "Unknown Youth" is a poster, affixed in today's careless manner. One of the ornate bedposts sports a "smiley" face. Worse, though, is that on the picture's upper right-hand border is a dragon's snout that, as we turn the page, appears to be Mother's face, as she wakes Kirsty. Now, back in reality, the alarm clock has gone, an Elvis Presley poster decorates the wall, and

Fig. 47. Anthony Browne, *Kirsty Knows Best*

From *Kirsty Knows Best* by Annalena McAfee, illustrated by Anthony Browne. Illustration copyright © 1987 by Anthony Browne. Reprinted by permission of Alfred A. Knopf, Inc. and Julia MacRae.

eyeglasses rest on the night table. Then plain, bespectacled Kirsty sits at the kitchen table and dreams of the breakfast party with her young parents—she herself pretty, without glasses. Back in reality, Kirsty walks to school. But soon—back in fantasyland—black, fearsome creatures roam far above her. When Nora is delegated to pulling the ricksha, in a round picture reminiscent of delftware, two birds high up hold Kirsty's glasses in their beaks. Now Kirsty envisions her parents' glowing future. Mother's dream is realized as a straightforward, glitzy photograph of a glamorous star, loaded with diamonds. Father's grandeur in his secret lab is an astonishing composition; it is a clearly portrayed agglomeration of dozens of items, a puzzle referring to art, science, and history, whose details ask to be identified (fig. 48). The general idea is comprehensible without going into all the details; however, they add depth and fantastic, ironic magnitude and fun. The poem to the left of the picture relates that Reg (this being Father's real, regal first name) pushes the frontiers of science ahead, having also set his heart on world domination. Following up this statement and heightening

Fig. 48. Anthony Browne, *Kirsty Knows Best*

From *Kirsty Knows Best* by Annalena McAfee, illustrated by Anthony Browne. Illustration copyright © 1987 by Anthony Browne. Reprinted by permission of Alfred A. Knopf, Inc. and Julia MacRae.

it, the picture shows Father as an all-embracing genius who spans the fields as well as the periods. He is the amazing scientist, the modern alchemist, standing in front of bottles and tubes filled with suggestive fluids. An opening in the ceiling (reminiscent of the Dutch artist Escher's painting "Another World") lets our gaze reach the moon and stars. At the same time, Father is a military hero and a statesman: Julius Caesar's bust and Napoleon's portrait vouch for that. A wrapped-up box (like Christo's style in art?) harbors unheard secrets. Still more forceful is the vision of Father standing in the foreground, while behind him a map of the world covers the wall—just as in many of the great Vermeer's paintings a map served as background for persons of distinction, as a metaphor of the Netherlands as a proud maritime power. (Vermeer came from Delft—does the plate allude to that?) Two overall metaphors unify the images found on this page: one is Father's eyeglasses. He wears them both in the real and in the fantasy realm; they serve to emphasize intellectuality; they are worn by Father himself; by Caesar, Napoleon, and Superman; and by the flying dog and the globe standing on the table. The other metaphor expresses the tendency to fly high, up and up. Close to twenty unrelated items represent flight: a flying hat and flying loaves of bread (both from Magritte); a witch, Mary Poppins, Santa Claus, two flying magic carpets, and many more. Father's smile tells of his elation. How valid is the prospect of his success in Kirsty's vision? It might be thought difficult to find some significance in such an incongruous but revealing assembly of elements. But the relevant flaw is right here: one of Father's conspicuous shoes is brown; the other is a blue slipper—irony in the foreground. Bettelheim wrote: ". . . the more insecure a man is in himself and his place in the immediate world, the more he withdraws into himself because of fear, or else moves outward to conquer for conquest's sake. This is the opposite of exploring out of a security which frees our curiosity.[17] This is the way Kirsty's father is represented by author and illustrator as seen by the daughter, with her usual behavior pattern of compensatory daydreams.

Now we are ready to take up the two continuous visual metaphors that persistently run through the story from beginning to end. Between them, these metaphors seem to embrace the story's message. The one is clad in the form of a pair of horns growing out of a head. It appears in a large number of pictures, some twenty times in all, mainly in those describing reality, looming large in Nora's upstanding pigtails, Nora's mother's car, a black cat, but also—in the form of chalk lines—on the blackboard behind Teacher's head, on the TV screen, and, in diminutive size, attached to a number of other objects, even a stain on the breakfast table. This metaphor constitutes a sign of evil—and one is strongly reminded of a detail in a well-known painting by Ambrogio Lorenzetti, done in 1338–39 and preserved in the town hall of Siena, Italy. The painting is called "The Allegory of Bad Government," and the detail referred to is a large face crowned by two horns and representing *Tyranny*. The other recurring image is a butterfly. On the cover, it flies away among the white clouds, close to a smiling Kirsty. On the title page, a caterpillar appears. Later, when Kirsty's boredom magically changes the classroom, the textbook on her desk takes on a butterfly's shape (fig. 49). Teacher's brooch also looks like a butterfly. At playtime, a butterfly lands on Kirsty's finger. In the last picture, Kirsty has become a butterfly, soaring high. The horns seem to have been transformed into her antennae. Fantasy triumphs. Kirsty's dream overcomes the wicked forces that cross her way, again and again, in her real world.

What is the message? What do McAfee's story and Browne's artistic fireworks want to communicate? There is, first of all, the proof of how reckless successful imagination can be when it is called up to transcend reality and to support a child's attempt to cope with what he or she recog-

17. Bettelheim, *The Uses of Enchantment*, 51.

Fig. 49. Anthony Browne, *Kirsty Knows Best*

From *Kirsty Knows Best* by Annalena McAfee, illustrated by Anthony Browne. Illustration copyright © 1987 by Anthony Browne. Reprinted by permission of Alfred A. Knopf, Inc. and Julia MacRae.

nizes as unbearable and unjust. Kirsty has learned early to escape whenever and wherever she wants into a realm of poetry. She does not make her peace with things as they are; correction is far reaching. She knows how to hate Nora's red-hot malevolence. She knows how to express attachment to her parents—though she is quite disappointed in them (and probably vice versa). She includes her parents in her daydreams, thus glorifying their aspirations and upgrading her lineage. It seems that she feels closer to Father: at the breakfast party she looks at him; his lab-dream of world domination is much more exuberant than her mother's singing scene. The motif of the eyeglasses—common to Father and daughter—hints at their closeness. Yet, the portrait Kirsty gives of her father also shows him as an insecure being, withdrawn and taciturn, who wishes to invent and to dominate not out of curiosity, but because overcompensation might bring security. Kirsty, herself, is an "ugly duckling" whose intuition knows better, and perhaps knows best.

The last illustration, Kirsty as a butterfly, shows her wearing her eyeglasses.[18] Does that suggest that the dream might come true? Still, behind this celebration of the power of the imagination, there exists a lonely, unloved girl, who suffers deeply by being plain—and bespectacled—and by being poor. Life is heavy—the butterfly is beautiful and light and bright. At this point, as in *The Visitors . . .*, a cultural comment again is made. This time, the comment seems to be social criticism, expressed in both illustration and text. The Littles are a very poor family. Who is to be blamed for Reg's unemployment and for the fact that Joyce's only treat is her monthly visit to the hairdresser? This poverty is set off by pretty, well-dressed Nora— riding in her mother's shiny car. School is depicted as detrimental to development. Teacher is pretty in the same cold way Nora is, and she's also hateful, in Kirsty's eyes, hostile as she is to daydreaming. Yet, interestingly, Teacher wears a butterfly brooch—could she, potentially, become a good force? Even without this association with "the allegory of bad government," the social comment seems clear. It adds a touching resonance to this girl's impulses and justification to her devaluation of reality.

Within the context of our theme—emerging identity—Kirsty is a girl in crisis. She is dissatisfied with who she is. As she perceives her situation, her surroundings are adverse to any attempt to change and develop. Feeling deserted, she cannot accept herself the way Julia or Shirley can. She overcomes her perplexity by evolving an ideal self-image. Yet the gap between her appearance and social status, on the one hand, and the wonderful intensity (a sense of humor and a talent for irony) she hides inside, on the other hand, is wide and may threaten self-realization. Let us hope she is an "ugly duckling," or, rather, an ugly caterpillar, and will one day be admired as a butterfly. She deserves it.

IDENTITY THREATENED

Continuing the motif of threatened identity, I wish to reconsider *The Bunyip of Berkeley's Creek.*[19] In *Ways of the Illustrator*, I used this story as an example of that growing trend—the picture book that helps to expand the limits of children's literature by offering different, if overlapping, messages to children and to adults. This trend was rather new in 1973, when *The Bunyip . . .* was published. I summed up what I had to say about the book by putting a question to myself and to the reader: "Have we already understood the skeptical message about humanity contained in [this book]?" Now my reply is: no. This is the place to reopen the argument and to correct or elaborate on a few observations. I need to go back to this story to examine three specific points on which it touches. But let me first quote from the passage that describes the bunyip:

18. See illustration on the title page of this book.
19. Jenny Wagner, *The Bunyip of Berkeley's Creek*, illus. Ron Brooks (Melbourne: Childerset, 1973).

The Bunyip of Berkeley's Creek is a fantasy creature born of the mud with a strong urge to know who he is and what he looks like. He is uniformly rejected by all animals whom he meets and asks about himself, because he is so horribly and disgustingly ugly. But he is persistent and goes on asking, until he meets a man who bluntly expresses his opinion that bunyips do not exist at all. Now the bunyip gives up. He retires to a deserted place where nobody can see him, and is content with looking at himself in the mirror. That very night the mud stirs once again and another bunyip is born, turning up to ask who she is and what she looks like. But now there is someone to reply. Joyfully, they are not alone, though they only have each other.

The illustrations intensify the melancholic mood. The Australian landscape is boundless and desolate. The bunyip is pictured as being ugly beyond belief. He is a fantasy creature; he wears trousers, owns a comb and a mirror, looks at a newspaper, lights a fire at night. There is something so modest and sad about him that one starts to like him quite early, in spite of his revolting looks. There is something softly funny about him and about Brooks's style, except for the horror when the bunyip meets *man:* the first sign of him is a technotronical, caged-in contraption with boilers, pipes, chimney, aerials; next comes the moment of pseudo-truth when a cold, indifferent researcher, backed up by closed circuit screens and panels computes the bunyip out of existence, without looking at him—for there is no one to look at. In style and intention, content and execution, and in quality this is, in spite of any doubts one might have, a picture book for children. But it is an odd one. Many ugly creatures rove about in children's literature; but either they are the protagonist's foes, to be vanquished by him or her, or they turn (as do Grimm's and Beaumont's beasts) into beautiful human beings. Here the ugly beast is delivered from neither ugliness nor lowliness; only his loneliness is alleviated by the female bunyip who joins him (surely they will multiply). So they find identity, contrary to what the most repugnant creature along the creek, man, thinks. This is not an easy message for children to perceive and assimilate. However, let us reiterate, this is, probably because of the inner logic of the straightforward story and the superior quality of the illustrations, an authentic children's book. It is a thoroughly contemporary one, influenced by motifs of the grotesque and of alienation in modern art. Its hero is an essentially ambiguous figure: are children to identify with the bunyip's indomitable belief in his existence and refusal to accept that he is ugly, or to be uplifted by the understanding that if even such a ludicrous lowly creature can find joy in life, so can they? A double-pronged, existentially true approach to what anxiety means characterizes the book."[20]

The first point refers to threatened identity in a way comparable to some of Lionni's stories, though more extreme and elaborate. In his search for his own identity, the bunyip has to overcome severe threats. When he arises from the mud and sits on the bank, he asks: "What am I?" A passing platypus offers a quick reply, telling him that he is a bunyip, thus seemingly solving the question. But the bunyip wants to know more about himself, such as is he handsome? Two of the animals he meets along the creek—the

20. Schwarcz, *Ways of the Illustrator,* 191–95.

emu and the wallaby—add a few signs when he asks them what a bunyip looks like, thus boosting his feeling of security. They are forced to tell him, at the same time, how horribly ugly he is. From the moment he appears, most animals refuse to look at him.

In this connection, it is important to cite from an extremely perceptive study on *The Bunyip . . .* done by two researchers, Bunbury and Tabbert.[21] They suggest that "Berkeley's Creek" may be an allusion to George Berkeley, the eighteenth-century philosopher, who is well known for his statement "to be is to be perceived." The bunyip's predicament is precisely the opposite—animals make an effort to avoid perceiving him. The nadir of his trip is reached when he arrives at the Environment Observation Post No. 1, and man, who denies the existence of bunyips, coolly looks through him, dis-perceives him. The bunyip is desolate—though, surprisingly, after he walks away from man's disappointing judgment, he is seen wearing short pants and suspenders and carrying his belongings on a stick. Does he aim at a semblance of identity by adopting human paraphernalia? He retreats to where no one can see him or speak to him. He looks at himself in his mirror, his eye inquisitive, not satisfied with what he sees (fig. 50). Self-reflection does not spell identity. However, there is no doubt that at this point he exhibits autonomous behavior, for he takes his fate wholly into his own hands. Only when the she-bunyip rises from the mud can the two perceive each other. When he lends her his mirror, does he look happier—and even a little more handsome?

Following Berkeley's definition, one is inevitably drawn to the concepts of identity formulated by psychologists and social philosophers such as Catherine Garvey, Margaret Mead, Harry S. Sullivan, and others, who held that personal identity, of the self, exists only in a social environment, being created by interaction with significant others. But what if the others decline to participate in interaction? Then identity is threatened. The bunyip is nobody until he is shared. Only he and the she-bunyip together can actualize each other. This is, according to existentialism, a basic condition of human existence. This existentialist point of view is also reflected in the text by the statement: "For no particular reason something stirred in the black mud" (referring to the origin of both bunyips).

The second point concerns what, elsewhere, I have called "cultural comments," that third level of communication (in addition to the aesthetic and the psychological levels). Turning to Bunbury and Tabbert's paper once more, we find that they explain that in Australian aboriginal mythology, the bunyip used to be a sacred, powerful, and terrifying being. Here, in the picture book, it has become "an uncertain being which is whimsical, romantic and a figure which draws on human capacity for compassion."[22]

---

21. Rhonda Bunbury and Reinbert Tabbert, "Ein Bunyip ist vieles, aber kein Umir," *Fundevogel*, no. 4–5 (1984); 25–28.
22. Bunbury and Tabbert, "Ein Bunyip," 27.

Fig. 50. Ron Brooks, *The Bunyip of Berkeley's Creek*
Ron Brooks *The Bunyip of Berkeley's Creek* from *The Bunyip of Berkeley's Creek* by Jenny Wagner and illustrated by Ron Brooks (Kestrel Books, 1973), copyright © Ron Brooks and Childerset Pty Ltd. 1973.

In other words, the bunyip is a symbol of the aboriginal people, who have become weak and whose strength and very existence are not recognized by the white man. The authors of the paper go one step further. They consider the bunyip when, after the man's lab tests, the bunyip avails himself of human equipment, reminding the viewer of the Australian swagman, and note that the front cover shows the dressed bunyip being supported by the wallaby and the emu in a heraldic stance; they thus conclude that these images might be the artist's individual and even ironic interpretation intended to convey that "the story of the bunyip's search for identity also suggests that idea of a nation. . . . its national identity, trying to fathom its place in the world."[23] So much for cultural comment.

DIGRESSION: FOCUS ON UGLINESS

The third reason for reconsidering *The Bunyip . . .* is in order to probe the issue of ugliness. Kirsty—that extremely rare, nonbeautiful protagonist—

23. Bunbury and Tabbert, "Ein Bunyip," 27.

made us aware of what it means to be a plain girl. Yet, the bunyip's story is an extreme case, both on the humorous narrative level and on the metahistorical one. It states clearly a question we have never been able to answer: why is it that we equate Beauty with Goodness and Virtue, and Ugliness with Evil and Inferiority? Over the centuries, religion, mythology, legends, fairy tales, literature, the arts, and advertising have been telling us that this is the way life is. We are aware that there is much validity in the Platonic assertion of a bond between Beauty and Truth, and of the antagonism between physical inferiority and spiritual perfection. It is common knowledge, confirmed by research, that good-looking, presentable people possess an attractiveness that makes life easier for them.

The child's own experience affirms the idea: does not Mother look uglier when she shouts at him or her than when she is pleased? The illustrators of children's books go out of their way to reinforce the concept and the belief. Are not most picture-book protagonists—from those in the Golden Books to Beauty and the Beast—either somewhat or very handsome, so that it gives the onlooker pleasure to be with them? Is not beauty the prize, the award, that both the legendary princess and the frog receive for coping with ugliness? (A notable exception is Snow White's stepmother, whose beauty is, however, often depicted with a certain reservation, to indicate her innate evil.) Yet, are not all these approaches and instances expressions of an evolutionary flaw that education attempts to correct because of its imperfection? Because we also know, although most of human fiction and fantasy tells us otherwise, that the ugly person can be and often is as virtuous or more so than the fair one. To think differently is an unethical condemnation of those who cannot help themselves.

Surely, these observations oversimplify the issue; the philosophical and psychological implications are too complex and far-reaching to be sorted out in the present context. Education is supposed to perform that function for children. Yet, every repulsive fictional frog that has to be saved is intended to weigh heavily on our conscience. We avoid or run away from ugliness in order to save ourselves. In any case, the bunyips are disadvantaged, and inferior, also because they are ugly in the eyes of others. They are portrayed as plain and will remain so—no redeeming kiss will change that. *The Bunyip of Berkeley's Creek* has demonstrated the humanistic dilemma to the eyes of children. It is an excellent story in terms of picture-book making, and it is a courageous one, about a courageous being. Certainly, it is also a humorous story. And the bunyip, as one advertising copy has it, is a being of portly demeanor—but the serious picture book goes deeper than the skin.

The plain or ugly protagonist, as represented by Kirsty (who longs for beauty) and the bunyip (who accepts his appearance as the price of being perceived), is a quite recent motif, one that picture books approach cautiously. The concept that the fictional hero, the model for identification, should be especially attractive is deeply and justifiably ingrained in our culture. The problem lies in the impact that trivially "innocent" glamour and pseudo-glamour has on global picture-book production. Reactions to that attitude are rare. *Adeli-Sofi* is the first adventure story about a very plain girl, who is kidnapped on the seashore by a Poseidon-figure, steadfastly refuses to be enchanted by his underwater kingdom and by his languid charm, and, erupting in a temper tantrum, is allowed to return home.[24] The book—containing a girl's firm stand against seduction (fig. 51)—is an early, tough, funny, sexually satirical takeoff on romantic and

Fig. 51. Björn Graf von Rosen, *Adeli-Sofi*

Björn Graf von Rosen: *Adeli-Sofi* from *Das Märchen von der Ungehorsamen Adeli-Sofi Und Ihrer Furchtbaren Begegnung Mit Dem Wassermann* von Björn Graf von Rosen, copyright © by Atlantis Kinderbücher bei Pro Juventute Zürich 1987

glamorous fairy tales. It was created by a Swedish author and artist, published in Germany in 1940, and immediately banned in that country. When the book was reissued in Switzerland in 1987, Adeli Sofi's adventures and ugliness still aroused opposition.

A milder, and therefore possibly even more significant, example of a not particularly handsome child is Stine of *The Girl Who Did Not Want to Go to the Kindergarten* (fig. 52).[25] Nor are her parents strikingly beautiful (fig. 53). But what a lovable family they are!

An author-illustrator whose work is gaining importance is Nikolaus Heidelbach, whose picture books are filled with children of homely countenance with large noses and ears, conspicuous lips, and attentive and inquisi-

24. Björn Graf von Rosen, *Das Märchen von der ungehorsamen Adeli-Sofi, und ihrer furchtbaren Begegnung mit dem Wassermann (The Tale about the Disobedient Adeli Sofi, and Her Terrible Encounter with the Man of the Sea)*, trans. Brigitta Wolf (Zürich: Atlantis/Pro Juventute, 1987).

25. Siv Widerberg, *Flickan som inte ville gå till dagis (The Girl Who Did Not Want to Go to the Kindergarten)*, illus. Cecilia Torudd (Stockholm: Rabén & Sjögren, 1986).

Fig. 52. Cecilia Torudd, *Flickan som inte ville gå till dagis*

Cecilia Torudd, *Flickan som inte ville gå till dagis*, Rabén & Sjögren, Stockholm. © Text: Siv Widerberg, 1986 © Bild: Cecilia Torudd 1986. Reprinted by permission of Cecilia Torudd

Fig. 53. Cecilia Torudd, *Flickan som inte ville gå till dagis*

Cecilia Torudd, *Flickan som inte ville gå till dagis*, Rabén & Sjögren, Stockholm. © Text: Siv Widerberg, 1986 © Bild: Cecilia Torudd 1986. Reprinted by permission of Cecilia Torudd

tive eyes.[26] These robust, stocky, often a little flabby common girls and boys, who are painted with empathy, experience strange adventures. They live in an environment as ordinary and drab as they are. Heidelbach seems intent on ridiculing the facile, sweet stories about handsome, innocent, well-intentioned children, whose exaggerated, well-meaning—often thoughtless—portrayal is promulgated in so many picture books. Against that attitude, Heidelbach (exaggerating no less, but with artistically forceful certainty) puts his "brats" (fig. 54). They are ungainly, but their wishes, dreams, fights, and relationships occur unmistakably in a child's world and are worthy of attention.

Even if one assumes that the attractive protagonist will rightfully continue to occupy his or her preferred standing in picture books (and in

Fig. 54. Nikolaus Heidelbach, *Der Ball, oder ein Nachmittag mit Berti*
Der Ball, oder ein Nachmittag mit Berti by Nikolaus Heidelbach, Beltz & Gelberg, Weinheim 1986

26. For instance, Nikolaus Heidelbach, *Der Ball, oder ein Nachmittag mit Berti* (*The Ball, or an Afternoon with Berti*) (Weinheim, Germany: Belz & Gelberg, 1986); *Vorsicht, Kinder (Caution, Children!)* (Weinheim, Germany: Belz & Gelberg, 1987).

children's literature in general), these authors' and artists' plain heroes and heroines constitute a healthy and refreshing departure. Children do not seem to have trouble accepting them; responsible adults would be wise to set aside their reservations and to accept them also.

SEARCH IN THE MAGIC CIRCLE

After these complex, partly troubling stories, we will conclude with a harmonious one—one told and painted in a magical spirit. *Do in the Red Boots* leads us back to earlier childhood and to an inner, psychological reality.[27] The story bears the imprint of a fairy tale: its narration reflects universal rather than individual characteristics. The fantastic and the natural mingle in an easy way. The plot consists of seven episodes, each of which presents a journey, in the course of which Do gathers experience, overcomes obstacles, and gains insights. Together, the magical happenings suggest—in symbolic pictures—a chain of events in which Do, sometimes hindered but most often aided by animals, travels along the road to identity. In psychological, especially Jungian terms, these symbolic pictures represent aspects of the subconscious. No other human beings intrude in text or pictures, a device that heightens the dreamlike mood of Do's adventures, which take her far and wide. Do sees, hears, and reaches toward the world of nature. As fits the mood, the text is restrained, emotionally neutral, yet lyrically descriptive of Do's wanderings. Each of the seven (the magical number) double pages follows Do as she sets out. She wants to get more than is possible, yet each encounter with nature results in a new achievement and then, with tension released, leads back to the security of home.

The illustrations closely synchronize with the text, paralleling the verbal journeys down to small details. The artist's creative contribution lies primarily in the overall structure with which he endows the action of Do's search. He envisions and organizes the journeys as taking place in circles, as recurring round-dances. Their rhythms are identical—starting out from the house in the lower left-hand corner, and in the end returning to it. This basic design varies from one picture to another, reflecting the events of the specific adventure. The artist's style is realistic with naive and expressionistic elements blended in, thus accenting the symbolic and—toward the end—the mythic significance of the phenomena Do comes across. The mood is already indicated by the picture introducing the plot, with Do wearing the traditionally magical outfit: hood, coat, and boots. The journeys are composed as "continuous narratives."[28] Do's figure is repeated several times in every picture and has to be followed as she moves along. The use of this technique, which turns a number of figures appearing before our eyes simultaneously into a dynamic sequence, solves the problem of how

27. Herzka, *Do in den roten Stiefeln.*
28. Schwarcz, *Ways of the Illustrator,* 23–33.

to avoid the adventures' becoming too static, or even repetitive. It is an interesting example of how to transform and visually interpret a text.

On the first journey, the white bird carries Do high up, past the sun and the moon. She gets down off a steep mountain by sliding on a spider's thread; then a snail carries her home. Do has learned that guileless carelessness may lead to disaster, but also that she can trust animals to help her. On the second journey, Do wants to pick flowers. A butterfly leads her into the woods, and she cannot find her way out; but an ant (the animal opposing the butterfly) shows her the way home. The third journey is spent on the water—a little brook and pond. Do's boat almost capsizes, the circle is threatened, but the ducks (in mythology associated with the Great Mother) save her and take her home (fig. 55). Do has experienced anxiety. On the fourth journey, Do wants to cross the wall that separates her from the fruit trees of paradise. She learns that there are limits and decides to plant a garden on her side of the wall: a reemergence of "homo faber" in miniature; so fascinated is she by her activity, that, this time, neither text nor illustration carry her home. During her fifth journey, Do tries again to overcome her limitations. This time she trusts a kite, a man-made artifact.

Fig. 55. Heiri Steiner, *Do in den roten Stiefeln*

Heiri Steiner *Do in den Roten Stiefeln* from *In den Roten Stiefeln* written by Heinz Herzka, ill. by Heiri Steiner © 1969 Artemis Verlag, Zurich und Stuttgart. Reprinted by permission of Mrs. Mary Steiner

But the kite, presented by the illustrator as a circle with an empty "smiley" face, only simulates the perfect golden sphere, the sun. The string is torn and the kite draws Do into a treacherous marsh. Here she meets two wise animals, a snake and a frog. The latter jumps ahead of her toward home. When she nears home, she finds the kite again because, persistent, she did not give up the search for it. The sixth episode is dominated by the contrasting of light and darkness. Do, candle in hand, ventures out into the clear night because she wants to see the stars. A toad trips her, the candle goes out, and only now does Do's gaze turn up toward the starry sky. Whoever can relinquish his or her own small light can reach for the far distance. A cat—the animal symbolic of femininity—accompanies Do; the glow of the stars surrounds her. Warm, yellow light streams through the open door toward Do, who returns home. On the seventh and last journey, Do sets out on the archetypical "night journey." She wants to find the golden ball—the symbol of the maturing personality, of the "self." She sets out during the daytime, yet sun and moon and stars all are visible in the sky. She frees a dove that is caught in a thornbush. For this act of compassion, she is rewarded with a green branch, which helps her enter a cave in the mountain. There she finds the golden ball. A pensive Do, carefully carrying the weighty ball, returns home for the last time. In a final illustration, Do takes off the hood and red boots (remember Max's final gesture in *Where the Wild Things Are?*). Only now do we see her red hair becoming visible.

Do has experienced the forces of nature, and she has come to know herself. The rhythmic events represent the child's development as a sequence of daring challenges that originate in the need, the will, to exchange his or her security for temporary uncertainty. Life, the world, and our own personalities are more complex and more confusing, but also richer and more open-ended, than we might believe. Ancient fairy-tale wisdom, as well as modern psychology, recognizes that errors committed are essential steps on the road to maturity, because they usually strengthen the child's inner forces. Is it true that—figuratively, in the case of the illustrator's conception—the circles following one another turn into a spiral, leading upwards?

The book *Do . . .* attempts to deal with stress by offering harmony, to counteract distortion by offering rhythm. The overall structure suggests the continuing circle. The author's strength lies in the psychological logic inherent in the sequence of images he has chosen; the artist's, in the configurations that clearly express direction, tension, and release. Unfortunately, at some points, the idea is stronger than its verbal and visual execution. However, the last three episodes in particular are executed convincingly.

The story operates on three levels: as a lyrical children's book; as a metaphorical and symbolic presentation of some stages in the child's development; and as an aesthetic expression of a pedagogical concept—the significance of individual growth. Do's vivid journeys into nature were supposed to be followed by two sequels: one, as yet unpublished, tells of her adventures as she meets people in both town and countryside; the other, for which text and sketches for the illustration have been completed (prepared by the illustrator shortly before his death), relates how Do finds a friend. Although the magical mood is sustained throughout the books, Do is far from being an escapist figure. She is a child, one representing many children gifted with the power to live her experiences intensely and intimately. As she finds out about nature and civilization and human relationships (in the books not yet published), her identity grows. Do symbolizes all children's ability to experience themselves and the world around them holistically and to achieve personal integration. Thus, the book is likely to help children strengthen their identities and to withstand stress—past, present, and future.

The present discussion is an uneven one for several reasons. The most significant among these is, as was already stated at the beginning, the theme of identity is a complex one, owing to the inspiring and at times confusing richness of concepts and definitions and their application in interpreting the way in which the personality grows and matures. Another reason is that there is a diversity of superior stories that dare to take up the subject. The ones introduced here are widely disparate. They approach different aspects of the theme and do so from extremely varying points of view. Even so, owing to the significance of the theme, it deserves to be treated. The stories included here offer pleasure and aesthetic value and a certain wisdom. They present to children's subconscious understandings growth processes that would be difficult to bring to their conscious attention.

CHILDREN'S BOOKS CITED

BROWNE, ANTHONY. *Gorilla*. New York: Julia MacRae Bks. and Random, 1983.

BURNINGHAM, JOHN. *Come Away from the Water, Shirley*. London: Jonathan Cape, 1977.

———. *Time to Get Out of the Bath, Shirley*. London: Jonathan Cape, 1978.

HEIDELBACH, NIKOLAUS. *Der Ball, oder ein Nachmittag mit Berti (The Ball, or an Afternoon with Berti)*. Weinheim, Germany: Belz & Gelberg, 1986.

———. *Vorsicht, Kinder (Caution, Children!)*. Weinheim, Germany: Belz & Gelberg, 1987.

HERZKA, HEINZ. *Do in den roten Steifeln (Do in the Red Boots)*. Illus. Heiri Steiner. Zürich and Stuttgart: Artemis, 1969.

JONAS, ANN. *The Trek*. New York: Greenwillow, 1985.

KEATS, EZRA JACK. *Peter's Chair*. New York: Viking, 1967.

———. *Whistle for Willie*. New York: Viking, 1964.

LIONNI, LEO. *Alexander and the Wind-Up Mouse*. New York: Pantheon, 1970.

———. *Cornelius*. New York: Pantheon, 1983.

———. *Frederick*. New York: Pantheon, 1967.

——. *The Greentail Mouse.* New York: Pantheon, 1973.

——. *Let's Make Rabbits.* New York: Pantheon, 1982.

——. *Little Blue and Little Yellow.* New York: Astor Bks./McDowell, Obolenski, 1958.

——. *Pezzettino.* New York: Pantheon, 1975.

——. *Swimmy.* New York: Pantheon, 1963.

——. *Tico of the Golden Wings.* New York: Pantheon, 1964.

MCAFEE, ANNALENA. *Kirsty Knows Best.* Illus. Anthony Browne. New York: Julia MacRae Bks., 1987.

——. *The Visitors Who Came to Stay.* Illus. Anthony Browne. London: Hamish Hamilton, 1984.

ROSER, WILTRUD. *Julia, oder ein Geschenk für Mutter (Julia, or A Present for Mother).* Ravensburg, Germany: Otto Maier, 1982.

SCHINDLER, EDITH. *Schlaf gut, Träum schön (Sleep Well, Have Pleasant Dreams).* Ravensburg, Germany: Otto Maier, 1982.

SENDAK, MAURICE. *Where the Wild Things Are.* New York: Harper, 1963.

VON ROSEN, BJÖRN GRAF. *Das Märchen von der ungehorsamen Adeli Sofi, und ihrer furchtbaren Begegnung mit dem Wassermann (The Tale about the Disobedient Adeli Sofi, and Her Terrible Encounter with the Man of the Sea).* Zürich: Atlantis/Pro Juventute, 1987.

WAGNER, JENNY. *The Bunyip of Berkeley's Creek.* Illus. Ron Brooks. Melbourne: Childerset, 1973.

WIDERBERG, SIV. *Flickan som inte ville gå till dagis (The Girl Who Did Not Want to Go to the Kindergarten).* Illus. Cecilia Torudd. Stockholm: Rabén & Sjögren, 1986.

8

A Sense of Place

Men and women, individuals and societies, live in environments. Over the ages, as humanity has evolved, its relationship with the environment has undergone radical changes. Horizons have widened, and ever more elements and structures have appeared. As humankind grows increasingly mobile, its surroundings become more complex.

Setting out from a primal state where the environment barely sustained and very much endangered humanity, we have reached, step by step, an altogether different one, with environment serving humankind in various fashions. Thus, as history rolls on, society becomes increasingly responsible for the spheres that it creates and maintains for its members.

Moreover, contemporary society is characterized by far-reaching dominance of the man-made environment, to a point where even large sectors of natural surroundings—green spaces, recreational areas, and national parks—continue to exist only by dint of socially engendered conservation. In the eyes of the majority of people today, including children who are growing up in our contemporary technotronic society, nature is a reserve. For better or for worse, the environment bears the imprint of human endeavor and aspirations.

However, apart from their manifold utilitarian functions, environments, both natural and man-made, fulfill aesthetic and ethical functions as well. Phillip Wagner, a noted American scientist, once suggested that all societies everywhere and throughout history have regarded some particular sort of environment as uniquely conducive to the good life, and have helped to create it.[1] For our era, this means a rich panorama of desirable, versus undesirable, environments whose influence on the people living within them is assumed to be considerable.

A large and fast-growing body of environmental research exists today, the purpose of which is to examine the relationships between people and their surroundings, and the influence of the physical background on rela-

1. Philip L. Wagner, *Environments and People* (Englewood Cliffs, N.J.: Prentice-Hall, 1974).

tionships between people who live, operate, and cooperate within those surroundings. People relate to each other in spaces. Space inspires and colors behavior and interaction. Environmentalists speak of a "cognitive map" in each person's mind—the sum total of the environmental elements and configurations he or she is aware of.

One of the conclusions of this research seems to be that aesthetically significant and satisfying environments have a beneficial influence on individuals and on groups. Some of this information has evidently been known and applied for a long time. However, modern developments, including industrialization, urbanization, and over-population, have made the issue an acute one.

In their studies on the environment, writers have spoken of "aesthetic welfare," to be distributed among all strata of society depending on the available supply of a specific society's aesthetic wealth, and of an "aesthetosphere" to be maintained on a benevolent level.

Within this intricate framework of issues and responsibilities, I propose to focus on one issue: the aesthetic and moral satisfaction that children are able to derive from their home environments. It seems that mental health depends, in part, on the bond created between the individual, the family, the peer group, and the place they live in—the rather confined area whose many facets are known from protracted personal experience. To live in a place signifies emotional involvement, for better or for worse. For the growing child, this involvement may mean not only the formation of aesthetic behavioral idiosyncrasies; it may also influence the formation of general attitudes as well. A sense of attachment and belonging to, of love for and pride in the hometown and in the close environment—of being rooted in that place—may clearly be part of identity development. Needless to say, the physical environment should be of a character conducive to favorable growth. Needless to emphasize, too, in societies as mobile as contemporary ones, this is an educational issue of prime significance and yet one entangled in endless doubts and problems, for it differs from one society to the next. In many countries, the majority of children still grow up in one place, or move only a few times during childhood and adolescence. In others, moving every few years is the rule. The trend is for most societies to become more mobile, in the social and in the geographic sense as well. The same events that make people move cause rapid, often radical changes in the physical environment. Such a change is described concisely in a passage by John Updike:

> I grew up in the Reading area. It was a grand place—thriving downtown . . . .
> It was a muscular, semitough kind of place. Now the downtown is a sort of empty, sad shell.
>
> I was brought up in two houses within one county. And so I've had a more stable life than most young Americans now, where there's a lot more moving around and a kind of placelessness that you feel in fiction written by young

people. There's not that sharp sense of locality that you get in Southern writers, who—above all others—are regionally attached.[2]

To promote children's progress through school, educators everywhere create and apply curricula, textbooks, and planning to further the children's affective and aesthetic attachment to their home region, or, in an education-ally wider context, to foster their perception of a sense of place (i.e., a sense of the beauty and wealth of the phenomena that make up a particular place, and also, where evident, its history). It is this perception and appreciation that Tuan has called "topophilia—love of place."[3]

Lutts, in an excellent paper, proposes much more.[4] In his view, a sense of place is not sufficient; the environment should be guarded and protected, protected and improved, just like a home. Stories, he believes, constitute a psychologically powerful tool for strengthening relationships with the environment.

It is in the context of this aspect of aesthetic education that one can see the role of the picture book. The representation of the environment by the illustrator is an artistic interpretation. In this connection, we have to touch briefly on a major issue in art. Researchers into art and psychology in our time—Gombrich, Weismann, Arnheim, Kenneth Clark, and others—have repeatedly stated that humanity acquires its attitudes toward nature, the landscape, and the environment through art, and not vice versa. If this is true, the representation of these in art-for-children—in books, television, films, etc.—must be of importance: *Vicarious experience creates the metaphoric and symbolic images of environment, and influences attitude formation and consciousness.* Pictures can alter and sharpen our perception of the world, as Novitz states.[5]

The importance of pictures and picture stories lies, of course, in the support they lend to a widening of children's horizons—from an attachment to their own area, children may be led to the appreciation of the concepts of a sense of place and of the spirit of environment in general.

Picture books presenting meaningful environments abound, and several approaches to the representation of a sense of place can be discerned.

STORIES INCLUDING THE ENVIRONMENT AS AN INTEGRAL ELEMENT

In the picture books we'll now consider, children go through experiences and mature in the specific environments they live in and, in a way, *because*

2. John Updike in "Conversations with Alain P. Sanoff," *U.S. News & World Report*, 20 Oct. 1986, 68.

3. Yi-Fu Tuan, *Topophilia: A Study of Environmental Perception, Attitudes, and Values* (Engle-wood Cliffs, N.J.: Prentice-Hall, 1974).

4. Ralph H. Lutts, "Place, Home, and Story in Environmental Education," *Journal of Environmental Education* 17, no. 1 (Feb. 1985): 37–41.

5. David Novitz, *Pictures and Their Use in Communication* (The Hague: Nijhoff, 1977); Compare: Schwarcz, *Ways of the Illustrator*, 55–64.

of where they live. The environment is felt to be not only a background for, but also an influence on the child's life and development. The text may scarcely mention the environment, but the illustrations portray it with care and with a high degree of authenticity. The story is the child's, yet the environment accompanies, or rather encompasses, him or her, containing the events, the places, the seasons, and their changing moods, and thus contributing to a sense of continuity. There is a serenity about many of the books, in spite of the dramatic situations and developments occurring in the plots. As with all good art, the convincing representation of specific environments has the power to create a more general appeal and to enhance sensitivity.

Barnaby and the Rocket is about a boy who lives on a farm in Australia (fig. 56).[6] He likes the quiet, but, being a boy, he likes noise, too. Cracker-night and the blaze of fireworks and a bonfire are pictured in vivid colors, contrasting with the flat, lean, barren landscape. The boy's closeness to the natural environment is well portrayed. *Walls Are to Be Walked* very attractively presents a small boy and three blocks of neighborhood in small-town America.[7] There is so much to do and to see that it takes him an hour to get from the schoolhouse to his home. The text describes the boy's carefree mood, which is matched by the illustrations (fig. 57). According to the illustrator, the lively depiction of that short stretch of neighborhood is probably also the outcome of the illustrator's own devotion to his task: prior

Fig. 56. Judy Cowell, *Barnaby and the Rocket*
From *Barnaby and the Rocket* by Lydia Pender, illustrations by Judy Cowell. Text © Lydia Pender 1972, illustrations © Judy Cowell 1972 by permission of William Collins Sons & Co. Ltd.

6. Lydia Pender, *Barnaby and the Rocket*, illus. Judy Cowell (London: Collins, 1972).
7. Nathan Zimelmann, *Walls Are to Be Walked*, illus. Donald Carrick (New York: Dutton, 1977).

to drawing the pictures, he rode his bike back and forth in just such a place for a number of days.

An outstanding example, in concept and in the depiction of the environment as an integral part of the story, is *Rain,* a textless account of a rainstorm.[8] Two children, brother and sister, don their raincoats and, carrying an umbrella, are allowed to run out into the rain to enjoy themselves. During an hour or so, they experience all the delights of rain that children can imagine. The events all happen to the two of them, who are cheerfully on the move; yet whatever happens is intimately connected with the small neighborhood—courtyard, street, home at nightfall—and with the rain, whose aspects are painted so well that we believe we can actually taste and touch the watery abundance: rain in drops and sheets, and in gushes and puddles and all (fig. 58). The book is a joyful celebration of what some eighty pictures, ranging from double-spread to miniature, can achieve without words, out of an apparently effortless empathy with children and the

Fig. 57. Donald Carrick, *Walls Are to Be Walked*

From *Walls Are to Be Walked* by Nathan Zimelman, illustrated by Donald Carrick. Illustrations copyright © 1977 by Donald Carrick. Reproduced by permission of the publisher, Dutton Children's Books, a division of Penguin Books USA Inc.

8. Spier, *Rain.*

smell of rain. I say "apparently" effortless, for there is much thought invested in structuring the book, and a closer look enables us to detect painstaking work.

These are instances of an approach found in many picture books, though rarely executed on such a high level. Illustrators in certain countries seem to be especially receptive to the idea of imbuing the representation of the environment with meaning, embedding, as it were, the story and its hero in natural surroundings. American, British, Swiss, Australian, and Russian illustrators furnish good examples. Books illustrated by the Australian Ron Brooks display an ingrained sense of landscape (fig. 59).[9] The Swiss Felix Hoffmann emphasizes the landscape even when illustrating the Grimms' tales (fig. 60).[10]

PANORAMIC BOOKS

Panoramic picture books present large scenes from environments. Their intention is to point out the character and the beauty of specific areas and

Fig. 58. Peter Spier, *Rain*.
Excerpt from *Rain* by Peter Spier, copyright © 1982 by Peter Spier. Used by permission of Doubleday, a division of Bantam, Doubleday, Dell Publishing Group Inc.

9. For instance, Jenny Wagner, *John Brown, Rose and the Midnight Cat*, illus. Ron Brooks (Harmondsworth, England: Penguin, 1977).
10. For instance, Jakob and Wilhelm Grimm, *The Sleeping Beauty*, illus. Felix Hoffmann.

Fig. 59. Ron Brooks, *John Brown, Rose and the Midnight Cat*

From *John Brown, Rose and the Midnight Cat*. Story by Jenny Wagner and illustrated by Ron Brooks (Kestrel Books, 1977), copyright © Jenny Wagner and Ron Brooks, 1977

The old man had heard from his grandfather that many kings' sons had already tried to force their way through the hedge of thorns, but had stuck fast and died a sorry death. Then the young man said: "I am not afraid. I will go and see the beautiful Briar Rose." The good old man tried to dissuade him, but he would not listen.

The hundred years had now passed by and the day had come for Briar Rose to wake again. When the King's son reached the hedge of thorns it turned into a mass of large and beautiful flowers which parted to let him pass unharmed, closing up into a hedge again behind him.

Fig. 60. Felix Hoffmann, *The Sleeping Beauty*

From *The Sleeping Beauty* by the Brothers Grimm, illustrated by Felix Hoffmann. © 1959 by Verlag Sauerländer, Aarau and Frankfurt am Main.

the manifold activities taking place in them. But there is no plot. Some of these books remind one of annotated catalogs of an exhibition of paintings; others, of a collection of sketches done during a trip. Yet, their texts and pictures reflect the interests and points of view of children. Very often, a poetic and humorous tone prevails.

Québec, je t'aime, I Love You is a collection of some twenty scenes of Montreal and rural Québec.[11] The naive style is appropriate to the depiction of the lives of ordinary people, both children and adults, at work and at leisure. The book's charm arises from the mood of vigorous activity reflected in the compositions and from the pleasant and nostalgic red-brick walls that dominate many of the illustrations (fig. 61). *Good Morning, King Zygmund* is

Fig. 61. Miyuku Tanobe, *Québèc, je t'aime/I Love You*
Taken from *Québèc je t'aime/I love you.* © 1976 Miyuku Tanobe, published by Tundra Books

11. Miyuki Tanobe, *Québèc, je t'aime, I Love You* (Montreal: Tundra Bks., 1976).

a Polish book of verses containing humorous stories about well-known sites in Warsaw, Poland's capital.[12] The illustrations characterize the buildings and statues embellishing the city. Realism mixes with fantasy: suddenly Chopin, the great pianist and composer, who lived in the nineteenth century, appears to be standing in the middle of a square. A simple sense of pride pervades the pages of this book. *Strange Animals in Milan* contains amiable, humorous nonsense verses and stories about sites in Milan "for children from five to ninety-five."[13] The pretext, the "organizing principle," of the book is that strange animals rove all over the city. The verses, which cleverly rhyme street names with animal names, and the simple, colorful sketches that depict the scenery, lightheartedly carry out an attractive idea.

While these three books are easy to read and to view, the following ones demonstrate more sophisticated approaches.

Heaven Is My Hat, the Earth Is My Shoe is made up of ten highly surrealistic pictures of great and complex beauty, each showing a different environment and each incorporating a different absurdity or visual riddle.[14] The book also includes forty-one stories written by children between seven and eleven years old, in response to the pictures. The stories prove how richly rewarding such a strange creative idea can be.

The Way to Start a Day is a collection of poems about the sun and sun worship in many cultures.[15] Parnall's pictures impart a dignified unity to the text, tracing the rise and progress of the sun throughout the day in radiant, increasing and decreasing hues of yellow, ochre, and brown, in an abstracted rocky desert landscape that is all arcs and concentric half-circles, imbuing the scene with festive solemnity.

FOCUS ON ENVIRONMENT—THE CHILD AS OBSERVER

In the category of "The Child as Observer," environments are presented by way of a plot and a protagonist. However, this is actually pseudo-fiction, a pretext for depicting sequences of environmental images through someone's eyes; thus, a viewpoint is introduced. The child in the story fulfills the role of an observer akin to that of the child who peruses the book.

The device of having a child observer is frequently employed in the representation of famous cities, whose history and cultural heritage are reflected in the present. *A Dream of Venice* begins with a grade-school teacher explaining to her class the greatness of their unique hometown, Venice,

12. Wanda Chotomska, *Dzien Dobry, Krolo Zygmuncie (Good Morning, King Zygmund)* (Warszawa: Nasza Ksiegarnia, 1973).

13. Maggiorina Castoldi, *Animali strani a Milano (Strange Animals in Milan)* (Milano: Mursia, 1985).

14. Anita Albus, *Der Himmel ist mein Hut, die Erde ist mein Schuh (Heaven Is My Hat, the Earth Is My Shoe)* (Frankfurt: Insel, 1973).

15. Byrd Baylor, *The Way to Start a Day*, illus. Peter Parnall (New York: Scribner, 1978).

Italy—born, like a dream, of the sea.[16] One day it will again be covered by water (fig. 62). The teacher asks the children to draw a picture of Venice underwater. That evening, Marco begins his drawing with the help of a siren who—lo and behold—enters by the window and offers to guide him. We glide through the waters, amid fish, medusae, and water lilies, and have a good "bird's-eye view" of the famous sights and of celebrations all over the city. Zavřel expresses his admiration for the city's architecture in a very personal style, romantic yet modern, with a strong flair for color. The enchantment is slightly sugary, but the glory of Venice and its unique character come through beautifully.

A similar device is employed in *How the Kingfisher Got Lost in Prague*,[17] a story involving a grandfather and granddaughter and a bird, flying about the city and spreading before one's eyes the impressive architecture of the capital of Czechoslovakia (fig. 63), and in *Susanna in Salzburg*,[18] which acquaints us with a girl who visits her relatives in the rococo city (fig. 64) and includes a dream sequence within which Mozart, the great composer,

Fig. 62. Stěpán Zavřel, *Un sogno a Venezia*
Stěpán Zavřel from *Un Sogno a Venezia* © 1974 Bohem Press, Zürigo. © 1977 Quadragono libri, Conegliano (Reviso) Stampa grafiche az. Verona. Printed in Italy by permission of Bohem Press, Zürich.

16. Stěpán Zavřel, *Un sogno a Venezia (A Dream of Venice)* (Zürich: Bohem Pr., 1974).
17. Miroslav Ivanov, *Jak Ledňáček Bloudil Prahou (How the Kingfisher Got Lost in Prague)*, illus. Zdeněk Mlčoch (Prague: Albatros, 1978).
18. Hans Gottanka, *Suzanna à Salzbourg (Susanna in Salzburg)*, illus. Annegret Fuchshuber (Augsburg, Germany: Brigg, n.d.).

plays for her. *Round Trip* is a much more sophisticated book, offering what could be called a visual adventure in environment.[19] With a minimal text, we journey from a rural place to a large town, and then, turning the book upside down, we are taken back home by the same black-and-white pictures. In other words, every picture presents two different views of typical American neighborhoods and of the roads connecting them. The

Fig. 63. Zdeněk Mlčoch, *Jak Leňáček*.

Zdeněk Mlčoch, *Jak Leňáček. Bloudil Prahou* from *Jak Leňáček. Bloudil Prahou* by Miroslav Ivanov, illustrated by Zdeněk Mlčoch by permission of the illustrator

19. Ann Jonas, *Round Trip* (New York: Morrow, 1983).

effect is achieved by the surprisingly flexible application of style and technique, using a few basic optical illusions to advantage. The effect is convincing (except for one page); the way mountain trails turn into flashes of lightning, or marshy inlets into fireworks, stuns us and is aesthetically satisfying (fig. 65). The views of towns, roads, the coastline, and so on, through which we hurry or linger for a short moment, are somewhat abstracted and generalized so that the field is open for our own imagination's creativity. The contrast between small town and big town, and the "round trip" arouse our curiosity and direct it toward conceptual thinking. This is one of those books that's about the environment and even more.

CHILD AND ENVIRONMENT AS CO-HEROES

In picture books featuring the child in tandem with the environment, the plot is slightly more substantial. In a way, the plot is still a pretext, for

Fig. 64. Annegret Fuchshuber, *Susanna à Salzbourg*
From *Susanna à Salzbourg* by Hans Gottanka, illustrated by Annegret Fuchshuber © by Brigg Verlag GmbH Augsburg.

without the wish to characterize a place, the book would not have been created. However, the child in the story experiences more than just pure sight-seeing. Two examples, one simple and one elaborate, will make the point. *One Day, the Eiffel Tower* tells of a little Japanese boy who loses his parents somewhere in Paris.[20] The Eiffel Tower transforms itself into a giraffe and helps Kazono to find Father and Mother. The book contains many views of the city and a number of funny situations.

Where the River Begins is another example of "environment and something more," namely, good art.[21] Two boys who live where the river flows into the sea set out on a camping trip with their grandfather. They walk upstream and uphill until they arrive at the source—the small pond where the river begins. They then descend again, with the river. The text is concise and descriptive. This is the first children's book illustrated, in oil and alkyd paintings, by the American artist Thomas Locker. In a style that owes much to romantic and academic traditions, he painted a series of stimulating landscapes, evocative of the vitality and dignity of nature (fig. 66). While the river's course—its life story—is the central concern, Locker also gives careful attention to the relationship between the boys and their grandfather, a bond strengthened by the experience related in the story. A rare Emersonian spirit of sanity pervades the book.

Where the River Begins provides an opportunity to introduce a pair of

Fig. 65. Ann Jonas, *Round Trip*
From *Round Trip* by Ann Jonas. Copyright © 1983 by Ann Jonas. Reprinted by permission of William Morrow & Co.

20. Victor Simiane, *Un jour le Tour Eiffel "sans oublier là jaconde" (One Day, the Eiffel Tower)*, illus. de Boiry (Paris: Grasset Jeunesse, 1984).
21. Thomas Locker, *Where the River Begins* (New York: Dutton, 1984).

concepts concerning modes of narration. The books we looked at before this one are essentially based on *synchronic* narration (*synchronic* meaning, here, "existing at one moment in time"). They portray an environment and the events occurring within it at the present time; for instance, even though the splendid buildings were erected a long time ago and reflect the past, they glorify today's famous city. Yet, *synchronic* is not synonymous with *simultaneous*, for, certainly, as we wander through Venice or Paris, acquainting ourselves with the remarkable and memorable parts of those cities through one picture after the other, we progress in time. However, the idea is that we become familiar with the respective environments as entities existing at a certain moment in time (at least at the time the books were created). *Diachronic* narration, on the other hand (*diachronic* referring to the historical development of a subject), emphasizes the way in which changes over a period of time led to present states and conditions. In *Where the River Begins,* the historical dimension is handled very subtly and rather indirectly: while throughout their trip up and down the river the boys and their grandfather remain in the present, we do follow the river up to where it is "younger" and back down to where it is more "mature." Time and space combine to convey a double meaning—explicitly from here to there and implicitly from then to now. This distinction applies, of course, to all picture stories and, more generally, to any work of art consisting of sequences of pictures.

Fig. 66. Thomas Locker, *Where the River Begins*
From *Where the River Begins* by Thomas Locker. Copyright © 1984 by Thomas Locker. Reproduced by permission of the publisher, Dial Books for Young Readers

THE SYMPATHETIC REPRESENTATION OF URBAN LIFE

The favorable representation of life in an urban environment is a theme to be treated separately, for the very reason that it does not seem to attract sufficient attention. It is one matter to give expression to pride in splendid cities; it is another to depict the ordinary urban sphere as conducive to the good life of ordinary people. Relatively few artists show the city (except stereotypically or perfunctorily) as a pleasing, meaningful place in which to grow up. No doubt, rural areas and historical sites are likely to arouse more interest in artists working for children; such places are aesthetically preferable to the frequently amorphous, sprawling, partly neglected conglomerates called towns or cities. But when we realize that in many countries—first and foremost, those where the picture book flowers—two-thirds or more of all children grow up in just such places, a need for balance becomes obvious. The following books demonstrate the agreeable aspects of life in towns.

Around and About in My Town is a series of large double-page pictures for small children.[22] Each of the seven panels presents a section in the town—a construction site, the harbor, a cross section of an apartment building, the swimming pool. Dozens of children and adults work or play or mill around in every picture, to be pointed out, followed, found again, and commented on. It's all very simple, mobile, in touch with children's interests—town as a nice place.

Two German books for older children take us fully into what we previously termed the diachronic dimension. In *Gatestreet,* large pictures with accompanying text trace the changes occurring between the years 1276 and 1980 on a single street in a fictitious town modeled on a Baltic port city (fig. 67).[23] In the last view, the street has turned into a friendly, though commercialized, pedestrian zone. *On the Footsteps of a Town—a Town Clerk Reports* chooses to turn diachrony around.[24] The historic trip begins with a view of the town center in 1985 and goes back, step by step, to the year 1000, when the (unnamed) town grew out of the remnants of a Roman citadel erected 1,000 years earlier.

Diachronic narration is also the technique used in a French book about the famous Luxembourg Garden in the center of Paris—*The History and Life of a Public Garden.*[25] The narrator comes from a family whose members have been gardeners in the Public Garden since its beginning in the early seventeenth century. In his eyes, the Luxembourg of today is a little para-

22. Ali Mitgutsch, *Rundherum in meiner Stadt (Around and About in My Town)* (Ravensburg, Germany: Otto Maier, 1968).

23. Heinz Joachim Draeger, *Die Torstrasse (Gatestreet)* (Zürich: Atlantis, 1977).

24. Edouard Bannwart, *Auf den Spuren einer Stadt, ein Stadtschreiber erzählt (On the Footsteps of a Town, A Town Clerk Reports),* illus. Marcus Herrenberger (Ravensburg, Germany: Otto Maier, 1985).

25. Jaques Barozzi, *Histoire et vie d'un jardin public (The History and Life of a Public Garden),* illus. Eddy Krahenbühl and Ruth Imhoff (Paris: Berger Levraut, 1984).

Fig. 67. Heinz Joachim Draeger, *Die Torstrasse*
Heinz Joachim Draeger. *Die Torstrasse* © 1977 by Verlag Pro Juventute, Zürich

dise, but its growth over the centuries reflects French history. The pictures include scenes demonstrating poignant events, emphasizing the people who took part in them, and depicting a few humorous situations attractive to children.

These last three books do not assemble overviews of cities as they exist today. They instead choose a particular sector—a street, the center of town, a public garden—and, strictly diachronically, examine its evolution over an extended period, focusing on significant links in a long chain of events. Rather than showing pride in the splendor of today's town, they reflect an affection, even an admiration for the spirit of the people who, in spite of wars and conflagrations and overcrowding, strove and still strive to develop their own places and turn them into congenial neighborhoods.

Public gardens are among the most stimulating and redeeming sections in any town. A Canadian artist, Warabé Aska, has been concentrating on them. In two volumes, *Who Goes to the Park*, depicting High Park in Toronto, and *Who Hides in the Park*, about Stanley Park in Vancouver, he develops an individual approach (by the time this book goes to press, he will have visited even more parks).[26] The framework of *Who Goes to the Park* is defined by the seasons of the year—from early spring to icy winter—with every picture presenting an activity appropriate to the season taking place in a different part of the park (fig. 68). Short poems on the left-hand pages

26. Warabé Aska, *Who Goes to the Park* (Montreal: Tundra Bks., 1984); *Who Hides in the Park, Les mystères du parc* (Montreal: Tundra Bks., 1986).

Fig. 68. Warabé Aska, *Who Goes to the Park*
Taken from *Who Goes to the Park* © 1984 Warabé Aska. Published by Tundra Books

introduce the scenes to their right, with the two final lines of each poem
rhythmically addressing the characters in each scene:

Boys and girls, boys and girls,
How very lighthearted you'll be!

or

Lean trees, lonely trees,
What dancers in the wind you are!

The composition is powerful. By thoughtfully arranging and interweav-
ing people, objects, and areas, the artist succeeds in emphasizing the essential spirit characterizing the season, the section of the park, and the activities
going on. Bright, warm colors sustain a joyful, even festive mood, with the
scene itself being sometimes intimate, sometimes loud and agitated, yet
always carefully executed down to the smallest leaf. Rhythmic configurations, color combinations, the light—glowing or glaring or dim—that im-

bues the scenes, and the skies crowning the views, all these deserve close study. High rises beckon on the horizon, however, and do not let us forget that we are close to the city.

Aska's style is modern and sophisticated, yet it carries the mark of earlier traditions. Henri Rousseau seems to be an influence: the controlled parkscape and, even more so, the rather static stances of the people enjoying themselves in the park recall his style; they contrast strongly with the almost choreographic rhythms of the clouds and the birds. A fantastic vein is worked into the stylized realism of the pictures by the imaginary appearances in the sky above, echoing and complementing the carefree happenings on the ground. The dominant motif throughout is the happiness that young people find in the park.

Who Hides in the Park basically continues the approach of the first volume. Playful, varied composition, fascinating color schemes, and a host of activities present scenes of the area. But, obviously, the artist, developing his style, also responds to the special character of the park. While we participated in High Park over the course of a whole year (diachronically), here we spend a single day, running along (synchronically) with a quartet of children—girls and boys, white, black, and Asian—who amuse themselves all over the garden. People enjoying themselves in the many recreational areas are portrayed as agile and active. A slightly mysterious mood pervades the park. The first three pictures let us peep inside through circular frames composed of strange creatures. Indian mythological and historical motifs hide everywhere—on the ground and in the apparitions in the sky above (fig. 69). Surrealistic forms lurk in unexpected corners. Fantasy reaches down into reality and aids children to leap high into the sky, with the fishes and the birds, with downtown not far off. Though more somber, this park, too, resounds with the joy and freedom it offers to young people.

The text, however, raises a problem. While in *Who Goes . . .* the lyrical verses help to uplift the pictures, in *Who Hides . . .* prosaic explanations ground them. Further explication at the end of the book tends to turn fantasy into geography; the contrast between the two elements becomes too strong unless one rushes back to the intense beauty of the pictures and lets their impact prevail. In fact, in both books, less comment would suffice.

On the whole, Aska's personal style radiates an attractive belief in youth and beauty. A few of the pictures are too dainty, and an occasional reminiscence of art-nouveau taste in children's books (the oak tree raising its baton as choirmaster of the birds) is unnecessary. Yet, these two books are among the most refreshing that exist in the field.

THE CITYSCAPE AS AN INTEGRAL ELEMENT

There are not too many picture books that depict the urban sphere as a meaningful background for the child's experiences. Usually the representation is stereotyped, boring, or nondescript. Downtown is generalized; the suburb, sleek and somewhat sterile, rarely arouses the illustrator's interest and powers. Bemelmans's *Madeline* books are among the earliest whose pictures express a tender affection for the town the heroine lives in—Paris (fig. 70).[27] The contemporary painter Mühlenhaupt has created a number of picture stories, such as *Turnips, Fish, Pancakes,* that present Berlin as a place where children can find corners to play in.[28]

Interestingly, it is the deteriorating, amorphous part of town that stimulates superior artists to find redeeming qualities in it. Frequently, E. J. Keats takes up dismal neighborhoods and turns them into magic places. The artist's brush reveals how, in the eyes of the children in the picture story, neglected buildings and streets metamorphose into colorful configurations; the ugly becomes expressive; the city is dramatized and endowed with dignity; living and growing up there is not the end of self-respect. Especially relevant to this motif are *Goggles* and *Apt. 3.*[29]

Fig. 69. Warabé Aska, *Who Hides in the Park*
Taken from *Who Hides in the Park* © 1986 Warabé Aska. Published by Tundra Books

27. Ludwig Bemelmans, *Madeline* (New York: Simon & Schuster, 1939).

28. Curt Mühlenhaupt, *Rüben, Fische, Eierkuchen (Turnips, Fish, Pancakes)* (München: Parabel Verlag, 1975).

29. Ezra Jack Keats, *Goggles* (New York: Macmillan, 1969); *Apt. 3* (New York: Macmillan, 1971).

Isadora's *Ben's Trumpet* reflects a similar attitude: a cheerless neighborhood is lit up and shines because of Ben's absorption in the sounds of jazz (fig. 71).[30] These artists help to save the urban child, and the urban educator, from a sense of apathy and frustration toward the city as a home environment.

What is it that converts the representation of an environment in illustrations into an aesthetic force? Very generally, this transformation will happen

Fig. 70. Ludwig Bemelmans, *Madeline*

30. Rachel Isadora, *Ben's Trumpet* (New York: Greenwillow, 1979).

Ben feels the rhythm of the
music all the way home.

Fig. 71. Rachel Isadora, *Ben's Trumpet*
From *Ben's Trumpet* by Rachel Isadora © by Rachel Isadora Maiorano. Reprinted by permission of Greenwillow Books (A Division of William Morrow & Co.)

when the artist focuses attention on the positive aspects of his or her subject and elevates the surroundings to a sequence of interesting configurations, where things happen to the people in the book. Thus, the artist creates conditions likely to arouse focal attention in the child looking at the pictures. Many of the books we have considered challenge children to open their eyes to the environments illustrated. One of the important means of achieving this result is the artist's special style of effectively moving the viewer through space and time in the region represented. In *Rain*, for instance, the two children and their activities produce the axis along which we progress. In *Where the River Begins*, direction is determined by the river's flow. In *Who Goes to the Park*, the changing hues of the sky seem to follow us wherever we go. In *Round Trip*, the intricate lines and shapes function as vectors inducing us to move on or stay for awhile. In *Susanna in Salzburg*, buildings generate a perception of a spatial entity. In the diachronic books, certain objects, a hill, a house, a street, preserve identity throughout the progress in historical time.

Not all the books we have examined here excel to the same degree. Some have charm, yet they lack depth. Others are beautiful, yet they are a bit too shiny, too ideal, too nostalgic, and consequently lack intimacy. The superior ones have that quality of "the environment and then something more." They not only denote a region and its characteristics; they carry connotations of moods, relationships and concepts connecting the background with the people acting and experiencing against it.

However, even the lesser ones embody more environmental meaningfulness within their pages than the average picture book. Leafing through quantities of the latter, we find that three patterns stand out: one is that in too many picture books, the background barely exists at all; the illustrators tend to create a sort of egocentric frame of mind for the people in the story. In a second pattern, the environment as background is sketched in as an afterthought, a series of cursorily applied stereotypes, lean and pale, or billowing and romantic—stage props, so to speak. The third and worst thing, however, that can happen to an environment is for it to fall into the hands of an artist of the Disney School—a school that by now seems to be established for all continents—because the environment then becomes subject to exaggerated manipulation.

All in all, good books of the types discussed here, especially the truly fictional ones, can become suitable partners in supporting the evolution of a sense of belonging. The increasing "medialization" of experience charges us with the need to choose our media with care. Books of this kind can partly compensate children for the lack of sufficient contact with, and also aid in creating new interest in, real environments. They can counteract the meretricious environmental images propagated by comics, animated films, and advertising. Such books have a role to fulfill in shaping the child's personal and social attitudes. Sam Shepard once said that the connection between physical territory and inner territory is a very strong one. Could it be that relatively small things such as picture books might offer some help toward saving a relationship endangered almost to the point of being lost, as Meyrowitz in *No Sense of Place* claims so authoritatively and convincingly?[31] The cognitive map evolving in children's minds may become richer and more meaningful.

The discerning reader will surely have noticed that a certain air of detachment prevails in several sections of this discussion. It is true that not too many of the books examined have excited the examiner's enthusiasm. A few have. The decisive point is that although the books in the field are, on the whole, not exciting, the field itself is. The manifold relationships between a human being and his or her environment form part of that person's individual and social makeup, and children need some open-ended guidance toward experiences and toward attitude formation in a field that has become too crowded. It is imperative to draw attention to the problem, even if, or actually precisely because, the simplicity and shallowness of many books we have looked at here impairs a feeling of warm involvement. The involvement rests with the issue.

CHILDREN'S BOOKS CITED

ALBUS, ANITA. *Der Himmel ist mein Hut, die Erde ist mein Schuh (Heaven Is My Hat, the Earth Is My Shoe)*. Frankfurt: Insel, 1973.
ASKA, WARABÉ. *Who Goes to the Park*. Montreal: Tundra Bks., 1984.
——. *Who Hides in the Park, Les mystères du park*. Montreal: Tundra Bks., 1986.

31. Joshua Meyrowitz, *No Sense of Place: The Impact of Electronic Media on Social Behavior* (New York and Oxford: Oxford Univ. Pr., 1985).

BANNWART, EDOUARD. *Auf den Spuren einer Stadt, ein Stadtschreiber erzählt (On the Footsteps of a Town, A Town Clerk Reports)*. Illus. Marcus Herrenberger. Ravensburg, Germany: Otto Maier, 1985.

BAROZZI, JAQUES. *Histoire et vie d'un jardin public (The History and Life of a Public Garden)*. Illus. Eddy Krahenbühl and Ruth Imhoff. Paris: Berger Levraut, 1984.

BAYLOR, BYRD. *The Way to Start a Day*. Illus. Peter Parnall. New York: Scribner, 1978.

BEMELMANS, LUDWIG. *Madeline*. New York: Simon & Schuster, 1939.

CASTOLDI, MAGGIORINA. *Animali strani a Milano (Strange Animals in Milan)*. Milano: Mursia, 1985.

CHOTOMSKA, WANDA. *Dzien Dobry, Krolo Zygmuncie (Good Morning, King Zygmund)*. Warszawa: Nasza Księgarnia, 1973.

DRAEGER, HEINZ JOACHIM. *Die Torstrasse (Gatestreet)*. Zürich: Atlantis, 1977.

GOTTANKA, HANS. *Suzanna à Salzbourg (Susanna in Salzburg)*. Illus. Annegret Fuchshuber. Augsburg, Germany: Brigg, n.d.

GRIMM, JAKOB AND WILHELM GRIMM. *Dornröschen (The Sleeping Beauty)*. Illus. Felix Hoffmann. Aarau and Frankfurt: Sauerländer, 1959.

ISADORA, RACHEL. *Ben's Trumpet*. New York: Greenwillow, 1979.

IVANOV, MIROSLAV. *Jak Ledňáček Bloudil Prahou (How the Kingfisher Got Lost in Prague)*. Illus. Zdeněk Mlčoch. Prague: Albatros, 1978.

JONAS, ANN. *Round Trip*. New York: Morrow, 1983.

KEATS, EZRA JACK. *Apt. 3*. New York: Macmillan, 1971.

——. *Goggles*. New York: Macmillan, 1969.

LOCKER, THOMAS. *Where the River Begins*. New York: Dutton, 1984.

MITGUTSCH, ALI. *Rundherum in meiner Stadt (Around and About in My Town)*. Ravensburg, Germany: Otto Maier, 1968.

MÜHLENHAUPT, CURT. *Rüben, Fische, Eierkuchen (Turnips, Fish, Pancakes)*. München: Parabel, 1975.

PENDER, LYDIA. *Barnaby and the Rocket*. Illus. Judy Cowell. London: Collins, 1972.

SIMIANE, VICTOR. *Un Jour le Tour Eiffel "sans oublier la Jaconde" (One Day the Eiffel Tower)*. Illus. de Boiry. Paris: Grasset Jeunesse, 1984.

SPIER, PETER. *Rain*. Garden City, N.Y.: Doubleday, 1982.

TANOBE, MIYUKI. *Québèc, je t'aime, I Love You*. Montreal: Tundra Bks., 1976.

WAGNER, JENNY. *John Brown, Rose and the Midnight Cat*. Illus. Ron Brooks. Harmondsworth, England: Penguin, 1977.

ZAVŘEL, STĚPÁN. *Un sogno a Venezia (A Dream of Venice)*. Zürich: Bohem Pr., 1974.

ZIMELMANN, NATHAN. *Walls Are to Be Walked*. Illus. Donald Carrick. New York: Dutton, 1977.

9

The Vicissitudes of Urban Life

While some picture-book stories are devoted to the security and acceptance that children and adults may discover in the urban environment, others demonstrate a lack of environmental beauty and dignity. The latter books depict dissatisfaction with the adverse conditions generated by contemporary technology for people living in the city. The authors and artists offer social criticism and, in many cases, propose concerted action, be it realistic or fantastic.

The societal background of these stories is found in broad developments—industrialization, urbanization, and overpopulation. It is also found, on the other hand, in democracy, with its demands for equality; in the scientific findings of ecology and in the claims of the ecologists and their public supporters in all the regions of the political map; and in movements, both religious and secular, promoting an alternative life-style.

Despite the weighty concepts they propound, many of these stories can be innocently entertaining, full of charm, and attractively colorful. Others, it is true, let their concern with the nature of things, their ironic modes or undercurrents, reach the surface; still others are quite openly serious, even desperate, about environmental states and developments that their authors consider that children should be warned against. Many are excellent picture books. Independent of the style chosen, the age group in mind, the specific situation attacked, the degree of naïveté or sophistication used, and the quality of execution, the books reflect an interest in improving the ecological and social quality of life in the city, for the benefit of growing children and, by implication, with children's future assistance and participation. Sympathy lies not with the environment, but with the people who suffer within it.

The books selected for this brief overview call attention to a number of phenomena treated in this manner.

POLLUTION

In *The Gray Witch and the War of the Corks*, industrial plants are erected near a tranquil town.[1] Dense fumes, taking the shapes of colossal witches, cover the town and enter people's noses. When confronted, the plant owners deny all knowledge. Doctors prescribe cork bottle-stoppers to be inserted in people's noses. The plant owners seize this opportunity and build another plant, this one producing corks. In the end, the boys in the town attack the witches with corks and drive them off. A successful competition for the invention of a gadget to hinder the witches from passing through smoke-stacks and pipes takes place, and the bosses are forced to install it.

The plot is crude; the text, clear-cut. The illustrations of air pollution overwhelming the town are dramatic in a small way. Action, even when vehement, is still funny. Eight years after its original publication, this book has been reissued by the same publisher. The format has become smaller; the text has been enlarged and become more explanatory, less dramatic, more didactic. A different, mediocre illustrator has drawn tame pictures; the strong primitiveness of the witchy vapors is gone; the boss counting the money received from the sale of bottle stoppers has been eliminated. Amusing protest has been toned down, and the book is presumably intended as a textbook.

The Fish is a gloomy treatment of water pollution.[2] One lone fish is left swimming in a muddy lake polluted by a nearby plant. The birds who sometimes come to visit him, one day weave a net of grass and carry him off. A paper dragon is caught in the net and tears it, but a gust of wind helps, and the fish lands in fresh water in a place where there are innumerable butterflies and beetles. But—how long will this lake remain fresh and clear? The illustrations are appropriately simple and lyrical.

Professor Noah's Spaceship tells of the animals on earth being frightened because the air has become sticky, the trees have paled, and the sun's rays have weakened.[3] The owl finds out about Professor Noah, who builds a spaceship and intends to reach a healthy planet that he has discovered. After the ship starts out, trouble with the "time antenna" causes it to return, after forty days and forty nights, and to land on earth as it was, fresh and green, eons ago. Happiness reigns in Wildsmith's rainbow colors.

Although on the surface the stories are pleasantly harmless and visually attractive, their statements are serious. Unbearable conditions cause "inhabitants" to rise in self-defense, with Zorzetti evoking frightening mythical

1. Nevio Zorzetti, *La strega grigia et la guarre dei tappi (The Gray Witch and the War of the Corks)*, illus. Nino Bon (Trieste, Italy: La Editoriale Librarie, 1977).

2. Heide Helene Beisert, *Der Fisch (The Fish)* (Mönchaltorf and Hamburg: Nord-Süd Verlag, 1982).

3. Brian Wildsmith, *Professor Noah's Spaceship* (Oxford: Oxford Univ. Pr., 1980).

figures and Wildsmith invoking biblical analogies of sin, abandonment, and redemption.

NOISE

In *The Mouse and the Noise*, a mouse approaching town attempts to strike up conversations, to make herself heard and to understand what others have to say.[4] But the infernal noise generated all about her by cars, trucks, airplanes, drills, and so forth frustrates any efforts at communication. Only in the country, where she came from, can she possibly connect with other people. In actualization of the old fable of the field mouse and the town mouse, the book makes its point mainly through the use of large "acoustic" insets—stars and rows of words, exploding vowels and consonants—that visualize, onomatopoetically, the sounds and noises encountered by the mouse. It's all an amusing game, especially if the text is read aloud; but the cautionary bias, the wish to frighten, comes out strongly.

CONSUMERISM

Joachim, the Streetcleaner is a much more serious story, in approach and accomplishment.[5] Some people in a town acquire goods, and they then go out and buy some more, because that is what all the other people do. Then they start throwing out everything that becomes spoiled or unneeded; soon squares and streets are heaped with garbage and the remnants of old gadgets (fig. 72). When the mayor seeks to solve the problem, Joachim comes forward and offers to clean the town without pay, on the sole condition that all the garbage will be his. Gleefully, the town council accepts the offer. Joachim clears the town of waste and dirt and, in the process, skillfully uses the materials to construct a castle, a submarine, and an airplane for himself. Instead of feeling or expressing anything like gratitude, the mayor and the councillors become suspicious; they are afraid that Joachim might become too powerful. Cunningly, they demand that he hand over his possessions to the town—patriotism coming before cleanliness. Joachim refuses. The town declares war on him. The citizens have no clear idea why they should march against the streetcleaner, but, anyway, marching and singing martial songs is a welcome change from watching television. The attack becomes mired in the garbage that has again accumulated. The mayor offers peace; Joachim has had enough and emigrates, accompanied by flocks of birds, hoping to find another town whose people will be more appreciative of his aid and goodwill.

On its own fantastic-ironic terms, Baumann's story (it is dedicated to "us

---

4. Anne Van der Essen, *Die Maus und der Lärm (The Mouse and the Noise)*, illus. Etienne Delessert (Köln: Middelhauve, 1975).

5. Kurt Baumann, *Joachim, der Strassenkehrer (Joachim, the Streetcleaner)*, illus. David McKee (Mönchaltorf and Hamburg: Nord-Süd Verlag, 1972).

Fig. 72. David McKee, *Joachim, der Strassenkehrer*
From *Joachim, der Strassenkehrer* by Kurt Baumann, illustrated by David McKee © Nord-Süd Verlag CH-Mönchaltdorf

soilers of the environment") has a convincing inner logic. The absurdity of consumerism is, of course, only one of the book's motifs. There are social ones as well. McKee pulls out all the stops of his register; as a cartoonist, he bitingly ridicules the bombastic craftiness of the establishment; as a painter, he dreams up numerous intriguing vistas of the town—his colors, ranging from muddy to lucid, spreading beauty over all, including the garbage. And as an experienced illustrator of children's books, he achieves vivid motion through dizzying variations of perspective and composition, with fleeting reminders of children's drawing styles thrown in: the town is represented from every possible viewpoint—as a place to live in, as the council's territory, and as Joachim's field of operations.

MASS TRANSPORTATION

Intercity takes its title from a European fast-train service.[6] As the train pulls out of the station, it gathers speed, traverses a stretch of country, and

6. Charles Keeping, *Intercity* (Oxford: Oxford Univ. Pr., 1977).

then slows down at its urban destination. The pictures alternately show the travelers in one compartment (six persons characterized by their individual behaviors) and the sights (industrial and pastoral, well-kept and neglected) that flash by the window. The alternating views have a swift fascination. In sharp contrast, the lack of contact between people who are so close together comes out strongly, offering a taste of the human isolation so typical in urban settings.

THE MANIPULATIVE POWER OF THE MASS MEDIA

Keeping has again created a book of ferocious beauty in *Sammy Streetsinger*, a story outstanding in its vehement protest against the delusions of stardom.[7] Sammy, a poor teenager who plays and sings for the people crossing a bypass (fig. 73), is put on the road to greatness by the impresarios: from circus clown he rises to being a rock star. His name fills the big halls. The press is jubilant. Television, records, and video follow. Yet, after a short while, everything turns hollow. Someone else is taken up by the media moguls. Lonely but at peace with himself, Sammy is back below the bypass, with the children and dogs he likes, playing and singing for a few coins. The story is quite melodramatic, but the illustrations endow it with credibility, especially the vertiginous, psychedelic mist of success and the lonely shame of the letdown.

The same theme is treated, in a mild and funny fashion, by Wildsmith in *Bear's Adventure*.[8] A bear is accidentally hauled into the big city, is caught up in a dress parade, earns a prize, wins a race, is feted by the masses and the media, and luckily escapes back to the mountains (fig. 74).

OVERSIMPLIFIED ECOLOGICAL ATTITUDES

Before continuing, we should briefly mention two books (typical of others) that take up environmental issues in ways exhibiting a lack of responsibility. *Barbapapa's Ark*, one volume in a popular series that over a number of years has left few issues untouched, is another book that latches on to the myth of Noah.[9] It relates how the Barbapapa family saves all of the animals from the pollution of air and water, from hunters for meat and hides, etc.—in short, from the malevolence of humankind—by escaping with them to another planet in an ark-spaceship. When the humans repent and purify the earth, the animals graciously return and have a party: all ecological evils are easily mastered. The humane nature of the animals overcomes brutish humanity.

The Tale of Manoah Who Used His Brains presents a man who wishes to

7. Charles Keeping, *Sammy Streetsinger* (Oxford: Oxford Univ. Pr., 1984).

8. Brian Wildsmith, *Bear's Adventure* (Oxford: Oxford Univ. Pr., 1981).

9. Annette Tyson, *Barbapapa's Ark*, illus. Talus Taylor (Amsterdam: Frank Fehmers, 1974, 1978).

Fig. 73. Charles Keeping, *Sammy Streetsinger*
Charles Keeping, *Sammy Streetsinger*. Oxford University Press, 1984

live close to nature.[10] When high rises crowd in on his small house (fig. 75), he moves on. When new apartment houses crop up, shutting out the view of fields and trees, he moves again. In the end, he gives up; he buys paints and applies them to his windowpanes, creating a pastoral view all of his own. As he adds another flower now and then, he feels quiet and satisfied. Neither text nor illustrations indicate tongue-in-cheek, ironic intention on behalf of author or artist. If the book were intended for adults, such an indication would have been superfluous; but this is clearly a book for children under ten, soothingly suggesting solitude (Manoah lives alone) and the closing of one's windows as a solution to all environmental troubles—solipsism as the model of the good life.

These are books that reflect misleading approaches to both societal issues and to the child's imagination.

10. Uri Orlev, *Ma'asseh be' manoah Schehif'il et Ha'moah (The Tale of Manoah Who Used His Brains)*, illus. Jiftach Alon (Givatajim, Israel: Massada, 1979).

Fig. 74. Brian Wildsmith, *Bear's Adventure*
Brian Wildsmith, *Bear's Adventure*. Oxford, Oxford University Press, 1981

ALIENATION

However incongruously represented in books such as *Manoah . . .* and *Barbapapa . . .* and with some sense of humor in *Professor Noah's Spaceship*, the idea that the good life cannot be found in urban surroundings also appears in eminently distinguished books. *The Little House* is probably the earliest significant picture book to handle this idea.[11] The story is about the little house with her telling eyes, who stood in the open country with nature close and meaningful until town encroached upon her and overwhelmed her with its skyscrapers and mass transport (fig. 76). She was then saved by being towed back to the country, where diurnal and seasonal cycles reign. This story has become a classic. The interplay of the transparent structures, the distinct depiction of neighborhoods and seasons, and the verbal and visual rhythms please to this day. Yet, text and pictures inti-

11. Virginia Lee Burton, *The Little House* (Boston: Houghton, 1942, 1969).

mately and forcefully interlock to communicate the message that life in town means unmitigated anonymity, abandonment, and alienation. Town frightens; salvation lies in a return to the countryside. Did the book have some influence on the suburban trend at the time it was first published in 1942, and during the years after, or did it just express this trend?

Müller's *Here a House Is Demolished, There a Crane Stands, and Always the*

Fig. 75. Jiftach Alon: *Ma'asseh be' manoah Schehif'il et Ha'moah*
From Uri Orlev, *Ma'asseh be' manoah Schehif'il et Ha'moah*, ill. Jiftach Alon. By permission of Massada Ltd.

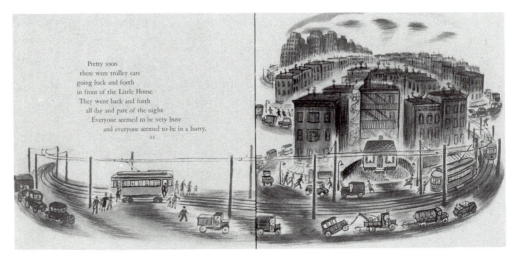

Fig. 76. Virginia Lee Burton, *The Little House*
From *The Little House* by Virginia Lee Burton. Copyright 1942 by Virginia Lee Demetrios. Copyright © renewed 1969 by George Demetrios. Reprinted by permission of Houghton Mifflin Co.

Dredger's Tooth Threatens, or the Alteration of the Town presents, in the diachronic mode, eight large-format panels depicting the changes taking place in a single corner of a town between 1953 and 1976.[12] The town is a composite model of developments typical of a modern city. What, in 1953, used to be a small, quiet square with a few trees and a bit of lawn and a statue of the blindfolded Goddess of Justice in the center; adjacent streets with small houses, some decorative, some deteriorating; and enough space for people to work and go about their business, and for children to play and run about has, step by step, undergone inexorable changes. By 1976 it has become an assembly of glaring walls of glass and concrete and neon lights, offices and movie theaters, with little space for people. Only the statue of blindfolded Justice still stands, squeezed in between an elevated highway and a parking-garage entrance (fig. 77).

Fig. 77. Jörg Müller, *Hier fällt ein Haus, dort steht ein Kran und ewig droht der Baggerzahn oder die Veränderung der Stadt*

12. Jörg Müller, *Hier fällt ein Haus, dort steht ein Kran und ewig droht der Baggerzahn oder die Veränderung der Stadt* (*Here a House Is Demolished, There a Crane Stands, and Always the Dredger's Tooth Threatens, or the Alteration of the Town*), illus. Jörg Muller and Heinz Ledergerber (Aarau, Switzerland: Sauerländer, 1976).

Yet, irony is kept low. It is the objective validity of the paintings that communicates, scene after scene, sadness, disappointment, and a feeling of growing danger to the future possibilities of a human life-style in the urban sphere. How children and young people are crowded out of the neighborhood is one of the book's central motifs, to be followed closely by contemplating one panel after the other. This is one of Müller's several outstanding books concerned with and expressing critical views on social issues.

Most of the books discussed here reflect a deep-seated dissatisfaction with contemporary environmental developments and strive to establish or modify basic attitudes toward "the good life." The vigorous and often militant protest against existing conditions displayed in these books is a healthy and necessary response to conditions requiring change. The call of these stories not to trust the establishment—economic, political, media— can be quite salubrious, too, if the book is a well-written-and-painted story, not a pamphlet. The problems and dangers condemned in these stories do exist in reality. It is the privilege of art to take these themes up and treat them in funny, fantastic, and dramatic ways. Most of the books that have been discussed here measure up to the requirement for aesthetic quality. Considering the age groups the books are attuned to, the concepts involved are communicated clearly and concisely. Whoever the protagonists are— children, adults, animals, individuals, or groups, or the one corner in town—they suggest ecological awareness in a childlike fashion. The stories do, however, raise a basic problem: with the exception of *Intercity* and *The Gray Witch* . . . , the books suggest one of two alternative options: either we stay in the city, which is undesirable (notably *Sammy Streetsinger* and *Here a House* . . .), or we leave the city and gain peace. In other words, a firm, persistent tone of pessimism accompanies us, an escapist tendency that does not overstate its point so much as it refrains from offering imaginary or realistic suggestions on what to do for city dwellers, similar to what *The Gray Witch* . . . proffers, though in more sophisticated terms: to encourage militancy in the service of urban change. It is true, no doubt, that urban development has often gone astray; children should know about that. It is less true that rural life or the cocooned way of life in the suburbs is unconditionally safer and sounder. Life in town can offer opportunities for personal and social growth in many respects. To repeat, the large majority of children will continue to grow up and spend their lives in cities; this means that the picture book should indeed be expected to encourage social awareness by giving expression to discontent and doubt as well as by offering opportunities to identify with efforts to improve the existing, predominantly urban social fabric.

CHILDREN'S BOOKS CITED

BAUMANN, KURT. *Joachim, der Strassenkehrer (Joachim, the Streetcleaner)*. Illus. David McKee. Mönchaltorf and Hamburg: Nord-Süd Verlag, 1972.

BEISERT, HEIDE HELENE. *Der Fisch (The Fish)*. Mönchaltorf and Hamburg: Nord-Süd Verlag, 1982.

BURTON, VIRGINIA LEE. *The Little House*. Boston: Houghton, 1942, 1969.

KEEPING, CHARLES. *Intercity*. Oxford: Oxford Univ. Pr., 1977.

——. *Sammy Streetsinger*. Oxford: Oxford Univ. Pr., 1984.

MÜLLER, JÖRG. *Hier fällt ein Haus, dort steht ein Kran und ewig droht der Baggerzahn oder die Veränderung der Stadt (Here a House Is Demolished, There a Crane Stands, and Always the Dredger's Tooth Threatens, or the Alteration of the Town)*. Illus. Jörg Müller and Heinz Ledergerber. Aarau, Switzerland: Sauerländer, 1976.

ORLEV, URI. *Ma'asseh be' manoah Schehif'il et Ha'moah (The Tale of Manoah Who Used His Brains)*. Illus. Jiftach Alon. Givatajim, Israel: Massada, 1979.

TYSON, ANNETTE. *Barbapapa's Ark*. Illus. Talus Taylor. Amsterdam: Frank Fehmers, 1974, 1978.

VAN DER ESSEN, ANNE. *Die Maus und der Lärm (The Mouse and the Noise)*. Illus. Etienne Delessert. Köln, Middelhauve, 1975.

WILDSMITH, BRIAN. *Bear's Adventure*. Oxford: Oxford Univ. Pr., 1981.

——. *Professor Noah's Spaceship*. Oxford: Oxford Univ. Pr., 1980.

ZORZETTI, NEVIO. *La Strega grigia et la guarre dei tappi (The Gray Witch and the War of the Corks)*. Illus. Nino Bon. Trieste, Italy: La Editoriale Librarie, 1977.

10

Social Action for the Disadvantaged

The five picture-book stories we propose to examine in this chapter tell of children or adolescents who are actively involved in exciting social issues. The common denominator is that each story centers on an acutely deprived or disadvantaged or even endangered group in society. The young people who intervene in states and processes that they perceive to be in need of improvement are successful in their efforts to achieve change. The stories are also quite effective at impressing the reader with the plight of the people who are to be aided. All of these books present clear and simple concepts of what wrongs ought to rectified, and in what ways. As we shall see, all of these stories bring forth various degrees of social criticism.

Beyond these common characteristics, a wide range of approaches exists. The improvement sought may be limited or rather utopian; solutions are arrived at realistically or else through magic or fantastic happenings; plots include mild protest or violent action. In three of the stories, the heroes act for the groups they themselves belong to; in the two remaining ones, they do so in the interest of others to whom the heroes feel close. Four of the plots describe the actions of both individuals and groups; one tells of a single child's efforts. An urban background clearly characterizes three of the stories.

THE GROWTH OF SOCIAL CONSCIOUSNESS

The Street Is Free is partly based on true events that happened in Barrio San José de la Urbina, one of the many barrack cities in the hills surrounding Caracas, the capital of Venezuela.[1] There, two million people, mostly former, poor villagers, have built makeshift houses for themselves and live in crowded conditions. The story relates how the children and teenagers of San José struggled for, and received, their playground. The idea behind the plot is to demonstrate the youngsters' budding understanding of how

---

1. Kurusa, *La calle es libre (The Street Is Free)*, illus. Monica Doppert (Caracas: Ediciones Ekaré Banco del Libro, 1981).

146

society operates and their growing awareness of how they might be able to help themselves. San José already has a library where the children can read and also do some artwork and play the guitar. But whenever they get bored and wish to run and play outside, the children are driven off by enraged adults with whose work they interfere.

One day, sitting on the steps leading to the library, they hit upon the idea of approaching the town council and asking for a playground. When they attempt to interest their parents in this request, the parents all are too busy with their own affairs. So, the children turn to Señor Bruno, the librarian. With his aid, they work out a proposal for the construction of a playground on an empty plot downhill near the road. They prepare a large placard, and, with some trepidation, they march down to the town hall. There, when they refuse to disperse, the guard calls the police. At the same time, the children's mothers appear, to take them home and punish them. When the children are about to be arrested, however, the mothers intervene and defend them (fig. 78). At this critical moment, a town councillor exits from the building, accompanied by the town engineer and a woman journalist. Being caught in the upheaval (in the presence of a member of the press), the councillor, all smiles and handshakes, listens to the mothers and children and promises to come and have a look, mañana. The journalist takes up the children's quest; her paper runs a report. Yet, the children are skeptical. Still, one day, when elections approach, the elegant councillor comes to the barrio and solemnly cuts the red ribbon at the entrance of the

Fig. 78. Monica Doppert, *La calle es libre*

playground-to-be. Weeks go by, and nothing happens. Finally, one of the children suggests that they construct their own playground. Slowly, this crazy idea takes root. Very slowly, too, the adults get involved. The shanty-town's community association calls a meeting. Putting aside earlier excuses, people decide to help in their free hours. The children have achieved their playground.

We have related the steps of the plot in some detail, for only thus does the main concept come alive—how children and youth may actively learn about some of the straightforward and some of the devious aspects of community life, gain experience, and even exert influence on adults. Against this background, the helpfulness of the librarian, the journalist, and those parents and adults in San José who are won over to the children's cause stands out in clear contrast to the workings of the political establishment. The fact that, to a certain extent, the events related are based on true happenings and that the children of San José took part in shaping the book adds credence and significance.

As a report, the story could well stand alone, without illustrations. The text blends documentation and dialogue with straightforward logic; it uses admirably sincere factual language. However, the pull, the force of the book is evoked by the textually inspired pictures. Stating this notion paradoxically but correctly, by molding an authentic visual shape of local people and their environment, the illustrations probably stimulated the universal appeal that caused the book to be translated into various languages. The pictures follow the text very faithfully, but they are large, and the text is placed in the corners of the pictures; so the illustrations take over, achieving not only depth but also a convincing continuity of their own, dovetailing with the verbal one. The illustrations do not aspire to be art but, rather, intend to record in an aesthetically satisfying and realistic way the children's environment and circumstances. The cover conveys the main theme: the three children, two boys and one girl, who will later lead both the defiant and the constructive actions, are sitting close to a dismal hovel and looking down on the bright high rises of the main town (fig. 79). Then a series of illustrations reveals how, over time, the verdant hill evolved into an ugly barrio. The crowded hillside houses with their makeshift roofs and narrow alleys are brought out well (possibly a bit too cleanly). The many people of San José exhibit genuine movement and expression. Several persons are characterized more fully than others: a few of the mothers; Bruno, the librarian; some boys; Camila, the girl with the sad eyes, who can also look very skeptical; and the town councillor with his spurious smirk. Groups and crowds are usually arranged convincingly, yet individuals are not lost in these scenes. Somehow, after a while, the illustrator's obvious personal involvement with the story makes the viewer feel close sympathy with the people to whom it happens.

In composing her pictures, the illustrator uses to advantage the contrast

Fig. 79. Monica Doppert, *La calle es libre*
From *La Calle es Libre* by Kurusa, illustrated by Monica Doppert. Copyright © 1981, Ekaré-Banco de Libro

between the wide horizontal space created by her double-page pictures and the barrio's hilly character. She emphasizes vertical and horizontal lines but then has diagonals interfere with them for dramatic effect. When Bruno and the children concentrate on preparing their proposal, they form a pyramid, with the librarian on top; when they arrive at the town hall, with the jitters, they spread out as an undersized horizontal group confronting the imposing vertical accents on the building and on the guardsman inside.

Doppert, who as an illustrator and an artist is used to expressing herself in varying stylistic forms, affirms, by the style she chose for this book, her social engagement and her sympathy for the children's cause. This is a sensible book, with a fresh optimism, but a book that is also realistically resigned, in content and in style, to what youth growing up in a disadvantaged settlement can accomplish on their first steps into community life.

WOMAN'S SOCIAL SIZE

The Story of the Sandwiches first shows us a beautiful village with little homes surrounded by flowers.[2] Then we read that the village has thousands of small houses where thousands of minuscule women and children live; that is why the village has no name. There Ita lives, too. We meet her as she is looking at a sandwich as large as herself—one of the sandwiches that every woman in the village prepares twice a day, each hoping fervently that hers will be the tastiest of all (fig. 80). The sandwiches are sent off to the Great House of the Men. One day, Ita, the girl with the dark braids, the sensuous mouth, and the intense eyes, leaning against a full cup of strawberries, each larger than her eyes, Ita, the most curious girl around, asks her mother about the unknown doings of the papas in Their House. Mother doesn't like the question. She doesn't know exactly, she says, and, anyway, girls should grow up to be obedient and pretty. But Grandma tells Ita that the papas write important documents, send registered letters, and compute statistics. Ita is not satisfied. She decides to find out about the papas.

Next, strands of highways hung on tall, spindly awe-inspiring pylons

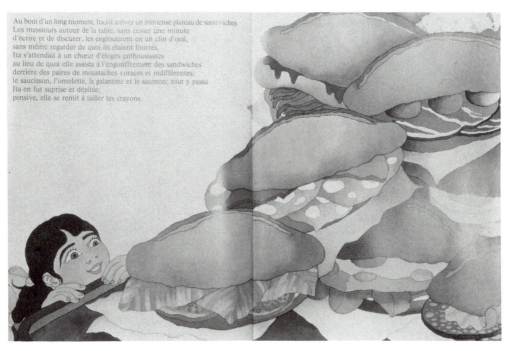

Au bout d'un long moment, Ita vit arriver un immense plateau de sandwiches.
Les messieurs autour de la table, sans cesser une minute
d'écrire et de discuter, les engloutirent en un clin d'oeil,
sans même regarder de quoi ils étaient fourrés.
Ita s'attendait à un chœur d'éloges enthousiastes
au lieu de quoi elle assista à l'engouffrement des sandwiches
derrière des paires de moustaches voraces et indifférentes;
le saucisson, l'omelette, la galantine et le saumon: tout y passa.
Ita en fut suprise et dépitée;
pensive, elle se remit à tailler les crayons.

Fig. 80. Margherita Saccaro, *Histoire de Sandwiches*
From *Histoire de Sandwiches* by Adela Turin, illustrated by Margherita Saccaro. Paris: Ed. des femmes, 1976

2. Adela Turin, *Histoire de Sandwiches (Storia di panini)*, illus. Margherita Saccaro (Paris: Ed. des femmes, 1976).

carry Ita, who is hiding in a van transporting sandwiches, toward the awesome Great House, whose tower bears the outlines of a human face. At the entrance, the man at the desk, whose gold-braided cap is the size of Ita, curtly informs her that the men are writing important dailies, weeklies, monthlies, etc. On the 199th floor, the men sit, talking and writing at the same time. Ita climbs on one of the tables and confronts a huge man, who notices her and condescendingly permits her to sharpen his pencil. When the enormous tasty sandwiches arrive, to Ita's growing surprise the men swallow them inattentively, without interrupting their work, still talking and writing at the same time. Ita, pensive, returns to her face-shaped pencil sharpener. At night, she falls asleep, amid rolls of paper, under the watchful eye and teeth of an enormous printing press. But she is satisfied, now that she has found work that's more important than preparing sandwiches.

The next day, as she turns and turns the sharpener, she listens (her eyes show how intently) to the news items coming in. Their importance strikes her as hollow. Becoming bored, she starts folding boats out of newspapers and starts thinking, why is it that the dailies, the weeklies, etc., never write about the women, the children, or the sandwiches? What goes on is not exciting enough. Indignantly, minuscule Ita faces the equally indignant giant, who is unable to grasp why the dailies, etc., should concern themselves with women and children (fig. 81). Ita escapes back to the village.

Fig. 81. Margherita Saccaro, *Histoire de Sandwiches*

From *Histoire de Sandwiches* by Adela Turin, illustrated by Margherita Saccaro. Paris: Ed. des femmes, 1976

Sitting on a table, scandal on her face, she tells and retells all the women what she found out in the Great House, especially about the demeaning of their work. They are dispirited. From then on, they prepare fewer and less tasty sandwiches, until one day none are prepared at all. The women stand around in the village square, arguing, expressing their indignation on the placards they carry. In the second-to-last picture, the unexpected occurs: on the left-hand side, a small Ita is standing in the tall grass; on the right, she has grown so much that her legs alone are longer than the whole girl used to be. Something marvelous is happening; within a few months, the village and its women and children grow to normal size. The men are stupefied. But, in the end, the fathers are seen together with the mothers, playing with their children. We are presented with a last view of the happy, colorful village.

This is perhaps the only story ever told where sandwiches serve as symbols. More than anything, it is a parable, demonstrating the diminutive and, by extension, abject status of woman versus the pompous, technological, bureaucratic importance of media-addicted man. The matter-of-fact text is expanded by bright pop-style illustrations, magnifying discrimination to emphatic, insistent, satirical Brobdingnagian proportions. But social change comes surprisingly easily, resulting from a change in female self-appraisal, engendered by just one curious girl.

Does the story exaggerate? It is a parable, isn't it? The story is a bit overpowering, but older girls will have no difficulty in identifying with Ita. Conceptually, the story is sound and sad. The issue of woman's low self-esteem in the face of male lack of recognition of her potential contribution to their common society, exists, on various levels, in any society. Ita comes out well as she moves assiduously, diligently through the stunning situations she encounters. She is pretty, energetic, and even a bit playful in spite of her seriousness. The anxiety that grips her every so often during her adventure is expressed by the recurring aggressively anthropomorphous objects.

Turin is an Italian feminist author who has frequently collaborated with women illustrators to create picture books advancing the cause of girls and women. This orientation might explain why, although the story attacks the media-stricken male writers, the final picture of the happy village includes signs raised on a few houses saying Children's Journal and Women's Publishing House.

SUDDEN UTOPIA, BODY AND SOUL

Allumette is a modern version of, or rather Tomi Ungerer's contemporary comment on, one of Hans Christian Andersen's saddest tales, *The Little Match-Girl*.[3] In that story, a destitute girl tries to sell matches on New Year's

3. Tomi Ungerer, *Allumette* (Zürich: Diogenes, 1974).

Eve, but the well-to-do people she accosts as they rush by pay no attention. They pursue their many errands. Soon they will spend the evening in peaceful, well-heated, and brightly lit homes. The girl dares not go home without having sold her matches; her father would be sure to beat her. Exhausted, she sits down on a corner. To warm herself, she strikes the matches, one after another; wherever their light falls, the walls become transparent: she can see warm rooms, filled with light and joy, and smell the apples and plums with which the roast goose is stuffed. She falls asleep and freezes to death. In her dream, her grandmother takes her to Heaven.

Ungerer's tale of Allumette (French for *match*), though transposed from the nineteenth to the twentieth centuries, starts out just like Andersen's. Dressed in rags, barefoot, and frightful to look at, Allumette tries to sell matches nobody needs. She is pushed around, feeds on garbage (fig. 82), and sleeps on doorsteps. On Christmas Eve, after all the people have gone home, she finds shelter at a building site. She lights a fire; soon it spreads, and she is forced to escape. Now the tale takes its modern turn. As, exhausted, she collapses and thinks her end has come, with her last breath Allumette starts to pray to "Somebody," asking to live a little longer, long enough to have a taste of cake, a slice of meat. At midnight, pandemonium breaks loose, and, with Allumette close to freezing, a cake, a turkey, and a ham crash down; blankets, sausages, and a tricycle follow; more lightning initiates another shower, a veritable rain of all conceivable consumer goods. News of the event spreads; in the morning—Christmas Day—the poor, the handicapped, the unemployed, the ill, and the weak-in-mind emerge to have their share. Looking at them, the rich feel cheap and selfish. Their reaction outrages the mayor, who calls in the riot squads. But as Allumette starts to sort out the goods that fell from the sky and as the rich people contribute gifts, the mayor is pacified. Nobody is able to explain the miracle. Allumette has no interest in explanations, only in the good that has come from the sudden downpour of gifts. From now on, the organization she initiates and heads will provide aid, through its volunteers, wherever disasters occur.

Ungerer characterizes the lines of development taking place simultaneously on the individual, the social, and the moral levels by thoughtfully combining verbal and visual means. A few persons stand out as representatives of change. When we see her first, Allumette is a scraggy, undernourished child. When her wish comes true over and above everything she could have imagined, she turns into a gleeful brat. In the last picture of the story, we glimpse her from behind, a slim, upright teenager who waves at the lightning and at the dark clouds on the horizon, a real heroine. She is happy with what she and her coworkers are able to do for suffering people everywhere. The mayor of the town is, as is to be expected, inept and fat; he quickly changes his hostile attitude toward the upheaval created by the fringe groups in the population, pragmatically endorsing the compassion that grips the well-to-do inhabitants. Even more significant is what happens

Fig. 82. Tomi Ungerer, *Allumette*
From *Allumette,* copyright © 1974 by Diogenes Verlag AG, Zürich

to the baker and his wife, who represent the greedy and wealthy in town. At first, on Christmas Eve, when Allumette presses her nose against the shop window displaying their cakes, the couple drive her off with a kick. The havoc created at midnight by the fulfillment of Allumette's wish catches the baker and his wife while they are counting money. They rush out to catch as much as they can of the goods pouring down and are hit by plumbing equipment and strawberry jam. The next morning, they fall on their knees before Allumette and become her faithful volunteers.

The changes taking place in society are depicted by a series of convincingly structured, large scenes—the pushy crowds buying and carrying goods; Christmas commercialized, presided over by a cardboard angel; the silent march of the meek and the weak who have come to feast on the miraculous gifts from above; and, near the end, volunteers operating at a disaster site.

Ungerer does not intend to make it easy for us to discover whether he wished to create a funny story or a morality tale. Entertainment and serious issues are inextricably mixed in a close, clever combination of text and pictures that only an experienced and superior artist would know how to accomplish. The events are represented, both verbally and visually, in a realistic framework. The miracle is, as it were, accepted by people as a not-quite-believable phenomenon, but after a short while, their attention is directed toward the changes it has effected. The surreal is easily assimilated, and not too much thought is given to cause and reason. On the one hand, we witness an utter change in the relationships between individuals in society and in society's attitude toward its weak and neglected members. On the other hand, the text and especially the pictures go out of their way to be funny, humorous, or satirical, The detailed account of the prosaic foodstuffs, fixtures, gadgets, and playthings coming down from the sky; Allumette's blissful gaze as she is surrounded by a garland of sausages; the mayor's taking action while, wearing a dressing gown, he bathes his feet in a very decorative tub; the woman in the fur who contributes a silly statue carried by her chauffeur—these and more scenes ridicule what happens and to whom it happens. Other pictures, such as the moment of Allumette's prayer, the parade (as the mayor calls it) of the lame and the hungry and the old, and the sight of the volunteers in action, are dignified and even touching.

The strongest contrast arises from the portrayal of Allumette herself: the final picture shows her, as we said above, as a serious teenager, conscious of her role in society. This image of the girl, who, ever since that Christmas night, feels close to the lightning in the sky and sees herself as the young bringer of light and justice to society, is derided (or reinforced?) by the caricaturistic jacket illustration presenting a scrawny and seditious Allumette holding up a big match like a liberating torch or a scepter (fig. 83). We are entertained by being moved from emotional involvement to caricature and back again.

Interestingly, the colors in the book do not change much throughout the story. Subdued yellow-to-brown hues dominate from the cover until the end. Thus, color emphasizes the somber, not comical, aspects of the story.

It is hard to believe that Ungerer took one of Andersen's gloomier tales and turned it around just for fun's sake. It makes more sense to assume that the idea of helpless pity demonstrated there seemed cheap to him, infuriated him. As one observer has put it, "Ungerer may have been greatly affected by the story as a child, and now he is rebelling against the awful burden of grief and sadness the story imposed upon him . . . he was driven to exorcise the pathetic match-girl from his mind by giving her a happy ending." So, he set out to show that the twentieth century has more to offer, or should be offering more, to the downtrodden. He is very experienced in

Fig. 83. Tomi Ungerer, *Allumette*
From *Allumette*, copyright © 1974 by Diogenes Verlag AG, Zürich

creating attractive picture books and knows well that ideas appeal to older children if they are put across in a funny way.

This view of purposeful ambiguity being employed by the artist in a mixture of crisp amusement and social concepts fits well with a few of Ungerer's less demanding stories, notably *The Three Robbers* and *Zeralda's Giant*.[4] There, too, children—girls again—easily, though not so suddenly, succeed in changing the ways of life of quite dangerous and unscrupulous types, who become civilized and helpful. Thus, indications abound that confirm what has been known for some time—that Ungerer is a satirist with a genuine bent for and a belief in social equality (among other inclinations), of which Allumette is one of the most adventurous expressions.

Allumette is a story about sudden economic utopia; it is, even more so, one about social and psychological utopia. One girl's prayer causes a rainfall of material plenty. She, herself, turns the cataclysm into an action against social injustice. She is also supported in this effort, far into the future, by

4. Tomi Ungerer, *Die drei Räuber (The Three Robbers)* (Zürich: Diogenes, 1963); *Zeralda's Riese (Zeralda's Giant)* (Zürich: Diogenes, 1970).

the change of heart of the wealthy and the powerful. The satirist is also an optimist, it seems; he believes that it is not very difficult to reform human individual and social behavior. He also reminds us that the starving beggar girl can turn out to be talented and socially valuable, and lead a humanly satisfying existence in the service of society. Her life should not go to waste.

RESPECT FOR THE AGED

The following two books provide views of how society treats and how it should treat old people. The issue has become, over the past decades, an urgent one, mainly because of the increasing longevity of the aged in many countries. Slogans such as "the fear of dying is being replaced by the fear of living too long" or polls asking people whether elderly parents should be placed in homes even if it is not absolutely necessary reflect the problems faced by many individuals and families.

It should come as no surprise, therefore, that this issue seeps down into the world of children and is taken up by courageous picture-book makers for the sake of children, and surely for the sake of the elderly, too. The two books chosen treat those we call "senior citizens" as a group in danger of being neglected. The stories differ in background and approach. The first presents old people as senior citizens who can still fulfill a small role in their families and enjoy life in the bargain. The second confronts us with old people, routinely cared for by the public, as being sickly, dependent, and shut away, until a child detects the dim human glimmer that's still there.

The cover of *Grandfather Thomas* presents double-spread urban land-scapes (fig. 84); there are large offices and apartment buildings, and rows of smaller houses, green hills, and a windowless tower on top of one of the hills; old people attached to improbable contraptions fly at night over this landscape, which is romantically lit by the moon as well as by lights from windows and headlights on the road.[5] In this book, Zavřel becomes even more naive than usual for him. He uses topsy-turvy compositions incorpo-rating motifs from children's art. Lots of likable, starry-eyed children and grown-ups are ever on the move; sometimes even the houses seem to move along with the people and the cars. Bright, friendly colors, *all* colors, overlay this small, motley world, often highlighting the center of attention in the picture with a warm yellow glow. Leaving Ita and Allumette, we are back in the magic realm of a story for pre-adolescent children, where things happen the easy way if only you use your imagination.

There is Grandfather Thomas, immensely loved by his grandchildren, with no end to his energy, his dedication, his creative ideas, and his treasure of games and stories. The children from the neighborhood come and listen to his bedside stories (fig. 85). However, one day the mayor goes on televi-

5. Stěpán Zavřel, *Grossvater Thomas (Grandfather Thomas)* (Zürich: Bohem Pr., 1984).

Fig. 84. Stěpán Zavřel, *Grossvater Thomas*
Stěpán Zavřel, *Grossvater Thomas* © 1984 by Bohem Press-Zürich, Recklinghausen, Wien, Paris. Lektorat: Kurt Baumann-Alle Rechte vorbehalten

sion (holding a smiling "good guy" mask in front of his own face) to declare that all the old people living in town will forthwith be transferred to an old people's home. Old-people-catchers swarm out to collect them, even by force when the elderly try to get away, and transport them to the windowless tower on the hill. Some time later, the television shows a program demonstrating how happy and well-adjusted the old people are in their new home. But the children notice that the grandparents look bored. The children conspire to free them at night while the parents are out and will not interfere, and to hide them in the children's own homes. The adventure centers, of course, on Grandfather Thomas. He is brought home and concealed under the bed (fig. 86). As always, he has the children spellbound

Fig. 85. Stěpán Zavřel, *Grossvater Thomas*
Stěpán Zavřel, *Grossvater Thomas* © 1984 by Bohem Press-Zürich, Recklinghausen, Wien, Paris. Lektorat: Kurt Baumann-Alle
Rechte vorbehalten

Fig. 86. Stěpán Zavřel, *Grossvater Thomas*
Stěpán Zavřel, *Grossvater Thomas* © 1984 by Bohem Press-Zürich, Recklinghausen, Wien, Paris. Lektorat: Kurt Baumann-Alle
Rechte vorbehalten

with his tales at night, when the parents are away. In the end, at Christmastime, Thomas reappears dressed up as Santa Claus, his white beard gleaming in the candlelight. Parents and children are happy to have him with them again.

For younger children, this is a buoyant modern adventure story, with vibrant, alert children, and adults who all look a bit strange, the way children see them. Older children and adults can scarcely overlook the criticism included in the fantasy. Society shortchanges the aged, who, though they may become a burden, are still attached to life as they have known it, and still may give and receive love, especially from children. The obvious grievance is directed toward the establishment. The mayor is characterized (once again) as a cynic and a crook. From behind his mask, he speaks of the dear old ones who need to be cared for and taken off the streets for their own good, adding that, anyway, they do not exactly adorn the town. The catchers, carrying out bureaucratic and autocratic orders, are nasty white-coated men using nasty contraptions to ferret out the helpless old ones and coercing them to board the buses to the tower during the night (as secret services are wont to do), when the burghers hear and see and say nothing, because they are sleeping—as the text and pictures convince us—the sleep of the righteous. Interestingly, however, more subtly but no less emphatically, the story also accuses the families of conniving with the rest of the citizens by not opposing the mayor's attitude and conduct. The parents do not ask any questions. Only later on, when Grandpa has already been confined under his bed for a long time, do they start to worry. The children have stopped mentioning Grandpa: have they forgotten him? will that also happen when they, the parents, grow old? But still the parents do not attempt to have Thomas with them again. Of course, in the end, tears collect in their eyes when they see him again amid a crowd of children, thus justifying what their children have managed to plan and carry out.

Two levels characterize the book. On the easier one, it is an imaginative, topsy-turvy story. On the deeper level, the social aspect stands out—the intention of opening children's eyes to what might happen in their homes and in their hometown.

It is interesting and gratifying to note that the children's, and Zavřel's, attitude assumes a general meaning, namely, that one of the elements supporting the evolution of a sense of place is the appearance of old people everywhere. It seems that their presence contributes to a general feeling of human continuity and variety. For children, the presence of the elderly might also mean—apart from the contact with their own "personal" old people—a softening of the dichotomous setup: children and a generation of adults in charge. Zavřel and his fictional children know that the establishment (the mayor) is wrong in attempting a schematic solution. Life prefers openness.

THE CHILD AS A SOCIAL WORKER

Opening *Wilfrid Gordon Macdonald Partridge* and leafing through it, we are taken aback, and are also possibly slightly shocked by the figures appearing on its pages: six very old people exhibiting signs of decrepit infirmity—bent, bloated, tottery.[6] Why should one give a book like this to children? For what purpose? Then we notice that those faces express changing moods. We sense the warm colors. We realize that a small boy on a skateboard flits in and out of the pictures. Our eyes move along with the words. The book has caught hold of us: it is *that* kind of book. Maybe we only now recognize Wilfrid Gordon—small, quick, attentive. We cannot help falling in love with him as we meet him for the first time, swinging from a beam, red hair, protruding belly, and all. He lives next door to an old people's home, going there and back through a hole in the high wooden fence. He knows all the old people. He has a special relationship with each of them. Best of all he likes Miss Nancy. As he hears his parents say that she has lost her memory, he tries to find out what memory is. It means something different to different people. Wilfrid Gordon collects small items he finds at home and in the courtyard and gives them, one by one, to Miss Nancy—a shell, a puppet on strings, a medal, a football (fig. 87); and she starts to remember things. The two of them smile.

Fig. 87. Julie Vivas, *Wilfrid Gordon McDonald Partridge*

From *Wilfrid Gordon McDonald Partridge* by Mem Fox, illustrated by Julie Vivas. Text copyright © Mem Fox 1984, illustrations copyright © Julie Vivas 1984, reproduced by permission of Kane/Miller Book Publishers

6. Mem Fox, *Wilfrid Gordon McDonald Partridge*, illus. Julie Vivas (New York: Kane/Miller, 1985; originally published in Adelaide, Australia: Omnibus Bks., 1984).

After one's initial reluctance has been overcome, it is easy to marvel at the strange idea of creating a book that recounts how a child can bring a bit of happiness to a few secluded old men and women (none of whom is Wilfrid's grandparent). It takes closer acquaintance to find out *why* the book is so beautiful. Certainly, the excellent, feeling characterization of the boy and of the aged (for instance, what goes on in Miss Nancy's face and with her hands) constitutes one impelling element. Another is the quiet glow of the watercolor paintings. Still another, a rare one in picture books, is the physical closeness Wilfrid G.M.P. permits himself to have with the aged. He touches them all, freely and naturally; tactile closeness complements visual closeness. In Wilfrid's eyes and for Wilfrid's hands, grown-ups and old people are not scary. They are playmates for whom he cares. Two adjacent pictures bring this idea out strongly: in the left-hand one, Wilfrid lies on the sofa between his parents, upside down, feet on father's shoulder, hand on mother's hip—a long-legged family keeping together. In the right-hand picture, he builds a tower of tiny blocks while snuggling up to Mrs. Jordan. By including Wilfrid's parents, the story discreetly but succinctly implies that they look favorably upon their small boy's involvement with the residents of the house on the other side of the fence (surely differing in their attitude from run-of-the-mill parents).

The compelling mood is lyrical. Brief verbal and visual rhythms abound in the book; correspondences, assonances, balances emerge and dissolve as quickly as a small child's attention span passes from one focus to the next:

Mrs. Jordan played the organ.
Mr. Hosking told him stories.
He ran errands for Miss Mitchel, who walked with a wooden stick.
Mr. Tippett, who is crazy about cricket, knows that memory makes you cry.

Also, Wilfrid loves Miss Nancy because, like himself, she has four names. For Mrs. Jordan, memory is "warm, close," and we get a close-up view of her blowing on a cup of milk; for Mr. Hosking, it is something from "long ago, remote," as he looks down the row of chairs; Mr. Tippet says memory makes you "cry"; Miss Mitchell, that it makes you "laugh"; Mr. Drysdale thinks it is as "precious" as gold, and Miss Nancy has "lost" hers.

The visual rhythms resound with and respond to the verbal ones: at first, we see the inmates of the home from behind, sitting on a straight row of chairs. Then rigidity melts; still seen as a group, the people acquire a personal note; later, they are portrayed singly. Most of all, of course, we get to know Miss Nancy. A structured sequence of five pictures depicts the return of her memory. As, aided by Wilfrid's gifts, she starts to remember, a small picture, with sharp perspective, removes her from us; as a young girl on the beach, she towers over the page; a small bull's-eye sketch shows her brother going off to the war; next, full page again, the tall girl dangles a puppet on strings; then, the day when she first met Wilfrid (short-term memory also returns, as usual, later than long-term memory!) presents another small view with focal perspective as a kind of passage back to the present. Memory plays with sizes and distances. And then we are struck by the way Wilfrid and Miss Nancy smile and smile!

There is a sense of pantomime, an inspiration of dance in the air throughout—in the manner in which everybody moves and in the way Wilfrid weaves in and out and about on his skateboard (fig. 88), crosses back and forth through the hole in the fence, and snatches Mr. Tippett's green belt. The choreographic spell is underscored by Miss Nancy's chair. In the beginning, she is shown from behind, sitting there separated from the

Fig. 88. Julie Vivas, *Wilfrid Gordon McDonald Partridge*
From *Wilfrid Gordon McDonald Partridge* by Mem Fox, illustrated by Julie Vivas. Text copyright © Mem Fox 1984, illustrations copyright © Julie Vivas 1984, reproduced by permission of Kane/Miller Book Publishers

others: as an outsider? as a special person in Wilfrid's eyes? Next time we see her, she is sitting on the chair sideways, with the boy hanging on to it, and at a similar angle later, as he gives her the things he has collected. Near the end of the story, when Miss Nancy is playing football with Wilfrid, the empty chair faces us; on it rest some of the things he has brought her. The 180-degree turnabout of the chair repeats and reinforces the changes happening in Miss Nancy herself. The cover picture, too, embodies a hint of the vigorous spin toward openness and hope.

The story does not portray a child's development; Wilfrid's interest, awareness, and involvement are there from the outset. He loves being with these old people. We are shown just a single instance of how he knows to find ways of helping them. Probably he will have learned something from the experience. But the important thing is that the boy is satisfied. *We* should be deeply moved by seeing how, in his eyes, and before our eyes, six sorry, gaudy clowns turn into persons commanding respectability. There is a fresh overall tenderness about this book, a sensitivity for human feelings and relationships, and for words and images and their relationships as well, which, far beyond the imaginative presentation of its specific theme, makes this story an inspired work of art.

In order to use books as a means of involving children in ideas concerning action for the disadvantaged, all sorts of styles and approaches are employed, ranging from the lifelike to the absurd. The selection found in the five books presented here is varied enough. The protagonists act in groups or singly. They may convince some adults to join them. They intervene in the adult world. Their adventures are narrated as realistic or as fantastic events, or as a mixture of both. The stories may relate to far-reaching changes in the social order, encompassing the whole of society, or to less inclusive alleviations of the suffering undergone by disadvantaged groups. As we noted above, the concern may be about self-help or about aid offered to others. *The stories variously emphasize a principle called social justice or a value called human dignity.* This theme—which focuses on the deprived, even the outcast group in society—is not one easily treated in picture books. The five books considered here demonstrate that it can be done successfully. They show how interest and compassion might be aroused. A key question here is, to what degree is the group whose conditions are depicted here authentically characterized?

Clearly, when the group is small–six aged persons, the children of San José, the grandparents in the town—the portrait may turn out to be more natural. In *Sandwiches* and *Allumette*, where anonymous crowds are also involved, schematization and exaggeration intrude. On the other hand, the concepts and contexts of these stories offer more excitement.

One might legitimately ask if these social-action picture books for older children are not a little too pat and optimistic, especially considering the solutions to social conflicts they offer. They are. But there is another side to the question. When, a few generations back, Andersen had the match-girl die of cold and hunger and fright, from all of which the dream delivered her, and hundreds of other stories described the pitiable fates of hundreds of other children, those depictions certainly reflected social and moral conditions that have not entirely disappeared from this world. Such stories told the truth, in a way, even if they did so in an outspokenly sentimental vein. However, they also reflected and thereby supported a social and moral attitude which held that the lot of humankind, and surely that of the poor, of women, and of children, was to suffer. The social order was to be accepted, and children were to be prepared for existing conditions. Fortunately, notwithstanding the disasters and atrocities witnessed by our age, in many societies the social scene has changed; social reform is on the agenda of any society for whose children the books examined here might be destined. No doubt, still better books can and, it is hoped, will be conceived. Yet, the present books serve a concept of progress that is an optimistic one. They do not actually offer fictionalized didactic notions; the only one of the books, the story of San José, that could in fact be emulated, is the sincerest of them all (while the didactic is not infrequently insincere). The books do have an ideological flavor, and the ideological tends, at times, toward tenuous optimism. In this context, one should view these stories as *études* toward the development of children's social attitudes and engagement.

The authors and artists whose works we have used as examples search in earnest for clarification of the issues and solutions within the grasp of young people's minds; their stories exhibit vitality, even vehemence; most important, *a spirit of hope pervades them*, a belief in goodwill and in the possibility of social improvement.

The two significant elements appearing in stories of this kind—the focus on neglected human beings and the realistic or fantastic portrayal of children's participation in efforts to recognize and remove social injustice—are likely to contribute significantly to older children's personality development, provided that the books also delight their readers and offer them aesthetic challenges.

CHILDREN'S BOOKS CITED

Fox, Mem. *Wilfrid Gordon McDonald Partridge.* Illus. Julie Vivas. New York: Kane/Miller, 1985. orig. Adelaide, Australia: Omnibus Bks., 1984.

Kurusa. *La calle es libre (The Street Is Free).* Illus. Monica Doppert. Caracas: Ediciones Ekaré Banco del Libro, 1981.

Turin, Adela. *Storia di panini (The Story of the Sandwiches).* Illus. Margherita Saccaro. Milano: Contact Studio, 1976.

Ungerer, Tomi. *Allumette.* Zürich: Diogenes, 1974.

——. *Die drei Räuber (The Three Robbers).* Zürich: Diogenes, 1963.

——. *Zeralda's Riese (Zeralda's Giant).* Zürich: Diogenes, 1970.

Zavřel, Stěpán. *Grossvater Thomas (Grandfather Thomas).* Zürich: Bohem Pr., 1984.

11

The Threat of War and the Quest for Peace

THE BACKGROUND

War is the most terrible form of human interaction and communication. It also is ubiquitous. It has always existed and will continue to exist for the foreseeable future. Adults who are responsible for the growing-up processes of children will find themselves in a painful predicament attempting to explain war, probably far more so than in dealing with the phenomenon of death. The latter is a natural occurrence (if we disregard, rightfully I believe, crime in this context). War is man-made. Neither can satisfactorily be explained to children, but death is ultimately beyond our power to control, whereas war depends on man's power. War is an abiding central motif and a persistent embarrassment in the framework of formal education. For, depending on one's circumstances and ideology, war can be seen—must be seen—as unavoidable, necessary, justifiable, defensible, or morally laudable if collective survival or the right to pursue a special way of life is at issue; or war can be viewed as an unethical, unjustifiable encroachment on another society's most basic rights and conditions. Always, values such as patriotism and good citizenship are involved. Always, war is perceived as an instrument of human behavior and, at the same time, as the ultimate horror. This double-edged recognition of war as an obligation and a disaster creates a dilemma for responsible adults who feel themselves at a disadvantage when they have to explain war to children— and consequently often attempt to retreat into trivialities. Yet, the beast does not go away. It is no doubt one of the tasks of education to inculcate, as an internalized value, in the growing individual the concept of sacrifices demanded by society and the personal readiness to sacrifice oneself. The teaching of subjects such as history, literature, Bible stories, and geography serves as formal education's most important means of achieving this goal, the emphasis being put, out of necessity, on heroism, on the fatefulness of war, and on collective processes and points of view.

However, ever larger sectors of human society are beginning to recognize that war is too effective an instrument, causing too much havoc on both the winning and the losing sides and leading to utter destruction. Beyond the terrible price in human suffering paid by individuals, the recognition grows that war creates invidious long-term damage to the fabric of society. Ethnocentrism, brutalization, the increasing disregard of physical and mental pain, the disruption of the family, poverty, and, above all, the deterioration of human contacts and interaction and the diminishing value of human life are not easily overcome or reversed. It seems that the insight is spreading that war as a phenomenon has to be fought against, even in the minds of children.

The purpose of the present discussion is to introduce picture books depicting the depravity of war unleashed, reinforcing the belief in the avoidability of war, and demonstrating ways in which individuals can try to influence public opinion.

Before we consider the books, we should confront a simple question: how dare a medium such as the picture book take up, or rather take on, so serious a matter, which is admittedly beyond the comprehension of even the older child? Possible responses are as simple and straightforward as the question itself. As we said above, the teaching of history (which no doubt also demands students to grapple with events, processes, and concepts beyond their comprehension) emphasizes the societal aspects. Only rarely is the human predicament spotlighted. Literature for young people supports and complements this tendency in many countries. New kinds of books containing outspoken antiwar statements are only gradually being published. When we come to children's books (not just a few isolated picture books in a few countries either), to novels, movies, comics, and TV series, to which the child and youth have easy access, a lighthearted glorification of war and phony heroism predominate. The terrible fact is that war has entertainment value. On the lowest level there exists the callousness (by now proverbial) inherent in the constant media news barrage—wounded soldiers and burning houses, at dinnertime—which habituates all of us to a minimalization of emotional and cognitive reactions. And there are too many wars—civil wars, uprisings, and acts of oppression —occurring simultaneously within our awareness for us to be able to sort them out. All these factors combine to raise the threshold of our ability, as adults, to recognize the danger signs.

Thus, the picture books we have in mind may turn out to be among the more important agents of society's attempt to scale down the abomination of war to a personal level, and to oppose it on that level. These books may, if their quality substantiates them, have a role to fulfill in aiding adults who have difficulty in coping with the issue. War as it is should not be discriminated against in picture books.

The books themselves present widely different approaches. The stories are of disparate origins, and there are few subjects for which the question of origin is of such importance: some children and families and picture-book creators exist who have been living with one kind of war or another for as far back as they can remember; others live with the threat of imminent war reverberating in their daily lives; still others live with memories of a past war that colors societal values and actions right up to the present. Then there are those for whom war is a disquieting concern, even though remote in both time and space. Finally, there is that nightmare, the radioactive war, overwhelming all boundaries. Yet, although the books differ in background, common to all is the implied or explicit argument for peace.

The works selected here can be arranged according to various categories. A few books treat past wars, while others probe the future. Conventional versus nuclear war is another division. The narrative background may also differ, since some treat the subject in a minor key, in a small setting, while others deal with an individual destiny against a backdrop of collective events. Conclusions are offered in more or less outspoken fashions. Levels of excellence vary. So do moods. After much thought, I believe that the prevailing moods of narrative presentation in word and picture will serve best as the guidelines for our examination.

IRONY

Is Leaf and Lawson's *The Story of Ferdinand* the first American antiwar picture book?[1] To our generation, this book appears to be pleasantly entertaining. When it first came out in 1937, at the time of the Spanish Civil War, the book was vigorously accused of giving expression to fascist or communist or pacifist leanings. Since it is now into its third millionth copy, a strong appeal must be hidden in this tale of Ferdinand, the bull, who, though not lacking in strength, refuses to fulfill his preordained role—to enter the arena, become incensed, find a vital interest in combat, and be killed as the climax of an amusing spectacle. Ferdinand also negates the spirit of competition, preferring nonchalant solitude with lots of time for ogling at flowers (fig. 89)—to all this, his loving and understanding mother acquiesces with a sigh.[2] The illustrations more than match the humor and sensitivity of the text. There is no doubt a sense of irony about this small volume—can one really believe that the nature of bulls and of those who organize bullfights can be changed? There is also a mild early whiff of the antihero, of flower children and nonviolent resistance movements.

A much later American antiwar book is the Emberleys' *Drummer Hoff* (fig. 90).[3] Under the guise of making fun of military ponderousness, there appears, as Lacy clarifies in her book on picture books, an antiwar statement

1. Munro Leaf, *The Story of Ferdinand*, illus. Robert Lawson (New York: Viking, 1936).

2. Remember how years later *Tootle* by Gertrude Crampton, illus. Tibor Gergely (New York: Simon & Schuster, 1946), the promising young engine, is ostracized by his teachers and peers because he falls in love with a horse, gets lost amid the flowers, and has to be coaxed back into the fold, to go on and become an outstanding long-distance engine?

3. Barbara Emberley, *Drummer Hoff*, illus. Ed Emberley (Englewood Cliffs, N.J.: Prentice-Hall, 1967).

Fig. 89. Robert Lawson, *The Story of Ferdinand*

From *The Story of Ferdinand* by Munro Leaf, illustrated by Robert Lawson. Illustration copyright 1936 by Robert Lawson, renewed © 1964 by John W. Boyd. Reprinted by permission of Viking Penguin, a division of Penguin Books USA

Fig. 90. Ed Emberley, *Drummer Hoff*

From *Drummer Hoff* adapted by Barbara Emberley, illustrated by Ed Emberley © 1967. Reprinted by permission of the publisher, Prentice-Hall, Inc., Englewood Cliffs, New Jersey

that was "popular with many Americans, coming as it did during the country's disquieting involvement in Vietnam."[4] The making of a cannon that is fired off and thereby destroyed without anyone being hurt, after which event birds and flowers reappear, is a metaphoric wish fulfillment way beyond the simple rhythms of text and illustrations. Lacy also cites Ed Emberley as saying that men sometimes return from war with wooden legs. She goes on to say that the pictures present a concern over the folly of humankind in building only to destroy, and ends with what, in my eyes, is a rather bittersweet consolation, "a faith in nature's endurance to reign triumphant in the end"—apparently because men cannot be trusted.[5] But can nature?

These books have a distant companion in the Italian Luzzati's *The Thievish Magpie*.[6] Again, the story is pleasant, even hilarious. Near a wood inhabited by scores of birds dwell three kings whose favorite pastime is making war. In these wars, as always, people die for nothing. One day, the kings decide to conquer the wood. But the thievish magpie moves into action (fig. 91), at first stealing the kings' crowns, then confounding the kings and tricking them out of one of their castles. Wearing three crowns on her head, the magpie returns to the wood, sharing victory with all the birds: the wood is free and secure; there is no need for fear anymore. Luzzati's rhymes and his naive and, at the same time, fiery theatrical pictures, reminiscent of stained-glass techniques, make for a swift pace. Yet, as Poesio has pointed out, the simple-minded delight affirms a single-minded attitude; common-ers can liberate themselves from the senseless egoistic wars of their amoral rulers.[7]

These three easygoing and, at first sight, innocent books evoke a common concept, one also found in other art forms: the belief that the vainglorious-ness, the seeming playfulness of war as a ruthless game can be shown up as pointless nonsense, that the age-old and still current ritual of combat can be fought by ridicule, by burlesque humor shielding irony.

VOICES: THE INTIMATE WHISPER

Efrat's Father is a slight book—small format, few pages, modest pictures.[8] It depicts war as experienced by a small Israeli girl and rendered in her own words. Her father used to be a writer. When she sneaked into his room, she inhaled the smell of books. One day, he dressed in khaki and left home.

---

4. Lyn E. Lacy, *Art and Design in Children's Picture Books: An Analysis of Caldecott Award-Winning Illustrations* (Chicago and London: American Library Assn., 1986): 64–103.

5. Lacy, *Art and Design*, 72.

6. Emanuele Luzzati, *La gazza ladra (The Thievish Magpie)* (Milano: Mursia, 1973).

7. Carla Poesio, "Lele Luzzati: Figure incrociate," *Schedario*, no. 196 (July/Aug. 1985): 127–31; "Messaggi per l'anno della pace," *Schedario*, no. 197 (Sept./Oct. 1985): 163–65.

8. Nira Keren, *Abba Schel Efrat (Efrat's Father)*, illus. Er'ela Hurvitz, photog. Hagai Eisenberg (Merchavia, Israel: Sifriat Hapoalim, 1971).

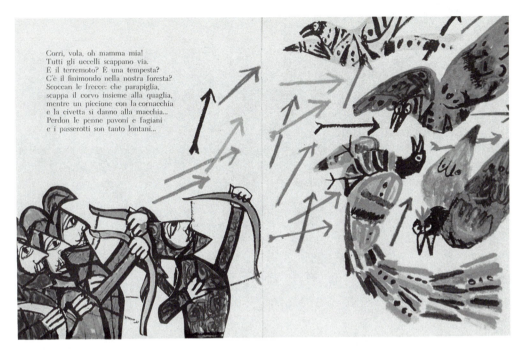

Corri, vola, oh mamma mia!
Tutti gli uccelli scappano via.
È il terremoto? È una tempesta?
C'è il finimondo nella nostra foresta?
Scoccan le frecce: che parapiglia,
scappa il corvo insieme alla quaglia,
mentre un piccione con la cornacchia
e la civetta si danno alla macchia...
Perdon le penne pavoni e fagiani
e i passerotti son tanto lontani...

Fig. 91. Emanuele Luzzati, *La gazza ladra*
From *La gazza ladra*, testo e illustrazioni di Emanuele Luzzati © Copyright 1964–1973 Ugo Mursia & Co., Milano

She and her mother went to visit him at his base. Some days later, nearby explosions made them descend to the shelter. When everything was over, only Father did not return. Grandmas came to visit, uncles brought Efrat presents, and Mother began to tell bedside stories. Now Efrat dreams of Father night and day. She imagines him as he throws her up high or is angry with her; she senses his strong grip when the neighbor takes her for a walk. Only the grown-ups don't see him.

Should the text continue one step further? As it stands, the story has a psychological completeness. It consoles. Efrat's surely slow and painful process of grief subsiding and acceptance overcoming her silent mourning should be left open, not be proscribed.

The illustrations are composed of black-and-white pen drawings mainly representing reality, alternating with photographs, in green and purple, evoking the dream. A few visual metaphors deepen our perception of the girl's suffering—Father's leaving home is depicted by five repeated photographs diminishing in size (fig. 92); the photograph of Efrat's hand resting in Father's covers the drawing of her walk with the neighbor; the last photograph, of Father playing with Efrat, is black, signifying that the illustration knows what the text conceals—that the dream will recede, and its enticing colors will pale.

War, in this case, is solely the girl's personal experience; only once do

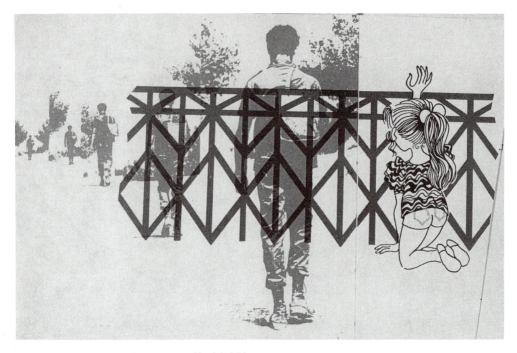

Fig. 92. Er'ela Hurvitz, *Abba Schel Efrat*

From *Abba Schel Efrat* by Nira Keren, illustrated by Er'ela Hurvitz, photography Hagai Eisenberg, published by Sifriat Hapoalim Publishing House of Hakibbutz Ha-Artzi Ltd. 1971

we see Mother's drawn face. No other images of war intrude. Efrat's whisper leads us to the remotest corner into which the curse of war can penetrate.

ROARING FIRE AND MUTED DYING

The Japanese book *Hiroshima No Pika (The Flash of Hiroshima)* is one of three works included here that treat nuclear war.[9] Immediately, doubt rises again: what sense does it make to bring before children this most inexplicable, most inconceivable of all forms of warfare? Yet, over the years the issue has been, on and off, in the center of public attention and of media coverage; waves of fear, of action, demonstrations, negotiations, and discussions come and go. How can children be left out of the picture? As early as 1982, R. J. Lifton, the Yale psychiatrist, was quoted as expressing his view that children as young as five had begun to fear that the world would be annihilated by a chain of events that the adults could not control.[10] The issue is on the minds of children and has to be dealt with. The question is, how?

Hiroshima No Pika is a fictionalized eyewitness account relating the fate

9. Toshi Maruki, *Hiroshima No Pika (The Flash of Hiroshima)* (Tokyo: Komine Shoten, 1980).
10. E. Salholz with J. Taylor and D. Gates, "Kids with Nuclear Jitters," *Newsweek* 11 Oct. 1982, 12.

of a family who lived in Hiroshima at the time of the first atom bomb. On August 6, 1945, Mii-Chan, the seven-year-old girl, and her parents are having breakfast when the bomb falls, the flash and the thunder engulfing them. When Mii-Chan comes to, flames issue from the darkness. Father, seared and hurt all over his body, emerges from the fire; the family starts out on its flight toward and across the rivers, as Mother bears Father on her back and holds her daughter by the hand, amid the others—the masses of the dead, the dying, and the ones who still have the energy to escape, with the swift fires at their footsteps. Four days later, the family is exhausted but safe. Even Father recovers. Then the story jumps forty years ahead. Father did not survive long. Like thousands of others, he died after some time. Mii-Chan and Mother live on. But Mii-Chan stopped growing on that day in 1945. She still looks like a seven-year-old girl. To this day, the dead are remembered and honored each year, on August 6. Red lanterns, each bearing a victim's name, are sent down the rivers to Hiroshima.

From the very first page, the book conveys an impression of dignity. Closer acquaintance reveals that this impression is the result of Maruki's success in balancing the elements of context and form employed in building up the story. The plot focuses on a small family whose individual fate is shown to be part of mass destiny. The text and pictures overlap in many ways, sharing and exchanging roles, to construct a narrative statement that is every so often overwhelmed by the unbearable nightmare underlying it. Taking upon herself the responsibility of documenting the events, Maruki keeps, over relatively long stretches of verbal narration, to a realistic style, while the pictures, too, reflect a sense of proportion. But then the text begins to cry out, and, not always simultaneously, the pictures become infused with fire and rain and the twisted suffering of the people (fig. 93), with expressionism being carried to the limits that a picture book can bear.

The text chronicles the days and nights following the bomb, from that summer morning in a city whose inhabitants had been used to war for a long time, through the flight and the mass dying, to the deceptive feeling of many that they have escaped death, only to be killed slowly, over years and decades. The pictures take up the roaring voices of the fires, whose tongues follow and engulf the fleeing thousands; then comes the vile radio-active rain, cold and oily, with the multitudes running and diving to get across the rivers, stretched out on the soil dead, or waiting for death, for the rain to stop, or for daybreak to arrive; and getting up again. By then, most people are stark naked, their clothes having disintegrated in the blast. Even as they are scorched, twisted, desperate, even in death, the elongated bodies have an aura of human decency about them; if it were not utterly out of place, one would be tempted to say that they reflect the beauty of man and woman that cannot be destroyed even *in extremis*. This is where Maruki reaches the climax of her expressionistic vein. Yet, even in the most harrowing scenes, she never loses control of composition. Rather than intending to shock us with visions of the impossible, she wants to over-

Fig. 93. Toshi Maruki, *Hiroshima No Pika*

From *Hiroshima No Pika* by Toshi Maruki. Copyright © 1980 by Toshi Maruki. Reprinted by permission of Lothrup, Lee & Shepard Books, a division of William Morrow, and by Nario Komine-Shoten Ltd.

whelm our emotions and our cognitive powers by informing us of the possible. The pictorially dramatic humanity of the dying woman offering rice to the weeping Mii-Chan is set off by the inhuman view of the dead Koreans whom nobody will bury. In all of the mass scenes, a personal focus interposes, with individuals standing out from the background; when a broad frieze of crazed people covers the upper part of the pages, below them hop a few swallows whose wings are aflame. Even though the inferno of fire clashes with the muddy, dark rain, we almost never lose sight of Mii-Chan and her mother: until very late into their escape from hell, the girl clasps the chopsticks in her cramped fingers, so that we shall be able to recognize her (fig. 94). In a few places, the pictures speak in metaphors. When we are told about the Koreans whose bodies will be abandoned, an ominous host of crows descends on them. As the text says that not only Japanese but also Americans, Koreans, Chinese, Russians, and Indonesians found their deaths on that day, do the nude bodies also wish to convey to us the thought, the conviction, that all humans are equal (fig. 95)? Does the rainbow appearing in the sky when the oily rain stops retract the promise that humankind will not again be annihilated?

Maruki's belief in the necessity of balancing the strains of impact against each other and her supreme power in achieving this effect explain the ending she has chosen for the story. At first, it is difficult to accept her choice. The anticlimax is too distant; after the dynamics of the atomic storm, the factual rendition of developments is dry, too dry. Coming immediately

Fig. 94. Toshi Maruki, *Hiroshima No Pika*

From *Hiroshima No Pika* by Toshi Maruki. Copyright © 1980 by Toshi Maruki. Reprinted by permission of Lothrup, Lee & Shepard Books, a division of William Morrow, and by Nario Komine-Shoten Ltd.

Fig. 95. Toshi Maruki, *Hiroshima No Pika*

From *Hiroshima No Pika* by Toshi Maruki. Copyright © 1980 by Toshi Maruki. Reprinted by permission of Lothrup, Lee & Shepard Books, a division of William Morrow, and by Nario Komine-Shoten Ltd.

on the steps of the intense account of how the living and the dead fared, between fire and water, during a few days and nights, the hurried summary spanning forty years hurts. Death—Father's after a short time, that of thousands of other people over the years—and Mii-Chan's arrested growth, with text and picture realistically, in neutral voice, so to speak, telling us how Mother extracts glass splinters from the skin of her (forty-)seven-year-old daughter, are strangely muted, played down. The effect disarrays. It shatters the aesthetic configuration. Only after going over the book several times are we able to comprehend that the aftermath is the worst—how human beings who overcame the unbelievable, who struggled on through the incandescent pandemonium, are betrayed, tricked out of their chance of living by the cold radiation remnants lodged in their bodies. Now, finally, documentation makes us shudder.

The message, it seems, is threefold. One lies in this shudder. Another is found in the figure of Mii-Chan's mother, who never wavers in her determination to save and care. The third might be found in Mother's remark, as she watches the memory lanterns adrift on the river, that such horror would not happen again if no one dropped the bomb—this, be it a warning or a circumspect expression of hope, is all Maruki wishes to offer. More would weaken the impact. It would, in the context, be insincere.

THE VEILS OF SILENCE

In *Rose Blanche*, we are in a small German town during the Second World War.[11] When we open the book to the first page, we see people cheering the troops passing through the town on their way to the front line. Trumpets blare, civilians and young soldiers smile, enthusiastic children wave swastika flags. A feeling of certain victory is in the air. Later, winter sets in. Still more convoys, tanks, trucks, and armored cars move through the streets (fig. 96). The flags are gone, but rousing slogans still adorn the brick walls of the old, well-kept, picturesque houses. As the war drags on, the convoys become tedious; the faces, dull; inhabitants stand in line for bread. Then the trucks and the armored cars return; now they carry wounded and exhausted soldiers. The townspeople—frightened, worn out—flee their homes, taking with them very few of their belongings. In the end, more vehicles arrive; this time, the soldiers wear slightly different uniforms that bear a red star—the victorious Russians. Their faces are no less haggard and their looks no less tired out than those of the Germans. The overall impression we get is, then, a panoramic view of the folly and sadness of war reflected in the main street of a single town.

Against this background, two figures stand out. The mayor of the town is portrayed as a burly Nazi, erect, convinced of his own importance, and

11. Roberto Innocenti and Christophe Gallaz, *Rose Blanche*, illus. Roberto Innocenti (Mankato, Minn.: Creative Education, 1985).

Fig. 96. Roberto Innocenti, *Rose Blanche*

From *Rose Blanche*. Text by Christophe Gallaz and Roberto Innocenti. Illustrated by Roberto Innocenti. Copyright © 1985 Creative Education Inc.

confident in the future. His is present throughout the story. In the end, he still has a car at his disposal as he escapes from the town, despondent and without his swastika armlet.

The other figure is Rose Blanche, a girl of ten or eleven. When the war begins, she happily waves her flag just like everybody else. As time goes on, she likes the noisy and smelly convoys crossing the town less and less. She takes to walking by the river and watching the trucks driving over to some place on the other side. One day, as she descends the stairs of her home, setting out for a walk again, she sees a van held up by engine trouble. A small boy runs away from it, trying to escape. While soldiers follow him, the boy runs straight into the outstretched arms of the mayor, who smilingly hands him over. The boy is pushed into the van, where more people can be seen. Rose Blanche, curious, decides to follow the van to find out where it will take the boy. She walks far into the fields and beyond. In a clearing in the woods, she detects a concentration camp—barracks surrounded by electrified barbed wire. In the yard, the inmates stand around in their striped uniforms, motionless, with a blank look in their eyes. Many wear a yellow star. Rose Blanche will not tell anyone of her terrible secret. But from that day on, her appetite surprises her mother. Surreptitiously, she takes food with her to school and later doles it out to the prisoners. When the townspeople flee, she runs to the dreadful camp for the last time. The prisoners are gone—killed by their tormentors? freed by the advancing Russians? Only torn barbed wire remains, and beams, antitank obstacles, collapse. Out of the fog appear soldiers who suspect the enemy is every-where, and shadows; a shot rings out. Rose Blanche will not return. Spring comes, trees are in bloom, and flowers begin to overgrow the spot where human beings were mistreated.

Although the book was originally published in French, by a Swiss pub-lisher, its creator is an Italian artist. My observations owe much to an extended talk I had with him. Roberto Innocenti was born in 1940 and, until the age of five, grew up while his country was at war, under a regime allied with Germany. As he tells it—and the American edition partly relates—when he was about five years old, two young German soldiers came to his house asking his parents to hide them until the coming of the English troops, to whom they would surrender. While the family was taking them into the house, a German truck drove by and took away a whole family. Not wanting to shock Roberto, his father gave evasive answers to the child's questions, making it more difficult for Roberto to make sense of the contradictory events happening around him and his family. Later, when the Allies entered Italy, Roberto got his first piece of white bread from the hands of a black American soldier. Ever since then, Innocenti believes, these early experiences have haunted him and impressed him with the cruel absurdity of war. Over the years, the idea grew within him to create an antiwar picture book whose protagonist would be a child.

The story's outline is Innocenti's; but not trusting his own narrative gifts, he had to find, and did find after some searching, a writer to compose the text. Innocenti emphasizes that his foremost intention was to create a book that speaks out against all, and any, wars. He chose the specific subject of Hitler's Germany and the persecution of the Jews and other minorities because, to his mind, that was the most terrible war ever. He wished to express the horror of war and the suffocating perception children have of war going on where they live. He also wanted to characterize the banality of fascism in a small place. As it turns out, the text—to which we will return later—serves as quite a problematic running commentary, describing only some aspects of the events taking place. The pictures dominate this book. They are large hyper-realistic paintings, executed with careful and consummate brushwork. The composition is complex, especially in those pictures replete with crowds and vehicles milling around and moving by in the small street; the style is also vivid and varied and unfailingly leads the eye toward the content and the mood each picture is intended to convey. This attention to focus is strongly supported and aided by an intriguing, ingeniously concealed interplay of double perspectives in several of the pictures. The pictures are painted with painstaking exactitude, down to the smallest detail. Glossy colors communicate the time-honored red-brick quality of the place, the grayish-green-khaki dreariness of war, the gloomy puddles of winter, the dark hues of the camp, and then the light of spring. The pictures are beautiful to look at, almost too beautiful. They transmit an overall impression of spotless, indeed ornate, static elegance that's strangely in contrast with the turmoil and the craze gripping the epoch they depict. This is photo-realism in the double sense of the term: it indicates Innocenti's characteristic style, and it also refers to the documentary sources used by the artist—authentic photographs of German architecture and of people belonging to the Nazi period.[12]

The exception to the refined depiction of the town and its population is the touching, intimate portrayal of Rose Blanche. This portrayal responds to every mood that arises, to any thought crossing the mind of the serious, sensitive schoolgirl, whose eyes courageously pierce the deception. She learns to act and to live with her lonely secret. Like so many children suddenly caught in the tangle of the terrible happenings of a war, Rose Blanche, a youthful and innocent girl, must grapple emotionally with what are unimaginable tragic events.

Some reviewers and some viewer-readers of the book have expressed negative opinions about it. They are disturbed by the stiffness of the people depicted, by a few particular scenes that these critics feel come close to what they would define as "kitsch," by the stereotyped mayor, by the use of a wartime photograph for the boy who is caught by the mayor, and by the scene in which Rose Blanche offers bread to a child in the camp. They

---

12. Gerhard Schoenberger, *Der gelbe Stern: Die Judenverfolgung in Europa 1933–1945, 196 Bilddokumente* (Hamburg: Rütten Loening, 1960).

criticize the book's ending, where spring sings and glibly, so it seems, overcomes the demons. They are offended by the improbability of the plot and by the crack in the narrative structure.

The book has, it is true, several flaws. No doubt, that picture of the girl offering a piece of bread to the child behind the wire fence is too sentimental. More importantly, however, no child could have ever approached a concentration camp so closely and managed to return there again. Camp inmates did not wear yellow stars. The mayor, by the way, derives from a real figure existing at the time. Yet, to my mind, the truly inexcusable imperfection lies in the change of narrators in mid-narration. The first part of the story is told by Rose Blanche herself. At a certain point, after she has discovered the camp, an omniscient narrator takes over. This incongruous shift—introduced suddenly, without any preparation, and obviously necessitated chiefly by the need to relate the girl's death—is no inspiring solution, nor is it conceivably the only possible one.

However, some of the other misgivings and reservations cited above are, I believe, caused by a misconception. The persistent photo-realism induces many viewers and readers to overlook the fact that the text, and especially the pictures, abounds with consciously conceived and employed metaphor. The key to it all is found in the picture on the book's jacket (or cover, in other editions). As the returning troops, tired out and with blood seeping through their bandages, are reflected in Rose Blanche's window, she pushes the curtain aside, wide-eyed, trying to understand what nobody will explain to her. This first picture, torn out, as it were, from the later part of the story, introduces the overall metaphor—the truth can be found out only through Rose Blanche's thoughts and actions. Veils of silence cover life in town— a silence and a veiling that everybody partakes in. As the boy tries to escape from the van and is caught by the mayor, we twice see ordinary citizens— a man and a woman—studiously turning their backs on the incident; they will know nothing. The girl walks toward the scene.

The double perspective applied in many places throughout the book is, then, a metaphor for the double standards people have become accustomed to living with, as society has become too dangerous for openness. There is the especially beautiful picture of Rose Blanche walking by the river, shortly before she stumbles upon the truth, where reality and its reflection become thoroughly mixed up, just as they are in her own mind. The sky can be seen only in its reflection at the base of the picture. Here, as in other pictures, perspective is kept low; the sky appears mainly in the ubiquitous puddles: the sky is debased, fragmented, and veiled. Only here and there, Innocenti says, did he allow the sky to penetrate from above, for, after all, this is a children's book. When spring arrives, after the war, the sky enters again.

Yet, even as the girl lifts the veil and learns about the unspeakable suffering that goes on behind it in the concentration camp and at the battlefront, she never breaks the silence. There is no one she would trust in this town where everyone watches everyone else. Seen in this light, the polished rigidity of the town and its inhabitants assumes a meaning of its own. It represents the outward spotlessness of an oppressive system. The hideous is hidden. People conduct themselves as if they were puppets acting out a scenario—the banality of daily life under fascism. Here, Innocenti's style fits the stereotyped endgame of totalitarian warfare.

In this view, the story's metaphoric character also embraces Innocenti's decision to name his protagonist Rose Blanche (French for White Rose), which was the name of a clandestine, short-lived group of German students who heroically stood up against Hitler during wartime and were executed in 1943. It also vindicates the use of the famous photograph of a little Jewish boy in the Warsaw Ghetto who fearfully raised his arms for the boy encircled by the three stereotyped but characteristic figures of the SS officer, the soldier, and the mayor. The photograph has been, over the years, adopted as a media symbol of the Holocaust. Why, therefore, should it be illegitimate for Innocenti to use it?

In this context, the improbability of the plot loses much of its importance. Innocenti makes a significant attempt to invent a story to which older children might find it possible to relate, even with an effort, and, as Innocenti himself adds, one that will force adults to give answers to children's questions, to push veils aside.

However, admittedly, the ending is still problematic. The text states that spring sang. The picture shows the remnants of persecution being rapidly obliterated by the grass and the flowers and the bright light. This victory of life is too sudden—the more so because Rose Blanche's mother is still waiting for her girl to return. The ending vexes us. It obstructs the message. Why should this be so? The artist says that he intended the exact opposite: spring with all its force is unable to hide the evil committed. In his notes, he still has the words he wanted to use to accompany the arrival of spring: "Mother is still looking for Rose Blanche and hasn't even realized that spring has come." It is regrettable that the writer and the publisher decided otherwise.

Surely, however, the wilting flower caught on the wire in the very last small picture bears out Innocenti's conception. It is his strong final statement. The message lies in the unsettling, haunting remembrance of the cruel absurdity of war suggested, rather than spelled out, to children— and even more so in the very slender hope personified in Rose Blanche's watchful eyes and her intense moral compassion.

THE COURTEOUS HOWL OF PERDITION

In contrast to *Hiroshima No Pika*, *When the Wind Blows* raises the specter of a future nuclear war.[13] By intention, it is an utterly British book, presenting Hilda and Jimmy Bloggs, an elderly, provincial couple. She is the

---

13. Raymond Briggs, *When the Wind Blows* (New York: Schocken, 1982).

typical housewife; her retired husband, still interested in what goes on in the world, usually spends his mornings reading the papers in the public library. As the couple sits down to lunch, an announcement coming over the radio informs them that three days' time is left to prepare homemade fallout shelters. While the woman is totally lost, her husband has an inkling of what the announcement might mean. Having brought home and studied some leaflets distributed by the authorities, he sets about converting their home into a shelter, with his wife protesting every step. As they labor on, following the instructions (which prove to be totally useless), turning everything upside down, and preparing all those little things one needs for short-term survival, such as food, blankets, and what have you, they reminisce about the previous war—the one that took place in the 1940s. After the blast, the couple finds out that they are totally isolated; they still try to make sense of what has happened. Then radiation sickness sets in, killing them within days.

The book is made up of hundreds of comic-style pictures, including profuse speech-balloon dialogues and reflecting feverish, often funny doings (fig. 97). The chatter of the two simple old persons continues without any respite. They get their home ready for an emergency they are unable to imagine except in relation to the Second World War. The ongoing dialogue—its diction and its reflection of habits, associations, and recollections—imbues the book with its British flavor. These oldies dearly love each other. Except for a few outbreaks of anger, mainly caused by the husband's use of bad language that his wife is not willing to sanction, even in an emergency, Hilda and Jimmy are unfailingly courteous and patient, and Jimmy's chivalry lapses only when he has to force Hilda into the shelter (as the bomb is launched somewhere and is expected to arrive within three minutes)—even though the cake will get burned. But far beyond that, whenever the couple ruminate about the services that have broken down, about the government, and about the enemy, both in the Second World War and in the present one (she cannot really tell the wars apart), husband and wife assume that, in fact, everybody has good intentions and that things will work out soon.

Briggs's sarcasm has no stronger tool in this book than this unshakable conviction of the two old people that the milk of human kindness has been imbibed by any and all. Occasionally, the sarcastic vein becomes double-edged: when, near the end, the husband quotes a book called *Armaggedon and You*, which he got in the public library, saying that reading aloud to pass the time would be a good idea; when "governmental" is written divided as "govern-mental";[14] and when Hilda complains that it is a shame that television doesn't continue to put on the serial people have been watching, and Jimmy reflects that science is still in its infancy; it didn't blow up the sun. The text is replete with dozens of quips, quotes, misquotes, and misunderstandings.

14. Briggs, *When the Wind Blows*, 23.

Fig. 97. Raymond Briggs, *When the Wind Blows*

Briggs's fury, his howl at madness, comes to the fore in the pictures. They lead us through a series of severe visual shocks. Interrupting and alternating with the small-scale cartoons, twenty or more to a page, there appear large full-page pictures—stark, violent, stunningly beautiful—recording the dark, ominous, silent approach of the bomb. Then comes the blinding white flash covering two full pages and, over more pages, the gradual cooling down, until we gain sight of the couple again, stretched out in their makeshift shelter. But probably the most harrowing impression this book creates arises from the gradual, inexorable transition in the color composition of the cartoon pages. In the beginning, we enjoy the warm, healthy green and red colors of the countryside and the couple's residence. Progressively, the tone dulls, and tints turn bleaker, until we confront the dreadful hues of radiation sickness and imminent death. The endpapers are black. Through this masterly conceived and executed color drama move the two ridiculously childish and innocently childlike, pitifully lost souls. The slow changes marking their faces and their gait, the drag on their bodies, provide one more shock.[15]

This is a ferocious book. It is consciously atrocious in its juxtaposition of unperturbable kindness and uncontrollable madness. It is also a true-to-life book, presenting quite an accurate account of what may one day happen. Thus, local flavor acquires universal significance. Are we all, like children, too simple-minded to cope with the macabre situations that might arise because of "the Authorities' " lack of responsibility? Are we misinformed, disoriented, lulled into acquiescence? Are we in danger of dying a slow, painful, solitary, hapless death?

Although *When The Wind Blows* induces us to smile in many places, the idea implicit in the plot, the dialogue, and the pictures—presented somewhat differently in each—is that we would be ill-advised to trust local, national, or international "Authorities" to save us from the destiny of this particular couple. The book clearly intends to stir up fear to the point where the reader is triggered into social, even political action. And yet, it dismisses us with a feeling of our own powerlessness. Does the book or does it not want to extricate us from the reign of the incomprehensible?

The three final pages take up Briggs's thesis once again. The pictures closely follow the Bloggs' macabre bodily decay until night comes and only the edge of the door, placed at an angle according to instructions, is left in our sight—a slender diagonal green bar crossing out all the rest. But it is really the text that takes over on that last day. The couple still carry on as usual, busying themselves with small things ("I'll pop down to the Chemist's in the morning"), acting out of the belief that soon things will become normal again. When the wife notices that her hair is coming out, the sudden recognition of approaching death grips Hilda and Jimmy. As daylight fails, they prepare for the end, trusting that the "Govern-mental Authorities" will know what to do with them. As the dark engulfs them, Hilda and Jimmy, solemn now, lovingly say good-bye to each other. He suggests that they pray ("It can't do any harm, dear." "Who to?" "God, of course."), and they start out with a polite "Dear Sir." Then they remember and thread together verses from the Twenty-third Psalm, one of those expressing

15. Suddenly, one cannot help recalling how lyrical Briggs can wax by using precisely the same techniques—consider his book *The Snowman,* for instance.

complete faith—"I shall fear no evil. . . . Lay me down in the green pastures (which were still there a few days and nights ago). . . . Into the Valley of the Shadow of Death. . . ." Composure enwraps them. Yet, with the very last phrase—the apocalyptic ". . . rode the six hundred . . ."—their minds leap to another valley of death. The phrase is a refrain in Alfred Tennyson's "The Charge of the Light Brigade" (1854), where

> . . . tho' the soldier knew
> Some one had blunder'd:
>
> . . .
>
> Theirs not to reason why,
> Theirs but to do and die:
> Into the valley of Death
> Rode the six hundred[16]

—most of whom never returned. The poem embodies Tennyson's admiration for the ultimate patriotic sacrifice. It is, at the same time, a testament to the malevolence of war and to the pitiless erroneousness and irresponsibility of the powers that be. We are torn away from acquiescence and forced back to the struggle between good and bad, to the evil forces surrounding us, to anxiety.

These final pages are a superior instance, an outstanding achievement in the realm of picture books and comics. They need to be studied in detail. Encompassed by an unfathomable lyrical mood ("Oh no more, love . . . no more . . ."), Briggs's sarcasm and fury ride on. Should we put our faith in the good forces? in ourselves? Once more: does the book or does it not want to extricate us from the reign of the incomprehensible? The decision is still ours. But surely Briggs assumes that we will be moved and will stop to think and, he hopes, become convinced of the necessity of defiant action against a possible atomic war.

The back cover of the American edition of *When the Wind Blows* offers a selection of statements praising the book, issuing from very different quarters and recommending that it be read by all of us, including young people. One readily concurs with this counsel. But we must also be aware that many young people will need guidance, not because of the shocks the book might cause them—these should serve as welcome antidotes to the melodramatic or glamorous treatment of similar themes and situations in all media—but rather because these two elderly people, with their roots in a specific past, are far removed from a later young generation's experience. It is important that young people be aided not to interpret irony and fun as mere cynicism. The cynic is impressed, smiles, and sits back. Briggs, being deeply involved, wants to involve us, too.

---

16. Alfred Lord Tennyson, "The Charge of the Heavy Brigade at Balaclava" in *The Poetic and Dramatic Works of Alfred Lord Tennyson*, Cambridge ed. (Boston and New York: Houghton, 1898), 501–10.

FAITH IN THE SANITY OF THE PEOPLE

The following two books have a common subject: peace. They also radiate a belief that ordinary people, such as you and me, can speak up and act and thus influence the shape of developments.

Lena and Paul—What's That about Peace? is a German story centering on a family.[17] Father is a press photographer; Mother teaches. They have two children. One day after the TV news reports tell of the outbreak of new hostilities in the Near East, Father is sent there. In the days to come, Mother is uncommonly tired and quiet. Then a telegram arrives—Father has been wounded and is hospitalized. Mother breaks out in tears, exclaiming, "This terrible war. Why do people have to make war again and again?" She remembers her mother's sufferings in the last war, which ended in 1945: Grandfather fell at the battlefront; they had air raids and spent nights in shelters; people were killed, and families fled their homes. "Everywhere war brought suffering for the people. For the victorious countries as well." Mother and the children talk about wars going on now, about bombs. Something will have to be done to avoid another big war breaking out. A letter comes from Father, who hopes to be home soon and away from a senseless war. One day, Mother comes across the information stand of a peace group and joins. Demonstrations take place (fig. 98): "When everybody will want peace there won't be any wars anymore." When Father returns and recovers, the entire family joins peace-group activities. The children, bored at first, are attracted by games, outings, and balloons to be painted. One evening, as the whole family helps with the dishes in the kitchen, the news announces yet another breakdown in disarmament talks. The parents are discouraged:

> "So you haven't achieved anything," Lena blurts out "and all the time you are away from home." "Yes, that's true," says Mother. "But the world should not be destroyed and wars should stop. . . ." Mother embraces Lena and holds her close.

In an unaffected fashion, the plot makes it clear how a normal, happy family living in a country at peace becomes increasingly worried about and involved with the issue of war. The past war is connected (though very cursorily) with present events and with the atomic threat. Father's personal suffering makes his wife and children more aware of the collective danger. The events in a faraway area, brought home to the family by Father returning and walking with a crutch, affect their happiness and prod the family into action, in the belief that they and many others like them can, though not in an easy way, try to change public opinion and, therefore, political decisions. The notion that war is not easily overcome is also underlined by small incidents that might make one think. Hostility is quick to

17. Gisela Degler-Rummel, *Lena und Paul, wie ist das mit dem Frieden? (Lena and Paul—What's That about Peace?)* (Ravensburg, Germany: Otto Maier, 1985).

Fig. 98. Gisela Degler-Rummel, *Lena und Paul*
Gisela Degler-Rummel, *Lena und Paul* reprinted by permission of Ravensburger Buchverlag Otto Maier GmbH

appear when a boy does not want to return Lena's ball and her little brother Paul arms himself with a stick to attack him, or when Lena and Paul have a row because he thinks her hot dog is larger than his: it is amazing how quickly irritation can develop into violence (it speaks for the good sense of the author that these incidents are not commented on).

The story is written with fluency. The situations effectively express the way of life of warm, simple people. Here and there, slight touches enhance authenticity—when Mother prepares to take the children to the airport, she spends a lot of time in the bathroom making herself prettier for Father's arrival.

The text dominates this book. The illustrations lend support to certain aspects, less to others. The author-illustrator's style is influenced by Matisse—large single-color areas, the placement of objects, the tilted perspective—and by German expressionism, as in the representation of the serious, simply dressed, rather stocky, quite likable people inhabiting the town. The people are, though, a bit too static for the dynamics of the story; their faces, especially, lack meaningfulness. Only in some scenes do the faces of the four members of the family become quietly expressive. We are compensated by the excellent dynamic composition of the illustrations. Whether we look at interiors or at outdoor scenes, we always gain the impression that the picture contains only part of a fuller, more extended scene or a more extensive background. Thus, the illustrator succeeds in encouraging the use of the viewer's own imagination. Colors come in strong, earthy hues. Perceptible changes in perspective, which tends to be either emphatically low or high, occur from one page to the next.

These three elements—composition, color, and perspective—effectively dramatize the text. In some key pictures, this effect is seen especially clearly, such as when Father packs his belongings, preparing to leave for his assignment in the war zone; or when Paul, wiping dishes in the kitchen, thinks of what Mother has just said about war.

The book represents a credible, sensible attempt to join the concepts of war and peace in the eyes of children.

Action in the American book *Nobody Wants a Nuclear War* starts with a little girl, her somewhat older brother, and their dog running down a hill.[18] They are scared because they know that a terrible nuclear war may break out one day. The urgency of fright drives them to their secret cave in the woods. Without telling anyone, they prepare the cave for the emergency: they smuggle in water, foodstuffs, and a picnic blanket; they cover the opening of the cave with branches so that nobody can find them (fig. 99). Only then does the girl, who tells the story in the first person, feel safe— and they fall asleep in the cave. All of a sudden, a loud crash wakes them up, and the girl thinks that the nuclear war has started. But it is only their mother, to whom the girl explains that they have made a hideaway, just in case. Mother calms the brother and sister: there is no need to hide, she says, because she and Daddy will always try to be with them, no matter what, and care for them. Then, at lunch, Mother tells them about the atomic bomb the United States dropped on Hiroshima—which brought an end to the war, but caused destruction more terrible than anyone could have imagined. She goes on to tell them of her own childhood, when, after 1941, children hid under desks during air-raid drills, and she herself was deeply scared. But no atomic bomb has been dropped since then, and grown-ups all over the world work to prevent a nuclear war. The president works toward this goal, too. She herself belongs to an activist group, and their neighbor writes editorial letters against the bomb. Next step: Mother suggests that together they use the picnic blanket to make a banner saying "Grown-ups for a Safer World to Grow Up In." A picture of Mother and the children with the finished banner is taken by the neighbor, to be sent to the president. The girl sums up the experience by avowing that she feels

18. Judith Vigna, *Nobody Wants a Nuclear War* (Niles, Ill.: Albert Whitman, 1986).

We thought we should build a hideaway,
just in case.
We went to the secret cave
in the woods behind our house.
We covered the opening with branches
so nobody would find us.

Fig. 99. Judith Vigna, *Nobody Wants a Nuclear War*
Judith Vigna, *Nobody Wants a Nuclear War*. Copyright © 1986 by Judith Vigna. Used by permission of Albert Whitman & Co.

a little safer now and that she will work hard when she grows up to ensure that her own children will feel safer, too.

Clearly, this is a book created in response to adults' widespread recognition of the anxiety produced in children by their exposure to media information and entertainment, to adult discussion of war-related issues, and to the activity of adults in peace groups. The plot starts out dramatically, with a psychologically genuine situation: the children reacting to a danger they have no means of understanding at all, trying to save themselves through acting out and overcoming anxiety with activity. The girl's startled awakening when Mother finds her and her brother reflects the strength of the girl's feelings. From this point, Mother, carefully and lovingly, leads brother and sister away, step by step, from their insecurity and makes her daughter feel safer. The plot, then, has a logical flow. However, it also has a psychological flaw. The early part grows out of an affective identification with the child's mind. Later, the story identifies with the adults' precarious cognitive belief in the simple ways by which children's worries can be laid to rest. If nuclear war is so terrifying (the whole world will blow up, her brother tells the girl; only a dark, smoky desert like the one they saw on television will remain) that children don't dare mention it to adults, then talking about it at lunch and going back to Mother's own childhood is an excellent beginning, to be followed up by more talks; and, yes, more action and information on adults' activities will do much to calm children's fears. But if, following lunch, an afternoon of cutting out letters and sewing them on the blanket, etc., takes care of the scare and can set the little girl's mind at ease, then apparently the atomic bomb isn't such a dangerous issue, after all. But it is. Mother plays it down. Why? Her children are old enough to interpret TV information in their own way. They know who the president is; they are able to appreciate, so it seems, the concept of time—when Mother was a child. The discrepancy between the two halves of the story is too wide. The first part of the plot builds up tension in a fashion commensurate with children's imaginations, but the latter half takes a didactic turn. It offers advice to parents on how to deal with children's anxieties the easy (too easy) way. It also offers sound advice to adults concerning what they should do about the danger of war threatening themselves and their children—go and act and let their children know about both danger and action.

The illustrations constitute faithful, realistic companions to the narrative. The first three pictures aid beautifully in introducing the dramatic, dynamic mood. First, there's the cover illustration, encompassing the book's front and back, with the little girl all alone, lost in thought, and the trees beckoning her, as it were, to get up. Second, there's the picture on the title page, with the blue, slightly disquieting sky; the wind getting stronger; and Brother running uphill toward the girl—he and his umbrella creating a countermovement to the trees, all urging her to move, and she responding to these forces. The third picture shows the sister and brother running downhill, away from the threatening angle created by the sky and the grass. This triad builds up a tension that still resounds in the following pictures, all through the children's preparations for their safety and through Mother's arrival. Then, further on, the illustrations fit the playfulness of the second half of the plot.

Why, by the way, should Mother look like a teenager? Why should pictures alternate between color and black-and-white? This budget-inspired device, applied all over the world, is an offense to children's imaginations. It should not be used for so serious an issue.

These last two books emphasize ways of achieving peace. Their stories are solid. Their makers wholeheartedly believe that it's possible for sanity to win out. Their approach is rational: children need faith in adults. And adults need support in their endeavors to deal with the subject. *Lena and Paul . . .* and *Nobody Wants a Nuclear War* are created in this spirit and embody this sort of advice. The question is this: are low-key books like these really strong enough to serve as antidotes to the pessimism that adults and their media send toward children?

QUESTS AND APPROACHES

War is an extreme situation and peace a precious state. Adults do not, individually or collectively, possess the acumen, the insight, or the means of avoiding the first and stabilizing the second. How, we ask, can such hazardous, risky issues and concepts be transmitted to children? How, again, can one possibly neglect to attempt to do so? Authors, illustrators, and publishers who create and produce picture books on war and peace take upon themselves a necessary yet awesome responsibility. Children and adolescents cannot really understand the issues involved in-depth (neither can many adults—can I? can you?). To be exact—they cannot understand the causes. But children *can* be informed about results and about choices. Fictional and artistic accounts like the ones we have discussed could well influence both children and adolescents.

All the books we have looked at present war as a threat and peace as a desirable goal. Outspokenly or tacitly, they are committed to that goal. What approaches do these books communicate? Disregarding the "Irony" books in this context, we can arrive at a few conclusions.

Most of the books examined have been created for older children, for adolescents, *and* for adults. This statement, as trivial as it is obvious, is necessary because of the occasional reviewers who desperately ask how one can possibly suggest putting *Rose Blanche* into the hands of preschool children, or what an eight-year-old boy is supposed to do with *When the Wind Blows*. Such exclamations come from critics who do not know what medium they are dealing with.

All the stories personalize the issue in one way or another. Fear, hope, and empathy arise by following individuals and the conditions of their existence.

Interestingly, many of the stories center on women or girls, or both, as protagonists. This focus may be the result of social change. It certainly is not a result of selection on my part. It may also reflect a deep-seated trust in women's potentially greater sensitivity and a recognition that it might be easier to influence audiences through female protagonists. The cover pictures of several books bring this idea out clearly, but none as incisively and solemnly as the image of Mii-Chan's mother—the upright woman, striding between fire and water, carrying her husband and guiding her child.

The books suggest, and argue for, a wide range of attitudes toward the common man's and woman's trust in government, in the establishment, and in the authorities. Between Vigna's basic assurance of these institutions' goodwill and Briggs's distrust, and between Vigna's and Degler-Rummel's affirmation of citizen's action and Innocenti's confidence in the lonely outsider, the chasm is wide and deep. This divergence is one of the reasons why the books also vary strongly in their implicit or explicit suggestions for social and political action by the people.

The most significant concept arising from the stories is that although their authors and artists come from such different personal and cultural backgrounds, *they minimize hate and are very careful about accusations.* Where perpetrators of atrocities are indicated, sometimes a balancing element is introduced. *Efrat's Father* mentions no enemy. *Hiroshima No Pika* names the United States as the country that used the bomb, but adds that many

Americans and people from other nations died because of it and that the Japanese themselves discriminated against the dead Koreans. Maruki also tells, in her postscript, how people in other regions of Japan hesitated, over the years, to aid the refugees from Hiroshima. In *Rose Blanche*, we meet the one flower that grows in the moral barrenness of the town, but Innocenti also makes it clear that all groups—Jews, Germans, Russians—were the victims of persecution and war. *When the Wind Blows* directs its wrath more against the men responsible at home than against the enemy, the Russians. *Lena and Paul . . .* totally refrains from accusing anyone specifically, stating that everyone suffers. *Nobody Wants a Nuclear War* specifically mentions the destruction caused by its own nation, without any "but. . . ." All of these books avoid any dehumanization of the enemy.

Such books, then, intend to combat the human suffering caused by war. They solicit for peace. This is their common message. These are the values they hold out to their audiences. This is their strength.

This is also their limitation. To show that war is not a fortuitous element in human history, one to be overcome mainly by applying rational controls, but that, on the contrary, humankind exists and develops with inherent, intrinsic, and basic ambiguities and contradictions; to admit that forces exist everywhere in the world that work for war, even nuclear war, forces that have to be fought—these are probably tasks that need to be fulfilled beyond the picture-book level.

Although, of course, the degree of optimism pervading books dealing with many other serious themes would not do for one such as war, it would be meaningful if in the future a picture book were to appear containing between its covers wrath and compassion and hope. In this regard, the girl Rose Blanche stands out as a lonely symbol.

The great psychologist and philosopher Viktor Frankl once said that the faculty of doubting the significance of his own existence is what sets man apárt from animal. In my mind, there is nothing in human existence that supports this doubt more strongly than the recurrence of war. Young people should know about that. But they also need to understand that another aspect exists that sets humankind apart from the animals and confirms our own significance—and that is the ability to entertain the thought of overcoming war.

CHILDREN'S BOOKS CITED

BRIGGS, RAYMOND. *The Snowman*. New York: Random, 1978.

——. *When the Wind Blows*. New York: Schocken, 1982.

CRAMPTON, GERTRUDE. *Tootle*. Illus. Tibor Gergely. New York: Simon & Schuster, 1946.

DEGLER-RUMMEL, GISELA. *Lena und Paul, wie ist das mit dem Frieden? (Lena and Paul— What's That about Peace?)* Ravensburg, Germany: Otto Maier, 1985.

EMBERLEY, BARBARA. *Drummer Hoff*. Illus. Ed Emberley. Englewood Cliffs, N.J.: Prentice-Hall, 1967.

INNOCENTI, ROBERTO AND CHRISTOPHE GALLAZ. *Rose Blanche*. Illus. Roberto Innocenti. Mankato, Minn.: Creative Education, 1985.

KEREN, NIRA. *Abba Shel Efrat (Efrat's Father)*. Illus. Er'ela Hurvitz; photog. Hagai Eisenberg. Merchavia, Israel: Sifriat Hapoalim, 1971.

LEAF, MUNRO. *The Story of Ferdinand*. Illus. Robert Lawson. New York: Viking, 1936.

LUZZATI, EMANUELE. *La gazza ladra (The Thievish Magpie)*. Milano: Mursia, 1973.

MARUKI, TOSHI. *Hiroshima No Pika (The Flash of Hiroshima)*. Tokyo: Komine Shoten, 1980.

VIGNA, JUDITH. *Nobody Wants a Nuclear War*. Niles, Ill.: Albert Whitman, 1986.

12

Sendak's Trilogy—A Concept of Childhood

Any picture book relating a story about a protagonist offers an implicit opinion on the nature of the child and the conditions of childhood. Whether this view is shallow or reaches deep down, whether it is narrow or ample, it is usually not difficult to sense and decode.

The work of superior authors and artists who create picture books over an extended period embodies clues that can be vital to our understanding of the child and childhood. Vistas widen and horizons open up as a result of the high level of creativity of the authors and artists and their strong personal associations with the experiences of the protagonists. In the course of their ongoing involvement with the circumstances of the child's life, a few outstanding storytellers (found predominantly among those who are both artist and author in one) create a body of work that communicates a comprehensive approach—a concept of childhood, Maurice Sendak typifies this phenomenon.

Several years ago, Sendak repeatedly stated that his three picture books *Where the Wild Things Are, In the Night Kitchen,* and *Outside Over There,*[1] constitute a trilogy.[2] Since then, this statement has been cited without comment by most authors writing on Sendak. The exceptions are found in an article by Scharioth, in which she speaks of "the sequence of picture books intended as a loose picture-book trilogy,"[3] and in a paper by Steig, who is not happy with Sendak's formulation.[4] Others writing on these

This chapter is an adapted version of Joseph H. Schwarcz, "Sendak's Trilogie" in *Maurice Sendak: Bilderbuchkünstler,* ed. Reinbert Tabbert (Bonn: Bouvier, 1987), 93–104.

1. Maurice Sendak, *Where the Wild Things Are; In the Night Kitchen* (New York: Harper, 1970); *Outside Over There.*

2. Selma G. Lanes, *The Art of Maurice Sendak* (New York: Abrams, 1980), 227, 235; Jonathan Cott, "Maurice Sendak—King of All the Wild Things" in *Pipers at the Gate of Dawn: The Wisdom of Children's Literature* (New York: Random, 1983), 67.

3. Barbara Scharioth, "Starke Bilderbuchkinder zum Beispiel: Maurice Sendak," *Informationen des Arbeitskreises für Jugendliteratur* (April 1985): 57.

4. Michael Steig, "Reading *Outside Over There,*" *Children's Literature* 13 (1985): 143.

books refrain from asking themselves if and why they are a trilogy. This fact should surprise us, considering to what extent Sendak's utterances are generally analyzed under the microscope and applied in order to better understand his work. We seem to be satisfied with accepting the statement that Sendak views the three works as a unit because his intention was to show "how children master various feelings . . . and manage to come to grips with the realities of their lives." Surely Sendak has carried out this intention in a fashion that has contributed to the enhancement and progress of children's literature.

To the central motif articulated above, we are easily able to add a few more characteristics common to the three books: the heroes solve their problems by dreaming of possessing magical omnipotence, their dangerous and very successful experiences carry them into faraway worlds, and they wander in and out of their dreams with great ease. They are, as Scharioth says, strong heroes. Oedipal relationships are important in various degrees for each of them.

These themes and motifs do not, however, make up a trilogy. We usually understand a trilogy to mean a work organized in three parts, whose unity is ensured by a number of selected elements. It may be the protagonist whose development we follow in three phases, possibly from varying points of view; or several figures whose lives are interconnected; or else a fictional realm where events take place whose interdependence reveals a comprehensive truth. Without infringing too closely on the identity of each part (otherwise the result is a serial), unity has to be somehow manifested by references and relations binding together earlier and later happenings and reflections. Also, structurally, we expect a trilogy to exhibit characteristic forms of style and composition that, whether being constant or changing gradually, aid us in bridging the parts and in better understanding their basic unity.

Examined with such criteria in mind, Sendak's three picture books do not prove to be a trilogy. They are too remote from each other. Their respective heroes live in real and dream worlds differing totally from book to book. Their allegoric spaces do not connect, nor do the relationships or the plots these spaces serve. For instance, Max sets out to regain his self-respect; the great danger to which he exposes himself is overcome early in the story when he tames the Wild Things with the magic trick of staring into their eyes. From then on, his anxiety lessens. In the end, he exerts some influence on the real world—in his view, is it not *because* he departed that he received his supper? By contrast, Mickey, awakened by noise, glides into the demonic kitchen of the father figures and into mortal danger, which he overcomes by gliding from there into performing a social task. Although it professes a merry mood and Mickey outwits his adversaries, there seems to be little doubt that the story conceals the weighty Judeo-Christian symbols referring to sacrifice, the Holocaust, rebirth, and resurrection that were detected by Hans Halbey.[5] In the third story, Ida introduces us to her family. During the course of the tale, she masters the bad conscience that was generated by her own imaginary neglect of her baby sister after successfully confronting grave dangers. In these three stories, in the end, Max has added to his sense of autonomy, Mickey is relieved and satisfied with himself, and Ida has quieted her conscience. Putting it another way: Max achieves balance; Mickey is content; and although her conscience has been quieted, Ida continues to be tense.

Or, let us look at parent-child relationships. In the background of Max's adventure exists mutual love between mother and son, delicately hinted at—a love that's stronger than the temporary conflict. By contrast, Mickey's parents scarcely exist as real persons. Ida's remote father communicates his grateful, and at the same time demanding, love from afar; and her mother expresses her gratitude by putting her hand on Ida's shoulder, obviously leaving Ida in charge of the baby and herself. In the penultimate picture, Ida ranks higher than her mother; she keeps this family together, being offered, so it seems, conditional love. When her father asks that she continue to watch over her mother and sister, the narrator hastens to add, in the last picture, that that is exactly what Ida does.

The differences in the styles of the three books emphasize how mutually dissimilar they are. The text in *Wild Things* is sparse, unerring, and subordinate to the pictures though parsing their rhythms; then come the fluent ribbons and speech balloons of *Night Kitchen*; while the text in *Outside Over There* lacks lyrical and narrative balance and becomes heavier still by its insertion, as white plates, in the illustrations. Similarly, the pictorial styles of these works differ. The fantastic realism of *Wild Things*, with its mildly wildly grotesque figures, is convincingly limpid and apt enough to serve the visual metaphors. In contrast, *Night Kitchen* exhibits an impressive synthesis of traditional comics and pop art. *Outside Over There* creates its magic realm by fusing elements of the Renaissance, Blake, English and German Romanticism, pre-Raphaelite art, and a contemporary movie (*The Marquise of O.*, after H. von Kleist's story).[6] Clearly, no literary or artistic associations or relations exist between the three stories.

Let us consider three arguments supposedly evincing the existence of a trilogy. The one is found in Steig's comprehensive investigation of *Outside Over There*, when he says, "this matter of losing oneself fits the pattern of all three works in Sendak's trilogy."[7] Is dreaming identical with losing oneself? Is it not also a process of finding oneself? Besides, in his dream, Max remains in control of himself, immediately adjusting to every magical transformation; whereas Ida loses direction and is never herself; but it is

5. Hans A. Halbey, "In der Nachtküche-zur Metasprache im Bilderbuch" in *Maurice Sendak: Bilderbuchkünstler*, ed. Reinbert Tabbert, 61–68.

6. Heinrich von Kleist, "Die Marquise von O." in *Sämtliche Werke*, vol. 3 (Leipzig: Max Hesses, 1902), 116.

7. Steig, "Reading *Outside Over There*," 143.

Mickey who, pushed into the oven, is in danger of losing himself. Another argument appears in Lanes's volume.[8] From the context, it is not entirely clear whether Lanes cites Sendak or herself as saying that each book has a place-name for a title—a fantasy locale where the major action of the story takes place. This reasoning is not really convincing, since titles of other books by Sendak include locales—*The Sign on Rosie's Door* and *As I Went over the Water*, for example.[9] And if locale is of such prime importance, why did Sendak accept that *Outside Over There* should be given, in translations into various languages, a silly title such as *When Papa Was Away*?[10] A third point is that the motif of how children master their feelings and come to grips with the realities of their lives also appears in several other stories created by Sendak.

There is, then, no trilogy to be identified, if we judge from appearances. Instead we have three outstanding picture books that have it in their power to give joy and suggest some thought to both children and adults, stories whose influence ranges wide, whose mere existence has enriched the picture-book scene—three gleaming pieces, but no mosaic.

One should put the issue to a test: would children and uninformed adults infer from viewing and reading these three works that the books belong together? Am I exaggerating when I suggest that readers would hardly guess that these stories are the work of one and the same author and artist? Would we be the poorer for not having been told that there is a trilogy about? Not up to this point.

However, Sendak has said—surely not arbitrarily—that the books constitute a trilogy. We will therefore have to look somewhere deeper for whatever we were not able to find or ascertain on the surface: sailing a private boat, swooping into a kitchen, entering caves—where signs become manifest. Sendak comes to our aid. When he had just begun work on *Outside Over There*, he confided the following to Jonathan Cott, who interviewed him:

> This last part of my trilogy is going to be the strangest. *Wild Things* now seems to be a very simple book—its simplicity is probably what made it successful, but I could never be that simple again. *Night Kitchen* I much prefer—it reverberates on double levels. But this third book will reverberate on triple levels.[11]

We may interpret this statement to mean that Sendak conceives of the three stories as successive steps in a gradual development: continuity is being created through growing complexity. This clarification is initially nothing but superficial. Of course, heroes, plots, fictional worlds, and styles become more complex as we go along from the first to the third book. And

8. Lanes, *The Art of Maurice Sendak*, 227.

9. Maurice Sendak, *The Sign on Rosie's Door* (New York: Harper, 1960); *Hector Protector and As I Went over the Water* (New York: Harper, 1965).

10. Sendak, *Als Papa fort war (When Papa Was Away)* (Zürich: Diogenes, 1984).

11. Jonathan Cott in Lanes, *The Art of Maurice Sendak*, 227.

yet, the concept he just proposed can serve as a key to unlocking deeper levels of meaning.

Psychological approaches could be considered first. Psychoanalytically oriented researchers tend to see the three children as representing Freudian stages of development—Max, the oral; Mickey, the anal; and Ida, the onset of adolescence. Similarly, it is possible to apply Eriksonian stages—the quest for autonomy, initiative, identity.[12] We may also reflect on a more recent theory of feeling proposed by the sociologist Agnes Heller, as quoted by Kalekin-Fishman:

> In explicating the significance of feelings for preserving and extending the ego, or for diminishing it, Heller describes a hierarchy. She traces its biographical revolution through various levels of consciousness from uncontrollable instinct to informed cognition. There are drives which are signals of need; "passions," which are fixed desires or thwarted needs. Complex cognitive-situational feelings, or "emotions," derived from more primitive, easily triggered "affects." Emotions are full-fledged "orientational feelings" in which affectivity and cognition are joined. They include evaluations of the self in what is perceived to be the context of reality.[13]

Do not our heroes pass through several phases of this hierarchy? Max's drives signal a need for self-esteem and love. Mickey's easily triggered affects turn into feelings, including the recognition that he is the one to save both himself and others. With Ida, passion (for the wonder horn) initially conflicts with cognition (of the dangers to her sister if she neglects her for even a short moment). Thereupon, in her fantasy, she acts with unflinching determination, guided by an orientational feeling—that of being recognized and valued by her family. This desire is fulfilled by the dream, as Roxbury's analysis of *Outside Over There* shows so well.[14]

Returning to the aesthetic context, we can discern in the *Wild Things* how the elements defining the structure of the story are set and combined with the utmost lucidity. The analogies on which the plot rests, the way in which residues of reality initiate the dream, the inner logic with which each and every aspect of ego violation is compensated for in the Land of the Wild Things, the widening and contraction of pictorial space, the evanescence of the word at the story's climax and of the image at the end—and the result of all these, the confident and elegant composition—have been examined over and over. They show that the book radiates a classical mood.

In the *Night Kitchen*, structure is still clear and obvious, and Mickey's expressive demeanor makes it easy to follow his wild gyrations. But the classical balance is gone. Space over-expands from the chthonic kitchen to

12. Erik H. Erikson, *Childhood and Society* (New York: Norton, 1950).

13. Agnes Heller, *A Theory of Feelings* (Assen, Netherlands: Van Gorcum, 1979), cited in Devorah Kalekin-Fishman, "Désalienation—Pour une conscience libérée dans l'éducation," *Cahiers de sociologie économique et culturelle* (Dec. 6, 1986), 122.

14. Stephen Roxburgh, "A Picture Equals How Many Words? Narrative Theory and Picture Books for Children," *The Lion and the Unicorn* (July/Aug. 1983–84): 20–33.

way above the stars. At one point, Mickey seems to feel societal pressure in his dream, even while he is seen stark naked inside the innocent white milk bottle.[15] The close interlocking of the funny with the ghastly—Hardy the comedian (of Laurel and Hardy) as triple-baker in the night kitchen, the merriment of shoving Mickey into the oven and Mickey's repeated exposure in the nude, the interchangeability of skyscrapers with baking-powder containers—arouses a disquieting, grotesque mood. The artistic styles, derived from comics and including pop art's insistence on the symbolic force resting within commonplace objects, are combined to great effect.

In *Outside Over There*, Ida's world is a scenic labyrinth whose passages are depicted in rich, satisfying pictures. Here and there, however, the richness is oversaturated. This excess is also true of some phrases in the text and, returning to the pictures, most significantly of Ida's facial expression. In several places, her face goes vacant. Her expression fascinates, more than it gives away what goes on inside her (except near the beginning of the story). All these elements of style do not happen by accident: the enigmatic ambiguity of expression and of symbols achieves a romantic, slightly mannered mood in this mythic thicket.

This evolution of Sendak's styles is not to be related only to the heroes' ascent from early childhood to puberty. It also reflects a change, a darkening in his perception of childhood. Sendak has always been an existentialist: "I think I had to find self-reliance at an early age . . . isolated from other children . . . it stimulated being an artist," is his way of putting it.[16] So, Max relies on himself (wasn't it this fact that shocked parents and educators when the book was first published?)—and yet he is aided by the smell of his supper. But Mickey is utterly alone. He escapes from his passive sacrificial role by trusting his own vitality. His act of deliverance—procuring the milk—is actually carried out in the service of evil companions. Does he have to help them so that things can go on? Pursuing this thought may well lead into the impenetrable. In *Outside Over There*, Papa does aid his Ida in finding the right direction—but he does no more than that.

I have attempted elsewhere to show how, again, what Sendak himself says, namely that *Outside Over There* is his homage to Mozart and to Mozart's opera *The Magic Flute*, makes it possible for us to come close to the central theme—the similarities and differences between the opera and the fairy tale.[17] Ida, the child on the threshold of adulthood, errs and repents, fulfills an arduous task and triumphs; she has done her duty and become more mature. Yet, she has not become liberated from the complex family relationship in which she is involved. Thus, Sendak the existentialist negates the sublime concept of *The Magic Flute*, the liberation and enlightenment

15. Reinbert Tabbert, "Literarische modelle von Kindheit und Jugend," *Informationen des Arbeitskreises für Jugendliteratur* (April 1985): 41.

16. Lacy, *Art and Design*, 109.

17. Joseph H. Schwarcz, "Die Darstellung des Geistes der Musik im Bilderbuch," *Librarium* (Dec. 1986): 3.

brought to young persons by bright rational forces. Even for a girl as beautiful and self-conscious as Ida, growing up is a lonely road, a process likewise furthered and endangered by archetypal forces and constellations pulsating in the unknown.[18] Sendak hints at this idea very clearly near the beginning of the story: as Ida starts playing the horn, the portrait of Kleist (an important German nineteenth-century writer and a representative of justice and severe conscience) looks down on her. In the following picture, this additional super-ego demonstrates open dissatisfaction. Sendak is certainly aware of Kleist's belief (expressed at the end of *The Marquise of O.*) that forgiveness should prevail because of the frail state of the world. This is what Ida gains: forgiveness and acceptance. She remains entangled in the static mythic bond that ties her parents. Her tale leaves us with a feeling that "There must be more to life" (the subtitle of *Higglety Pigglety Pop*).[19] DeLuca, too, in her comprehensive paper on the exploration of the levels of childhood in Sendak, sees no liberation for Ida at the end of the story.[20]

The adventures in the course of which the three children extend their personalities turn out to be increasingly more complex: Max's adventure inspires him with hope. Mickey experiences an illusion of grandeur. Ida goes through a rite of passage that leads her back to her point of departure. Ambiguity grows, in text and picture. Sendak communicates an existentialist, complex vision of childhood. This emerging view of a young person's growth (which has by now been adopted by so many) is, I believe, a remarkably truthful one. It is not, by any means, the only existentially possible one, nor is it easily accepted; however, it is significant for the child of our time.

Should we, though, consider Sendak's dictum on the trilogy a mere autobiographical anecdote? The impulse, the wish to fathom the artist's personal and creative development is too deeply rooted in our civilization to permit us to leave it at that. Besides, as Bosmajian has written, "Children's literature is a complicated artistic, psychological, and social phenomenon, in some ways more so than adult literature because the author projects memories and libidinal releases through forms pretending innocence."[21] Childrens' literature is too significant to be disregarded in this respect. We may, then, legitimately interpret Sendak's opinion on his own work and apply it toward a better understanding and appreciation of what he is

18. Schwarcz, "Die Darstellung," 201.

19. Maurice Sendak, *Higglety Pigglety Pop, or There Must Be More to Life* (New York: Harper, 1967).

20. Geraldine De Luca, "Exploring the Levels of Childhood: The Allegorical Sensibility of Maurice Sendak" in *Children's Literature*, vol. 12 (New Haven, Conn.: Yale Univ. Pr., 1984), 18.

21. Hamida Bosmajian, " 'Charlie and the Chocolate Factory' and Other Excremental Visions," *The Lion and the Unicorn* (Sept. 1985): 36.

contributing to the range and depth of this art medium for which we still possess no term but "picture book." The scintillating fashion in which Sendak disperses throughout his books quotations from art, literature, music, and reality affirms that he is well aware of the importance of children's literature and does not pretend to innocence (though on occasion he deprecates the value of his own quotes). Let us just give one example: decidedly, no banality is intended when, after the rumpus in the *Wild Things* is over, Max is seen sitting in front of the royal tent in a pose reminiscent of Shakespeare's King Henry V as he appears in Laurence Olivier's filmed version, *before* the Battle of Agincourt (fig. 100), in which he decisively defeated his enemies—and immediately afterward, the news of Max's own victory (the smell of supper) wafts across the world. It is a metaphor for adults, of course.

Fig. 100. Maurice Sendak, *Where the Wild Things Are*
From *Where the Wild Things Are* by Maurice Sendak. Copyright © 1963 by Maurice Sendak. Reprinted by permission of Harper & Row, Publishers, Inc.

This example furnishes an occasion to argue once more that the trilogy is imperceptible to children and to most of their adult educators. No further dimension is added to children's experience by these concealed motifs and associations, which are of vital concern to Sendak in his own personal sphere and to those wishing to discover what his deep creative attachment to the reality and the imagination, the power and the suffering of the child might mean to all of us.

This conclusion in no way belittles the value of the stories. It does, however, outline (or delineate) the scope of their influence. As *art*, they are outstanding; *psychologically*, they introduce protagonists and narratives that transform basic insights of depth psychology into incisive, attractive symbols. In the *educational* sphere, though, matters differ. The stories' magic, kinetic appeal; their uniqueness; and their quality ensure that the three books will be with us for a long time. And yet, in spite of its roving range, *In the Night Kitchen* does not seem to be a really essential book from the educational point of view. *Outside Over There* is a many-faceted book embodying an astonishing intuition of the female psyche. We will want to study this work for many more years. However, only *Where the Wild Things Are*, the perfect jewel, could have been credited with achieving a turning point in the educational influence of the picture book. This work's validity is as yet unblemished.

At this point, a suspicion takes hold of us. When Sendak was informed by his publishers that *Outside Over There* was scheduled to be sold on both the children's and the adults' book market, the artist was gratified "to be taken out," at long last, "of kiddy-book land and allowed to join the artists of America."[22] It is not at all difficult to appreciate his joy. Still, does his reaction mean that Sendak, who has so often spoken of his unseverable ties with his own childhood, views the "trilogy" as the termination of his role as an interpreter of children for children and adults? His works since 1981 (when *Outside Over There* was published)—*Nutcracker*,[23] stage designs, promotional designs, illustrations for his father's story *In Grandpa's House*[24]— seem to support this suspicion.

It would be sad if the creator, who, out of compassion and admiration for the child, has given us so much, were from now on to be silent on how children cope with their inner and outer realities.[25] We are ready to listen, from trilogy to heptalogy.

As we leaf through the three books once more, one picture in each arrests our attention—three pictures that together create a common trilogic motif, thus disclosing Sendak's involvement: Max as victorious Henry V; Mickey the Savior, inside the bright halo of the morning sun (fig. 101); and Ida as the Madonna, pointed to by her sister (fig. 102) in the very last picture. The artist who three times solemnly presents children in the hour of their triumph and glory, communicates an apotheosis, a homage to the child. Whoever accomplishes this effect reveals deep understanding, compassion, admiration, and also love. He should not turn away.

We have to return, for a brief moment, to what we said earlier about

22. Lanes, *The Art of Maurice Sendak*, 235.

23. Maurice Sendak, *Nutcracker* (story by E. T. A. Hoffman) (New York: Crown, 1984).

24. Philip Sendak, *In Grandpa's House*, illus. Maurice Sendak (London: The Bodley Head, 1985).

25. Reinbert Tabbert, "Ein Sonntagskind als Alltagsheldin? Anmerkungen zu deutschen Kinderbüchern des Jahrgangs 1983" in *Neue Helden in der Kinder- und Jugendliteratur*, ed. Klaus Doderer (Weinheim and München: Juventa, 1986), 64.

Fig. 101. Maurice Sendak, *In the Night Kitchen*
In the Night Kitchen by Maurice Sendak. Copyright © 1970 by Maurice Sendak. Reprinted by permission of Harper & Row, Publishers, Inc.

Sendak's existentialist vision of childhood. It is true that dependence of the child can be resolved, and his or her personality extended, by dialectic processes. Yet, dialogic processes, offering somewhat less conflict and more openness and support, also lead to growth.

It would be good if a mature Sendak, who now creates in the intermediate region of works that openly appeal to both children and adults, would retrace his steps and return to the locale of a more hopeful existentialism, to the very place where Max is at home, and would guide us there with new heroes.

I hope the foregoing analysis has substantiated a number of points. First, the stories operate on several levels. On the uppermost, we have three magical adventure stories, adventures experienced by three different children in three utterly different fictional worlds. No common denominator exists among them except for the very general one just mentioned.

On a deeper level, Sendak's consciously formulated intention to show how children master various feelings and manage to come to grips with the realities of their lives constitutes a unifying element. Its meaning is most clearly stated in the three pictorial metaphors representing the "apotheosis" of the child.

On a still deeper level, there appears the probably unconscious expression of Sendak's evolving existentialist view of childhood. This view is represented by the plots, the protagonists' personalities, and the changing styles.

These levels interlace—with mythical, psychological, and philosophical associations and motifs floating between them. Many young people sense and are being influenced by the more complex elements found in these stories. Only adults, however, are able to appreciate the full impact of Sendak's literary and artistic sophistication.

Fig. 102. Maurice Sendak, *Outside Over There*

CHILDREN'S BOOKS CITED

SENDAK, MAURICE. *Als Papa fort war (When Papa Was Away)*. Zürich: Diogenes, 1984.
——. *Hector Protector and As I Went over the Water*. New York: Harper, 1965.
——. *Higglety Pigglety Pop, or There Must Be More to Life*. New York: Harper, 1967.
——. *In the Night Kitchen*. New York: Harper, 1970.
——. *Nutcracker*. Story by E.T.A. Hoffmann. New York: Crown, 1984.

——. *Outside Over There*. New York: Harper, 1981.

——. *The Sign on Rosie's Door*. New York: Harper, 1960.

——. *Where the Wild Things Are*. New York: Harper, 1963.

SENDAK, PHILIP. *In Grandpa's House*. Illus. Maurice Sendak. London: The Bodley Head, 1985.

Bibliography

Arnheim, Rudolf. *Visual Thinking*. Berkeley: Univ. of California Pr., 1971.

———. *Art and Visual Perception: A Psychology of the Creative Eye*. Berkeley: Univ. of California Pr., 1974.

Bader, Barbara. "A Second Look: The Little Family." *Horn Book* (March/April 1985): 168–71.

Berger, John. *About Looking*. New York: Pantheon, 1980.

———. *The Sense of Sight*. New York: Pantheon, 1985.

Bettelheim, Bruno. *The Uses of Enchantment: The Meaning and Importance of Fairy Tales*. New York: Vintage Bks./Random, 1977.

Bosmajian, Hamida. " 'Charlie and the Chocolate Factory' and Other Excremental Visions." *The Lion and the Unicorn* (Sept. 1985): 36–49.

Bunbury, Rhonda, and Reinbert Tabbert. "Ein Bunyip ist vieles, aber kein Umir." *Fundevogel*, no. 4–5 (1984): 25–28.

Cianciolo, Patricia. *Illustrations in Children's Books*. Dubuque, Ia.: Brown, 1974.

Clark, Kenneth. *Landscape into Art*. Harmondsworth, England: Penguin, 1949, 1961.

Cott, Jonathan. "Maurice Sendak–King of All the Wild Things." In *Pipers at the Gate of Dawn. The Wisdom of Children's Literature*. New York: Random, 1983, pp. 39–89.

De Luca, Geraldine. "Exploring the Levels of Childhood: The Allegorical Sensibility of Maurice Sendak." In *Children's Literature*, vol. 12. New Haven: Yale Univ. Pr., 1984, pp. 3–24.

Dreyer, Sharon Spredemann. *The Bookfinder: A Guide to Children's Literature. About the Needs and Problems of Youth, Ages 2–15*. 3 vols. Circle Pines, Mich.: American Guidance Service, 1977, 1981, 1985.

Erikson, Erik H. *Childhood and Society*. New York: Norton, 1950.

Halbey, Hans A. "In der Nachtküche—zur Metasprache im Bilderbuch." In *Maurice Sendak: Bilderbuchkünstler*. Edited by Reinbert Tabbert. Bonn: Bouvier, 1987, pp. 61–68.

Heller, Agnes. *A Theory of Feelings*. Assen, Netherlands: Van Gorcum, 1979.

Herman, Gertrude. "A Picture Is Worth Several Hundred Words." *Horn Book* (July/ Aug. 1985): 473.

———. Letter to *Horn Book* (Jan./Feb. 1986): 3.

Herzka, Heinz S. *Play as a Way of Dialogical Development*. Leiden, Netherlands: Postacademisch Onderwijs Sociale Wetensschappen, n.d.

———. "The Dialogics of a Doctor-Patient Relationship." In *Doctor-Patient Interaction*. Edited by Walburga von Raffler-Engel. Amsterdam and Philadelphia: John Benjamins Pub., 1989.

Jeanhenry, Josiane. "Einige Gedanken ueber Zärtlichkeit, über liebevolle Zuwendung." *Jugend Literatur* (Feb. 1986): 20–29.

Kalekin-Fishman, Devorah. "Désalienation. Pour une conscience libérée dans l'éducation." *Cahiers de sociologie economique et culturelle. Ethnopsychologie* (Dec. 1986): 109–29.

Lacy, Lyn E. *Art and Design in Children's Picture Books: An Analysis of Caldecott Award–Winning Illustrations.* Chicago and London: American Library Assn., 1986.

Lanes, Selma G. *The Art of Maurice Sendak.* New York: Abrams, 1980.

Lutts, Ralph H. "Place, Home, and Story in Environmental Education." *Journal of Environmental Education* 17, no. 1 (Feb. 1985): 37–41.

Marantz, Sylvia and Kenneth Marantz. "An Interview with Anthony Browne." *Horn Book* (Nov./Dec. 1985): 696–704.

Meyrowitz, Joshua. *No Sense of Place: The Impact of Electronic Media on Social Behavior.* New York and Oxford: Oxford Univ. Pr., 1985.

Moles, Abraham A. *Information Theory and Esthetic Perception.* Urbana, Ill.: Univ. of Illinois Pr., 1968.

Novitz, David. *Pictures and Their Use in Communication.* The Hague: Nijhoff, 1977.

Poesio, Carla. "Lele Luzzati: Figure incrociate." *Schedario* no. 196 (July/Aug. 1985): 127–31.

———. "Messaggi per l'anno della pace." *Schedario* no. 197 (Sept./Oct. 1985): 163–65.

Roxburgh, Stephen. "A Picture Equals How Many Words? Narrative Theory and Picture Books for Children." *The Lion and the Unicorn* (July/Aug. 1983–84): 20–33.

Salholz, E., with J. Taylor and D. Gates. "Kids with Nuclear Jitters." *Newsweek,* 11 Oct. 1982, pp. 43–44.

Scharioth, Barbara. "Starke Bilderbuchkinder–zum Beispiel: Maurice Sendak." *Informationen des Arbeitskreises für Jugendliteratur* (April 1985): 56–59.

Schoenberger, Gerhard. *Der gelbe Stern: Die Judenverfolgung in Europa 1933–1945, 196 Bilddokumente.* Hamburg: Rütten-Loening, 1960.

Schwarcz, Joseph H. *Ways of the Illustrator: Visual Communication in Children's Literature.* Chicago: American Library Assn., 1982.

———. "Die Darstellung des Geistes der Musik im Bilderbuch." *Librarium* (Dec. 1986): 190–202.

Shepard, Sam. Interviewed by Jonathan Cott. "The Rolling Stone Interview: Sam Shepard." *Rolling Stone,* Dec. 18, 1986–Jan. 1, 1987, pp. 166–72.

Steig, Michael. "Reading *Outside Over There.*" *Children's Literature* 13 (1985): 139–53.

Tabbert, Reinbert. "Literarische modelle von Kindheit und Jugend." *Informationen des Arbeitskreises für Jugendliteratur* (April 1985): 29–43.

———. "Nichtsichtbares sichtbar machen. Ein Interview mit Annalena McAfee und Anthony Browne." *Informationen des Arbeitskreises für Jugendliteratur* (Jan. 1986): 8–13.

———. "Ein Sonntagskind als Alltagsheldin? Anmerkungen zu deutschen Kinderbüchern des Jahrgangs 1983." In *Neue Helden in der Kinder- und Jugendliteratur,* ed. Klaus Doderer. Weinheim and München: Juventa, 1986, 63–73.

Tennyson, Alfred Lord. "The Charge of the Heavy Brigade at Balaclava." *The Poetic and Dramatic Works of Alfred Lord Tennyson.* Cambridge ed. Boston and New York: Houghton, 1898, 509–10.

Tuan, Yi-Fu. *Topophilia: A Study of Environmental Perception, Attitudes and Values.* Englewood Cliffs, N.J.: Prentice-Hall, 1974.

Updike, John. "Conversations with Alain P. Sanoff." Interview in *U.S. News & World Report,* Oct. 20, 1986, pp. 67–68.

von Kleist, Heinrich. "Die Marquise von O." In *Sämtliche Werke*, vol. 3. Leipzig, Germany: Max Hesses Verlag, 1902, pp. 83–116.

Wagner, Philip L. *Environments and People*. Englewood Cliffs, N.J.: Prentice-Hall, 1974.

Weismann, Donald L. *The Visual Arts as Human Experience*. Englewood Cliffs, N.J.: Prentice-Hall, n.d.

Index of Illustrators

by Carol Nielsen

Italicized numbers refer to illustrations.

211

General Index

by Kristina Masiulis

The late Joseph Schwarcz, author of ALA's award-winning *Ways of the Illustrator* (1983), was an internationally known educator and lecturer on visual education and children's literature. A resident of Israel, he was a lifelong advocate of all the world's children.

Chava Schwarcz has taught English literature at the University of Haifa and Hebrew University in Jerusalem. She is a former principal of a girls' vocational school.